To Edward and Sarah,

so happy to have got to know you.
Thank you very much for all,
and hope you enjoy my writing!

love,

Zoe

Living Boundaries

Frontiers and Identity
in the Basque Country

P.I.E.-Peter Lang

Bruxelles · Bern · Berlin · Frankfurt am Main · New York · Oxford · Wien

Zoe BRAY

Living Boundaries

Frontiers and Identity
in the Basque Country

"Multiple Europes"
No.28

To Rodrigo

To my parents

To the people of the Basque Country, in the hope that this book may contribute to a better understanding of the richness and complexity of their daily lives.

With the financial support of the European University Institute.

Cover illustration by the author.

© P.I.E.-Peter Lang s.a.
PRESSES INTERUNIVERSITAIRES EUROPÉENNES
Brussels, 2004
1 avenue Maurice, 1050 Brussels, Belgium
info@peterlang.com; www.peterlang.net

Printed in Germany

ISSN 1376-0904
ISBN 90-5201-212-1
US ISBN 0-8204-6620-4
D/2004/5678/11

*CIP available from the British Library, GB
and the Library of Congress, USA.*

Bibliographic information published by "Die Deutsche Bibliothek"

"Die Deutsche Bibliothek" lists this publication in the "Deutsche Nationalbibliografie";
detailed bibliographic data is available in the Internet at <http://dnb.ddb.de>.

Map 1. The Basque Country in France and Spain.

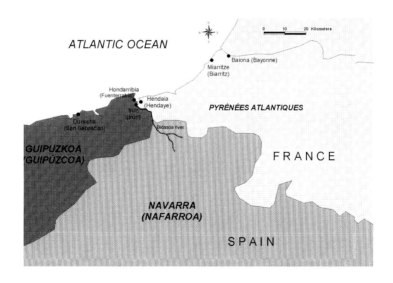

Map 2. Bidasoa-Txingudi: Hendaia, Irun and Hondarribia on the Franco-Spanish frontier in the Basque Country.

Spanish border controls booth in Irun, now empty.
Note the graffiti in support of ETA.

French border controls booth
on the Hendaian side
of the International Bridge,
similarly derelict and graffitied.
Note also the attempt by
graffitists to write 'Euskadi'.

A supporter of *Euskal Presoak Euskal Herrira*, the campaign to bring militant prisoners back to the Basque Country, stands on the Spanish side of the frontier area brandishing her flag at passing traffic.

French paramilitary troops stand on their side of the frontier carrying out one of their sporadic controls. In the foreground, the modern *mugaria*, or frontier marker stone, was made by the sculptor Jorge Oteiza.

Roadsign welcoming drivers to Hendaia with details of twinning arrangements with towns in Scotland and Portugal. There is no mention of the cross-frontier cooperation agreement with Irun and Hondarribia.

Author standing on the Hendaian side of Santiago Bridge, with a view of Irun and the Aiako Peñak in the horizon.

Entrance to Muara bar, in Hondarribia.

Author at the bar inside Muara. Notice the numerous posters calling for independence for the Basque Country and portraits of incarcerated activists.

A participant in the Korrika shouts "Euskal Herrian Euskaraz! Mugarik Ez!" ("The Basque language in the Basque Country! No frontier!") at members of the French paramilitary police force near the train station of Hendaia.

The Irunian rock star Fermin Muguruza takes the baton surrounded by fans and *Euskal Presoak Euskal Herrira* campaigners.

Participants in the traditional Alarde of Irun gather in front of the town hall.
Note the Basque flag in the square and the Irunian and Spanish flags
in front of the town hall.

A poster on a bus stop in Irun advertises the shopping center called
Txingudi, using the theme of the Alarde.

Cover of a pamphlet
for the Partzuergo's Euro
campaign in 2001 (courtesy
of the Partzuergo
Bidasoa-Txingudi).

One of the covers for the
magazine Bidasoa-Txingudi,
illustrating the Partzuergo's
logo (courtesy of the
Partzuergo Bidasoa-
Txingudi).

Contents

Preface

The removal of frontier controls between many European Union countries is forcing border communities on either side of state frontiers to reassess their relationships. This book focuses on a border area in the Basque region that straddles the Franco-Spanish frontier at the point where the Pyrenees meet the Atlantic Ocean. Known as Bidasoa-Txingudi, often shortened to Txingudi, it brings together people of Spanish and French nationality, speaking Basque, Spanish and French and identifying in a range of different ways with Basque, Spanish and French symbols. Since the late 1990s, a project of cooperation, with some financial assistance from the EU, has been initiated by the three towns that make up Txingudi: Irun and Hondarribia on the Spanish side of the frontier, and Hendaia on the French side. It operates in an environment in which contrasting and sometimes conflicting issues of identity, nationality, language and culture mingle and interreact.

This book contributes to an ongoing debate in the social and political sciences about issues of identity, ethnicity, culture, nationalism and frontiers. Based on anthropological fieldwork, it examines how the inhabitants of frontiers construct and express their identities. Focusing on Txingudi, it explores a process of institutional attempts to create a new sense of local identity and unity drawing on notions of 'European belonging'. Challenging notions of fixed identity among members of groups often perceived as homogeneous, this book presents identity in terms of a configuration of boundaries that are constantly drawn, crossed and reinterpreted by individuals in the course of everyday social interaction. It concludes by pointing out the difficulties inherent in attempts to forge a new sense of local and European belonging in a complex sociocultural and political context such as that of the Basque Country. The analysis is also relevant to any area in which institutional initiatives seek to foster new notions of self.

During the four years that I have taken to carry out this research and produce this book, I have been able to proceed thanks to the strong support and confidence of the many people around me who in different ways provided encouragement and inspiration. I thank my family, and in particular my father who was always there to support and advise me with his sensitivity and natural anthropological insight. My gratitude goes to my close friends, and to Stuart. In the field, I could not have gone ahead without the openness and warmth of the people who welcomed me there. I thank them all for accepting me into their lives, talking to me so openly and, in many cases, for allowing me into the intimacy of their world. Not only did I learn about them but also about myself. This research was funded by generous grants from the European University Institute, the Madariaga Fund and Eusko Ikaskuntza, for which I express my gratitude. I would also specifically like to thank Professors Michael Keating and Bo Stråth at the EUI, Christian Joppke at the Russell Sage Foundation, Jeremy MacClancy at Oxford Brookes, Joseba Zulaika at the University of Nevada, and Hastings Donnan and Thomas Wilson at Queens University, Belfast.

Zoe Bray

Introduction

Since 1985, when France, Germany, Belgium, Luxembourg and the Netherlands signed what came to be known as the Schengen Agreement, state frontiers within the European Union have progressively ceased to be barriers to the movement of people. Called after the town in Luxembourg where the first agreements were signed, the 'Schengen area' has gradually been extended to include, as of 2003, all of the EU member states apart from Ireland and the United Kingdom. In parallel, the launch in 1993 of the European Single Market has led to the removal of customs controls at state frontiers. By allowing both people and goods to cross national frontiers without having to go through passport and customs checks, these two developments have meant the disappearance of many of the visible signs of borders. One result has been to oblige numerous communities located in border zones to reassess their sociocultural, economic and legal relationships with neighbouring communities on the other side of state frontiers.

This book is concerned with issues of identity and the ways in which individuals constantly shape their personal expressions of identity to take account of circumstances. It focuses on an area straddling the Franco-Spanish frontier at the point where the western Pyrenees meet the Atlantic, whose inhabitants have had to adapt to a new environment in which the frontier has been transformed from a dividing line into the axis of a newly conceived project of unification. The promoters of this project are the municipal authorities of three towns with a combined population of around 85,000 straddling the Franco-Spanish frontier at the point where the western Pyrenees meet the Atlantic: Irun and Hondarribia on the Spanish side; and Hendaia on the French side. The progressive disappearance of frontiers between them, while creating new conditions for social, political and economic interaction, have simultaneously raised new questions with regard to the way in which their inhabitants experience and express their identity.

Though close to each other, these three communities continue to display many different characteristics. The French and Spanish states have left their imprint on the political, cultural and linguistic landscapes and on economic and social development. In Irun and Hondarribia, the Spanish influence is clearly evident; in Hendaia, the environment is unmistakably French. At the same time, however, all three towns have in common a visible Basque cultural heritage, reflecting their location in the Basque Country. The result is an intermingling of cultural influences that is a source of both stimulation and tension. With the removal of border controls, people on either side of the frontier have had to reassess how they express their 'selfhood' in relations with each other and with their neighbours across the state divide.

Historically, relations between the three communities have shifted between tension and cordiality, interspersed by indifference. Against a background of change at a European level, political leaders in all three towns recognised during the 1980s and 1990s that changing conditions called for a gearshift in cross-frontier links. In 1999, a decade of efforts to formalise closer institutional relations between the three towns bore fruit in the launching of a 'consortium' to undertake cross-frontier projects in the area. The 'Bidasoa-Txingudi Cross-Frontier Consortium' takes its name from a newly coined name for the area in which the three towns are located. In Basque, it is known as *Bidasoa-Txingudi Mugaz Gaindiko Partzuergoa*, in French as *le Consorcio Transfrontalier Bidasoa-Txingudi* and in Spanish as *el Consorcio Transfronterizo Bidasoa-Txingudi*. The French version of the name, using the Spanish word *consorcio* rather than the French *consortium*, reflects the fact that it was set up using a Spanish legal vehicle for co-operation between local authorities.

At the root of many human actions is the desire to exercise and retain power, and the Consortium is no exception. It owes its genesis to elected officials anxious to maintain their supremacy in a changing economic and social environment. From the start, the individuals behind the Consortium have faced the challenge of winning and maintaining the support of the local population. They have attempted to promote a new common sense of local belonging across a state frontier, based on a combination of existing regional and cultural ties. But they have also had to contend with the disillusion and antagonism provoked by the continuing presence within local society of violent Basque nationalism, with all that this entails in terms of dissemblance and ambiguity of identifications.

In this book, I have set out to analyse a range of different ways of understanding, expressing and instrumentalising identity among representatives of the Consortium and other individuals and groups in Bidasoa-Txingudi. I take as my point of departure the observation that the fact of sharing a common nationality, in a frontier area like Bidasoa-Txingudi, does not necessarily imply membership of a discrete cultural group whose dominant characteristics are reflected and replicated in the behaviour of individuals. Equally, I shall show that belonging to a given linguistic group does not necessarily entail the sharing of identical social and political values. Instead, I shall argue that the state frontier and the linguistic barriers that are evident on either side of it are just some examples of the many boundaries used by individuals to form and define identities, and that the deployment by individuals of a multiplicity of boundaries, many of them permeable and changing in nature, is a constant feature of social interaction.

By analysing these boundaries and the ways they are perceived and used by people in the construction and expression of their selves, I aim to contribute to current debates on the nature of identity. Fundamental to my approach is the use of the concept of boundaries as a tool for perceiving the way in which individuals construct and express their identity. Rather than viewing identity as a result of a fixed configuration of symbolic markers and boundaries, such as the use of one language rather than another or the choice of certain types of clothing or other attributes, I suggest that individuals constantly engage in the erection of markers and the drawing up of boundaries in order to construct the expression of their selves. Identity thus becomes the product of a fluid and changing application of these symbolic markers and boundaries.

In the context of a society that is still struggling to resolve deep-rooted conflicts, represented at their most virulent by the continuing murderous violence of the Basque armed nationalist group *ETA*[1] and the often excessively authoritarian attitude of Spanish and French government officials, my objective is to shed light on the multiple facets of what it means at the level of individuals to 'feel Basque'. In analyzing the use of boundaries, I also examine the way in which individuals engage in struggles for the control of symbolic markers in order to obtain and consolidate power. My analysis of identity constructions leads me to question not only the existence of a clearly definable 'Basque identity' but also the 'reality' of 'open borders' and the validity of assumptions concerning the likely emergence of new forms of identification characterised by such concepts as 'supranational consciousness', 'postnationalism' and 'transnationalism'.

In the long run, projects like the Consortium may pave the way for the development of a European ideal of 'multiple identity' attachments. A new sense of common belonging based on an alliance of distinct cultural expressions in a wider European setting may produce a shift from the nationalist sentiments of yesterday to a new form of regionalism and European supranationalism. On a local scale, that is what some people in Bidasoa-Txingudi, including the promoters of the Consortium, are trying to achieve. In addition to launching projects to inject new vigour into the local economy, the Consortium has given its backing to a range of ventures designed to foster a new local sense of identity, a so-

---

[1] ETA stands for *Euskadi ta Askatasuna*. This is Basque for 'Basque Country and Freedom'.

called 'Txingudi spirit',[2] and a sense of 'Txingudi citizenship'.[3] In doing so, its leaders seek to manipulate symbolic boundaries in order to create a new cultural identity, in an area where spatial and social boundaries are in the process of being redefined.

Their pursuit of this objective is hampered, nonetheless, by the ambiguities and contradictions that result from differing uses of boundaries in a context in which identities and allegiances are highly contested. In Bidasoa-Txingudi, despite the efforts of the Consortium's promoters, different notions of self continually emerge among the local population. At a broader level, I suggest, this is equally true for other cross-frontier projects in areas where multiple ethnic, cultural and social allegiances exist.

In light of this, an understanding of the dynamics of identity formation and expression clearly becomes essential for anyone trying to promote an eventual 'Europe without frontiers'. In Bidasoa-Txingudi, if the Consortium project is to work effectively and enjoy popular support, its backers will have to take account of the manner in which individuals constantly adapt aspects of their identity and behaviour to different contexts, company and circumstances. Similarly, at a European level, identifications based on shifting symbolic boundaries may result in new kinds of identity formation that do not go neatly in the direction of either regional, nationalist, or European ideals. If the ways in which symbolic boundaries are used and understood can vary from one person to another and according to the social context in which they are expressed, the ways in which individuals experience notions of belonging and identification are equally variable. The challenge facing politicians and policy-makers is to take these differences into account in any attempt to group people under a particular banner or category, so as to ensure that such projects are open, flexible and harmonious.

The twelve chapters that follow combine an account of my personal observations of social interaction in the area with theoretical considerations and analysis in relation to issues of identity. Chapter One provides a description of Bidasoa-Txingudi as I experienced it, drawing on sensory impressions of sight, sound and smell. Its aim is to give the reader a feel for the place, highlighting both similarities and differences between the three towns and the two sides of the frontier. Among other things it highlights differing and sometimes conflicting social and political perceptions of space depending on whether the viewer regards himself or herself as being in the Basque Country, France or Spain.

---

[2]   This term appears often in communiqués of the Consortium. See for example in the *Présentation du Txingudi Eguna*, Town hall of Hendaia, October 1999, p. 4.

[3]   See for example in the Consortium's monthly magazine *Bidasoa-Txingudi*, October, 1998, No. 9, p. 13.

With the help of an ethnographic vignette, Chapter Two elaborates on the boundaries evoked in Chapter One. It explains the political and socio-cultural tensions existing in the Basque Country and in Bidasoa-Txingudi. Chapter Three uses ethnographic vignettes to review various experiences and expressions of Basque identity on the part of individuals. It links the issue of Basque identity to that of Basque nationalism, broaching the problematic of identity as a political project. This chapter then briefly explains the concept of identity as it developed in the social sciences (a more elaborate account is included in Annex 1). Chapter Four looks more closely at experiences of local space with a particular focus on the frontier as a social and political boundary, highlighting the different and sometimes conflicting views that individuals have of the frontier in the context of Bidasoa-Txingudi and various forms of nationalism.

Subsequent chapters explore different empirical observations of boundaries at work in Bidasoa-Txingudi. Chapter Five focuses on language as a symbolic boundary in the construction and expression of identity in Bidasoa-Txingudi, while Chapter Six looks at the use of space in the context of a night out in Irun. Chapter Seven focuses on a ritual component of the annual town fiestas of Irun and Hondarribia whose role in the expression of local identification has been magnified in recent years by a conflict over who has the right to participate. In reviewing the tensions that result from this, I explore their significance for the possible construction of a Bidasoa-Txingudi sense of belonging.

Having seen how a variety of symbolic boundaries are drawn by individuals and groups in different ways and in a range of different situations in the common context of Bidasoa-Txingudi, I look in more detail at the cross-frontier cooperation project led by the Consortium in Chapter Eight. An ethnographic vignette depicting a meeting of the Consortium illustrates the interaction of the various participants from Irun, Hondarribia and Hendaia. Chapter Nine is a discussion of how the Consortium seeks to go beyond the symbolic boundaries existing in the area, in its attempt to construct a common sense of Bidasoa-Txingudi belonging. I describe and analyse the discourse and the various social, cultural and economic projects of the Consortium from an anthropological perspective. In Chapter Ten, I evaluate the impact of the Consortium, examining both the perspectives of those involved in its organisation and the reaction of other members of the local population to its actions. This examination, revealing as it does a number of paradoxes and contradictions, paves the way for the Conclusion of this book, which can be briefly stated as follows: While the members of any kind of social group distinguish themselves through the drawing-up of a selection of symbolic boundaries, the usage and interpretation of these symbolic boundaries can differ according to the individual and the nature of social interaction. Reflecting such varying usage and interpretations, individuals experience notions of belonging and identification in different ways. Only when these differences are taken into account can any attempt to group people under a particular banner or category be open, flexible and harmonious.

CHAPTER 1

Introducing Bidasoa-Txingudi

Seen from the air, the area known as Bidasoa-Txingudi looks like a self-contained urban community, wedged between the mountains of the Pyrenees and the Atlantic Ocean at the point where the river Bidasoa joins the sea. On the north side of its estuary, Hendaia covers an area stretching from the river to an extensive beach area. On the south side, Irun sprawls along the river bank while Hondarribia, at the tip of the estuary, looks over to Hendaia and out to the Atlantic. Conceptualisation of the area as a particular space has been stressed since the late 1990s by road signs in Basque and Spanish saying "welcome to Txingudi" and "Bidasoa-Txingudi" as one approaches Irun and Hondarribia on the motorway or Spain's *Carretera Nacional 1* highway from San Sebastian, the main town of Gipuzkoa, known as Donostia in Basque.

But appearances are deceptive. Until recently, Irun and Hondarribia had relatively little to do with each other and even less with Hendaia. The place-name Bidasoa-Txingudi combines the name of the river Bidasoa, which here provides a natural frontier between France and Spain, with that of a bay on the French side of its estuary, the Bay of Txingudi[1]. Its invention as a spacial and social concept marks a deliberate appropriation of geography for purposes of self-identification on the part of the people and institutions that use it.

The use of place-names is both a cultural and a political act with rich implications for individuals and groups in matters of identity. In this book, I shall use the standardised Basque, or *Batua*,[2] version of place names, except in a few cases where the French or Spanish equivalents are better known to an international audience. In speaking of the three towns of Bidasoa-Txingudi, I shall refer to Hendaia instead of the French Hendaye, to Hondarribia instead of the Spanish Fuenterrabía and to Irun, without the accent on the u found in the Spanish version of the town's name, Irún. I shall also henceforth refer to the Consortium by its Basque

---

[1]   The name was originally applied to an area of tidal marshes alongside the Bay of Hendaia on the estuary of the Bidasoa, known in French as Chingoudy. In recent years, use of this name in its Basque-icised version, Txingudi, has been extended to the bay and subsequently to the entire area around it.

[2]   Batua means 'united' in Basque.

name, as the Partzuergo.[3] In doing so, I am aware that these terms have particular political connotations – and are therefore one of the objects of my analysis. Equally, however, I know that whatever term I choose will be open to accusations of contributing in some way or other to the particular symbolic power struggle existing in the Basque Country. When quoting individuals, I shall follow their usage for place names and other symbolically loaded vocabulary, in an effort to take into account the importance of names and vocabulary as an element in the process of self-expression. Reflecting growing public acceptance of a new geopolitical reality, the term Bidasoa-Txingudi is now increasingly giving way to 'Txingudi' in local parlance as a shorthand designation for the area, and I shall use that term as well.

It is useful here to say a few words about the Basque Country and its component parts. According to Basque nationalists, the Basque Country covers the territory occupied by the seven historic territories of Gipuzkoa, Bizkaia, Araba, Nafarroa, Behe Nafarroa, Lapurdi and Siberoa.[4] This territory has no unanimously accepted name, however, and the terms used by different people with different cultural and political identifications to describe the region – Basque Country in English; *Euskal Herria, Eskualherria* or *Eskualerria* and *Euskadi* or *Euzkadi* in Basque; *País Vasco* in Spanish; and *Pays Basque* in French – all have different connotations. The word 'Basque' comes from the Latin *Vasconia*, the name given by the Romans to the people living in this region.

Euskal Herria and its variants refer to the Basque Country as a linguistic and cultural territory, ignoring political and administrative frontiers. As such, they are often used by Basque nationalist sympathists to avoid Spanish and French political conceptualisations of the Basque space. The phrase *Zazpiak Bat*, meaning "the seven (provinces are) one", which first appeared towards the end of the nineteenth century with the emergence of traditional Basque nationalism, refers to this whole Euskal Herria. But although traces of Basque etymological roots have been found in place names across a much wider area than that covered by today's Basque Country, not all of the area supposedly forming the Basque territory today can clearly be identified as Basque. Much of Nafarroa (known in English as Navarre) is Spanish-speaking, rather than Basque-speaking, and its southern parts have little that is obviously Basque about them. Bayonne, the main town of Lapurdi, known as Baiona in Basque, has Gascon, as well as Basque, cultural

---

[3] The letter 'a' at the end of Basque words serves as the definite article. Since I say *the* Partzuergo, the suffix 'a' is not necessary. In ordinary parlance however, many people used the word Consorcio rather than Partzuergo.

[4] Archaeological, biological anthropological and linguistic researchers claim to have found evidence of a broader extension in former times of Basque characteristics.

roots. In both Bayonne and Bilbao, or Bilbo, the capital of Bizkaia, as well as in the province of Araba, only a small portion of the population is Basque-speaking.

People with Basque nationalist motivations talk of the French part of the Basque Country as *Iparralde*, which means the North side, and the Spanish part as *Hegoalde*, meaning the South side. Thus they transmit a certain vision of Basque space transcending the state frontier, in their desire to see the Basque Country as a whole. Neither of these areas has any official or administrative status, however. Hegoalde is a loosely defined conceptual area of Basqueness, covering Gipuzkoa, Bizkaia and Araba plus Nafarroa, a separate autonomous region within the Spanish state, known in Spanish as the *Comunidad Foral de Navarra*. As for the three historic provinces that make up Iparralde, with a combined population of 258,000 inhabitants, they have no self-standing administrative structure but form part of France's *département des Pyrénées Atlantiques* and the larger region of Aquitaine. Since the late 1970s, Basque nationalists in Iparralde have sought unsuccessfully to obtain the creation of a *département du Pays basque* with its capital in Bayonne, through the division of the département des Pyrénées Atlantiques which combines the three historic provinces of Iparralde with the non-Basque speaking historic province of Béarn, into two new départements. Successive French governments have rejected such a plan, however, effectively refusing any institutional recognition of Basque identity.

The term Euzkadi, invented by Sabino Arana Goiri, founder of the first Basque nationalist party, *Eusko Alderdi Jeltzalea*[5] (EAJ) in the late nineteenth century, to refer to a notional Basque homeland, has since been dropped in favour of Euskadi, with an "s" rather than a "z", to conform to the standardised Basque word for the Basque language, *Euskara*. According to Letamendia (1976) and Conversi (1997), this orthographical shift reflects both a desire to mark distance from Arana's racial vision of a Basque homeland and the political context in which the Basque government, or *Eusko Jaurlaritza* in Basque, was born in 1978. Today, the word Euskadi is the Basque name for the autonomous region known in Spanish as the *Comunidad Autónoma Vasca*, or Autonomous Basque Community, which covers only Araba, Bizkaia and Gipuzkoa.

The Spanish term *País Vasco* is commonly used to refer to this restricted definition of Euskadi. For French people, meanwhile, the term *Pays basque* is often taken as referring to the part of the Basque Country in French territory, made up of the three provinces of Lapurdi, Behe Nafarroa (or Lower Navarre) and Siberoa. When referring to Euskadi, *Pays basque espagnol* is often used. As for the English 'Basque Coun-

---

[5]   This is the party's name in Basque. In English, it is the 'Basque Nationalist Party'.

try', although it is a literal translation of Euskal Herria, País Vasco and Pays basque, it does not refer to a clearly defined territory. Without entering into the merits of the various arguments in this geopolitical confusion, I shall refer in neutral terms to the Basque region as the 'Basque Country' since this is how it is referred to in English, irrespective of political and cultural identifications. Straddling the Pyrenees, this wedge-shaped area of more than 20,600 square kilometres, with a population of over 2,870,000, stretches along the Atlantic coast from Bayonne at its northern extremity to Bilbao in the west and inland at its deepest point for some 120 kilometres. I shall also use the terms Iparralde and Hegoalde to refer to the areas north and south of the frontier.

Following this geopolitical definition of space, Hendaia is located in Lapurdi and Iparralde, while Irun and Hondarribia are in Gipuzkoa and Hegoalde. As a conurbation straddling the state frontier, Bidasoa-Txingudi is unique in the Basque Country. An important transit point for centuries, the area has been marked in the past by frequent confrontations between the communities and states on either side of the frontier. Victories against the French army involving the militias of Irun and Hondarribia in 1522 and 1638 continue to be celebrated in each of these two towns in an annual parade known in both Spanish and Basque as the *Alarde*.

Hendaia

Driving in a southerly direction along France's *Route Nationale 10* from the village of Urruña, one descends a steep hill to a built-up area where roadsigns in French point left to the *frontière d'Espagne*. To the right, a road leads along the northern bank of the Bidasoa to Hendaia, a sprawling town with a population of around 18,000. Across the river, Irun and Hondarribia are separated from the rest of Euskadi and Spanish territory by more mountains, the *Aiako Harriak*, or *Peñas de Harria* in Spanish, and *Jaizkibel*. In the middle of the Bidasoa are several uninhabited islands, one of which was the site of the signing of the Treaty of the Pyrenees in 1659 to delimit Spanish and French territory. Over the centuries, ownership of this island, known today as the Island of the Pheasants (in Basque *Faisaien Uhartea*, in French *Île des Faisans* and in Spanish *Isla de los Faisanes*), switched between the French and Spanish states. Since 1902, the island has changed jurisdiction between the two states every six months, on February 1 and August 1, under the authority of the two countries' navies.

Hendaia is cut off from its hinterland to the north by hills rising to a high plateau. From vantage points around the area – the clifftop by the *Château d'Abbadie*, a mansion on the coast to the north of Hendaia, the chapel of the Virgin of Guadalupe at the top of Jaizkibel near Hondarribia, and the chapel of San Marcial near Irun – one can see all around the bay and beyond. To the north, on a clear day, one can see up beyond Biarritz, twenty-five kilometres away, to the *département des Landes.* To the east, one can see the mountain of Ruña, an impressive peak on the French side of the state frontier. To the west, beyond Jaizkibel, the rocky coastline stretches into the distance, past the port of Pasaia to the city of San Sebastian. Along the mountain tops are watchtowers built in the sixteenth and seventeenth centuries to look out for enemies coming from France or from out at sea.

Entering Hendaia from the road that branches off the Route Nationale 10, the visitor is greeted by a sign in French announcing the town's twinning arrangements with Peebles in Scotland and Viana do Castelo in Portugal. In visual terms, first impressions of Hendaia clearly demonstrate its Basque character, with red-roofed, white-walled houses and Basque names on shops and road signs. But it is also very clearly a French town. At its centre, the Place de la République is lined by neatly pollarded plane trees and parked cars. Around this square, as in many other towns in France, are the town hall, the church and the state tax office, as well as a café and a few shops. As in other small towns across France, most shops in Hendaia open from 9.00 a.m. until noon, when they close for lunch, and from 3.00 p.m. until 6.30 p.m.

The town hall is a modern two-storey rectangular building with white walls, red-painted doors and shutters, a balcony and a red-tiled roof, in keeping with an architectural and decorative style typical of Iparralde. Past automatic sliding doors, visitors are greeted by a receptionist in French. Fluent in Spanish, she can also deal with Spanish-speaking visitors. She does not, however, speak Basque. Other than on Wednesday mornings, when market stalls are set up in the square, the centre of Hendaia is quiet. In fine weather, a few people sit having a drink outside the Café de la Bidassoa, which uses the French spelling of the river in its name. Inside, French television and the Spanish Basque Radio Euskadi blare out simultaneously and customers can be heard chatting in French, Spanish and Basque.

On the Rue du Port leading down to the Bidasoa estuary where fishermen worked until the 1990s, a shop called Au Petit Paris sells books, incense and semi-precious stones. Opposite, the Pharmacie Franco-Espagnole advertises its beauty and medical products only in French, despite its name. Nearby, a branch of the French bank Crédit Agricole stands alongside a branch of the Hegoalde bank Kutxa Donostia-Gipuzkoa. Next door, a bakery with a Spanish name, Alonso, sells delicate French pastries, chocolates and *"gâteau basque"*, a crumbly cake with a custard filling typical of Iparralde.

At the other end of the square, smells of roast beef and other French meat dishes emanate from the butcher's Arruabarrena, named after the family that has owned it for over half a century. Beside it stands the main church of Hendaia, a small early eighteenth century building with a rectangular steeple dedicated to Saint Vincent, or San Bixente in Basque, the patron saint of Hendaia. In nearby streets are two other buildings of central importance to the spatial organisation of any French town: the post office and the municipal library named after the late Socialist president of France, the *Médiathèque François Mitterrand.*

Opened in 1998, this building is of a minimalist and spacious architectural style, with typical French Basque features in its clean white walls and red-tiled roof. Following the more varied colour scheme of the "nouveau Basque" style, the balcony and windows are painted dark blue. Above its entrance, big blue letters spell out the library's name in French. Staff members address visitors in French but are ready to answer in Spanish if necessary, though not in Basque, having no knowledge of the language. The library offers a selection of mainly French books and newspapers, as well as the main Spanish-language Hegoalde newspapers.[6]

The Boulevard Charles de Gaulle, named after another former French president, leads from the town centre to the beach area, with roadsigns sometimes in both French and Basque and sometimes just in French. Past a few commercial establishments, a bar called Maitena owned by a Basque-speaking man originally from a rural part of Iparralde is a regular rendez-vous for local sympathists of the Basque left-wing nationalist movement. Further on, one of six schools in Hendaia is housed in a nineteenth century building which still bears inscriptions in French designating what were formerly separate sections for girls and boys. The boulevard runs along the estuary, with a view across to Hondarribia on one side and a line of Basque-style villas with Basque names like 'Ongui Ethorri' (Welcome'), 'Etche Ona' ('Good House') or 'Gure Ametza' ('Our Dream'), in some cases following the Gallicised orthography customary in Iparralde, on the other. Halfway along the boulevard, a small roundabout is decorated with flowers arranged to spell "*Txingudi*", an innovation that dates from 1999.

On the ocean front, the most sophisticated part, Sokoburu, is a short distance from Hondarribia on the other side of the estuary. It consists of a few smart hotels and a conference centre. Nearby, the fishing port has recently been redeveloped to provide mooring facilities for yacht-

---

6   It does not, however, have the French-language left-wing Basque nationalist weekly, *Enbata*, on the grounds, according to the library's French-speaking director, that it is "too political". In making this judgement, he seemingly overlooked the fact that the other newspapers there could also be regarded as political, particularly the Spanish-language Hegoalde paper *Gara*, whose name means 'we are' in Basque and which has a similar left-wing Basque nationalist stance.

owners. Close to the sea-front, a street is lined with a series of bars, including the rustic-looking Txirrimirri, from which Basque rock music is blaring out, the Ouf! with its decorations of old French rock stars, the Océanic, with a minimalist glass interior décor and rugby trophies behind the counter, and the more psychedelic Krypton with its bright colours and techno music.

At the other end of town, road signs indicate the way past a few old and once grand-looking shops to the railway station and the state frontier. The old-style boutique Le Palais du Crystal, a gem of late nineteenth century architecture, is a reminder of more prosperous days when Spanish shoppers flocked here to buy French goods. It continues to sell odd bits and pieces to a now much diminished clientèle. Further down, a small toyshop with a dilapidated façade advertises '*petardos*', Spanish for fire-crackers. Its main business is with young Spaniards who come to Hendaia especially to purchase fireworks, banned under Spanish law. In the station, some of the staff speak Basque but there is no public indication of this. Notices and loudspeaker announcements advertise the train times in French, Spanish and English.

Next to the station is the terminus of the *EuskoTren*, a narrow-gauge rail service known locally as the *topo*, meaning mole in Spanish, which since 1912 has transported people from Hendaia along the coast to San Sebastian, stopping on the way in Irun and other towns. A bus service also stops at the station, linking Hendaia to Bayonne. Since the early 1990s, the company running this service and another bus company from Irun have also provided a summer-time service between Irun and the beach of Hendaia. Beside the station, a small building on which are written the words "*Centre d'Accueil*", French for Welcome Centre, provides shelter for homeless people, many of whom come from the Spanish side and who, during the day, wander back and forth across the frontier. This building was formerly an office to welcome immigrants mainly from Spain, Portugal and North Africa who entered France in great numbers during the 1960s and 1970s to work.

Opposite the station, a number of cafés have names like Bar du Midi, Bar Le Terminus, Café International and Café de la Frontière. Beyond, in front of some recently built houses, a sign advertises newly built residential flats and villas in Spanish on behalf of a Hendaian estate agency. Other signs with 'Irun' and '*frontière*' written on them show the way along the Avenue d'Espagne to the so-called International Bridge, an example of late nineteenth century architecture linking Hendaia across the Bidasoa river to Irun. Halfway across, an iron post bears the blue, white and red colours of France and the insignia of Napoleon III, Emperor of France from 1852 to 1870. Opposite it, another post bears the red and yellow colours of Spain with the insignia of Isabel II who reigned as Queen of Spain from 1843 to 1870. Now closed to traffic, the bridge is a haven for anglers and tramps. At either end, the old customs booths stand derelict and covered with graffiti.

Across from the station, the Route de Béhobie leads inland to the neighbourhood of Pausu[7] and the Route Nationale 10, while another road takes traffic across the Bidasoa via the more modern Santiago[8] Bridge to Irun. On the right-hand side of the Route de Béhobie, just beyond the road leading to Santiago Bridge, an imposing three-storey building resembling an old Basque farmhouse with a wooden front door and red-painted shutters, is the headquarters of Sokoa, a firm which produces office chairs and which we will have occasion to visit later on. Further along, a residential area alongside the Bidasoa is composed of villas with red-tiled roofs and red or green shutters, and white-walled apartment buildings with tidy gardens. Most of the cars parked in the streets are registered in the département des Pyrénées Atlantiques. But some have Spanish plates showing that they are registered in Gipuzkoa.[9] Back on Santiago Bridge, at mid-point, a Spanish flag flies from a flag-pole. Across the bridge, beyond an open area filled with trucks and shops selling souvenirs and liquor, the Iparraldeko Hiribidea, or Avenida de Iparralde in Spanish and formerly known as the Avenida de Francia, leads up to the centre of Irun.

Irun

Though directly across the Bidasoa from Hendaia, Irun is markedly different in character and appearance. The town was formerly a major base for the *Guardia Civil*, Spain's paramilitary police force, and this combined with the numerous job opportunities provided by the customs service and the railway led to an influx of people from other parts of Spain during the 1950s and 1960s. An active industrial and commercial centre, Irun has a population of around 56,000 inhabitants. Much local activity focuses on rail and lorry transport services and on light industry, capitalising on cross-border trade.

---

[7]   Béhobie is the French name of Pausu.

[8]   Santiago is Spanish and Basque for Saint James. Irun, Hondarribia and Hendaia are located on one of the many pilgrimage routes to St James of Compostella.

[9]   During summer 2000, a new series of number plates was introduced in Spain which no longer show in which province the car is registered. When these were first issued, I interviewed people in Irun and Hondarribia who had different viewpoints about this change. Some expressed nostalgia, saying they liked being able to tell where a car and its driver come from and they were proud to be able to show that they come from Gipuzkoa. Others were indifferent, while a third group saw advantages in the change: some referred to a perceived risk of being the object of derogatory remarks in other parts of Spain, where some people have a negative image of the Basque Country due to the nationalist conflict and the activities of ETA.

Public signs mark the names of the streets and squares in Basque and Spanish. The formal centre of Irun is an open space known as San Juan Plaza in Basque or Plaza San Juan in Spanish, dominated by the town hall at one end. The town hall, dating from 1763, is typical of Hegoalde, built in stone with arcades at ground level and above them a balcony and the foral crest. A flag with the arms of Irun, composed of a castle with a helmet on top and flanked by ostrich plumes and two storks,[10] flutters above the façade. In May 2001, black and white banners declaring "*ETA no. ETA ez*", meaning "No to ETA" in Spanish and Basque, were hung from the balcony, and they were still there over two years later. The entrance, open to the public from 8.00 a.m. to 1.00 p.m. every weekday, is guarded by the municipal police who ask in Basque and Spanish to see visitors' identity cards before allowing them through.

Shops in Irun open at 9.00 or 10.00 a.m. and shut for lunch at 1.00 p.m., opening again at 4.00 p.m. and closing at 7.30 p.m. or 8.00 p.m. Opposite the town hall, the pastry shop and bakery Gaztelu Mendi advertises in Basque and Spanish its Spanish-style white bread and creamy buns. Alongside it is a rich variety of shops and bars. Down one street, the main church of Irun is of imposing size and appearance, contrasting with the 1990s urban park installation around it. Built in local sixteenth century Gothic style, it is dedicated to Our Lady of Juncal, the patron saint of Irun. Nearby, around Urdanibia Plaza, the nineteenth century narrow three-storeyed houses with the woodwork showing and small balconies are among the few surviving remnants of pre-Spanish Civil War Irun. A few have names like 'Gure Etxea', meaning 'Our House', or 'Ongi Etorri', meaning 'Welcome', painted in Basque on their façades, using the orthography of Batua, the unified version of the Basque language that is nowadays taught in schools throughout Euskadi. On Saturdays, Urdanibia Plaza is home to a lively market where vendors from the nearby Gipuzkoan and Nafarroan countryside sell local produce. In the evenings, the numerous bars on this plaza, decorated in rustic Basque style, provide a meeting place for many Basque-speaking youths identifying with the left-wing Basque nationalist cause.

Beyond the square, a street leads through residential areas dating from the 1970s out into the countryside, eventually ending up at the chapel of San Marcial from where the visitor can look out over Irun to Hendaia and Iparralde beyond. At the other end of San Juan Plaza, another pastry shop, named Aguirre after the family who founded it over a century ago, is a popular day-time rendez-vous for elderly ladies taking coffee and pastries together in a cackle of Spanish. At another

---

[10] The castle symbolises defence against enemies, the storks represent vigilance and prudence, the helmet nobility in battle and the feathers the trophies of war.

extremity of the square, which has also managed to preserve nineteenth century buildings, the high street leads past the municipal library, which has a rich selection of newspapers in Spanish and Basque. The only newspaper from Iparralde, however, is the French-language *Sud-Ouest* which, when I came to consult it, I often found untouched.

The street at this end of the square becomes the busy Kolon Ibilbidea (in Basque) and the Paseo Colon (in Spanish), named after Christopher Columbus and lined with late 1950s style apartment blocks, clothes shops, banks and supermarkets, one with a Basque name, Eroski, and another called Consumer. There, as in most public places in Irun, customers often get addressed in Spanish unless they speak first in Basque. Billboards at bus stops advertise the Centro Comercial Txingudi,[11] a shopping centre built in 1996 just outside Irun on the road to San Sebastian, popular with people from Hendaia because of its wide array of choice and lower prices.

A short distance along the avenue, Ensantxe Plaza/Plaza de Ensanche, formerly known as Plaza de España, is another popular meeting place for old people and families with young children, lined with pollarded plane trees and with a band-stand in the middle. At one corner, a stand sells sweets and lottery tickets while a kiosk beside it sells newspapers, including Sud-Ouest. Alongside a café and bars serving Spanish Basque style *pintxos*,[12] to the sound of the Ser Radio Irun, a local branch of a Spanish radio station, are the offices of the Spanish postal service. Round the corner is the town's municipal information point, the SAC.[13] Off this part of the square is a street of apartment buildings and trendy modern bars.

The Kolon Ibilbidea carries on with more shops, cafés and an EuskoTren stop. One of the streets off it is the Aduanak Karrika/Calle de Aduanas, which formerly housed customs control booths where freight destined for France first had to be checked and now is a base for numerous transport agencies. The Kolon Ibilbidea continues over the railway line towards Hondarribia, changing its name to Hondarribia Karrika. To the left, road signs in Spanish and Basque indicate the way to the train station past two hotels called Bidasoa and Los Fronterizos.

Down the hill, the street reaches a roundabout leading into the municipal territory of Hondarribia. Also joining the roundabout are the road to Irun's mainBasque-language school, called Txingudi, housed in a

---

11   This shopping centre is part of a franchise of the French supermarket chain Auchan, known in Spanish as Alcampo.

12   Pintxos are small prettily assembled bits of food. Another more Spanish word for this is *tapas*.

13   *Servicio de Asistencia al Ciudadano*, meaning 'Assistance Service for Citizens' in Spanish.

1980s concrete building, and the highway from Behobia, bypassing the center of Irun. Along the highway, brown and white signboards welcome visitors to Bidasoa-Txingudi. One of the buildings along the road is the Villa Ducourau, the former French consulate, which in 2002 was undergoing restoration in order to house the offices of the Partzuergo. Further back, road signs saying *Francia* and *Frantzia* indicate the way along the Iparraldeko Hiribidea to the frontier and Hendaia. Close to the frontier, a commercial exhibition area is being built as a project of the municipality of Irun, with the financial backing of the Basque government, the provincial government of Gipuzkoa and the Partzuergo. Opposite it, cars with French and Spanish registrations and lorries from various countries queue at a Repsol petrol station which advertises its prices in Basque and Spanish. As customers replace the petrol pump nozzles in their holders, a recorded voice says "Muchas gracias y buen viaje. Eskerrik asko eta bidai on bat" – Spanish and Basque for "Thank you very much and have a good journey". Beyond, opposite an open area formerly occupied by the Spanish customs authorities and now used as a parking area for lorries, are a couple of small hotels, some restaurants and shops selling alcohol, tobacco and Spanish products, many of their wares advertised exclusively in French. The last of the customs booths that once dominated this area was pulled down in November 2001. Vehicles now drive freely back and forth across the frontier.

Hondarribia

Once a fortified town, Hondarribia has two centres – one within the city walls and another just outside. Compared with Irun, Hondarribia has more of a traditional Basque character, and more Basque can be heard spoken on its streets. Thanks to its picturesque fishing port and medieval fortress, Hondarribia draws significant revenues from tourism. In 2001, in an effort to raise Hondarribia's touristic profile, the beach was refashioned to include a big leisure port and a big multi-sport complex. The town's small-scale fishing industry, though less attractive today as a source of work for young Hondarribians than it once was, still plays an important socio-cultural role. Although Hondarribia also has some light industry, it is less developed than Irun, where many of its nearly 16,000 inhabitants work. Since the late 1980s, the population of Hondarribia has grown significantly due to the increasing numbers of people from other parts of Gipuzkoa who use it as a residential base from which to commute to nearby towns for work.

Here too, road signs are written in both Spanish and Basque. The town hall is located within the medieval part of the town, on a narrow cobbled street called Kale Nagusia/Calle Mayor that leads from a medieval gateway into the town up to the main square, Armak Plaza/Plaza de las Armas, where a small fortified castle has been converted into a sophisticated hotel. The town hall is a sixteenth century stone building with arcades on the ground floor and the municipal and foral crests emblazoned above. At the reception desk, marked in Basque above the door on a side entrance under the arcades, a receptionist greets visitors in Basque, switching to Spanish if necessary.

All the buildings on this street are of a similar period and style, tall and narrow, built in brown stone. Some have shops on their ground floor, most of them with signs in both Basque and Spanish. Further up on the left, a building with the Basque name Zuloaga Etxea, or Zuloaga House, after a famous painter of the early twentieth century, houses the municipal library. This is open from 10 a.m., when most other shops in Hondarribia also open, until 7.30 p.m., with a three-hour break for lunch. The librarians generally address visitors in Basque, unless the latter speak first in Spanish. A wide selection of books and newspapers is on offer but, unlike in Irun, no French papers are available.

The main church of Hondarribia is a seventeenth century building dedicated to Our Lady of the Assumption and situated further up the street, just before the square. A few small bars, restaurants and hotels surround it, also of antique appearance. The streets off Kale Nagusia and Armak Plaza are narrow and cobbled, lined by stone-faced buildings divided into small and dark apartments, with the oak beams typical of seventeenth and eighteenth century architecture. Sections of the old part of town, in ruins until recently, are now undergoing restoration.

Beyond the city walls, the fishing port or marina area provides the main social focus for both Hondarribians and visitors. This is reached by walking down the small cobbled streets off the other side of Armak Plaza. In one of these, is located Muara, a bar run by members of the left-wing Basque nationalist movement, whose entrance is marked by a large metal insignia of a black eagle[14] on the wall and a big white, green and red Basque flag, or *ikurriña*, hanging above it. Further down, the tourist office, opened in 1999, displays in its window a big aerial photo of Irun, Hondarribia and Hendaia. The designation "tourist office" is written beside it in Spanish, Basque, French, English, German, Portuguese and Italian, in that order. Pamphlets at the desk advertise touristic and cultural events taking place in Hondarribia, Irun and Hendaia and other parts of Iparralde and Hegoalde. But a map provided by the assistant only features Irun and Hondarribia.

The centre of the marina area is a street called San Pedro Kalea/Calle San Pedro, lined by three-storey buildings in the Basque style with

---

[14]   The black eagle is the symbol of the medieval king of Nafarroa, Sancho the Great. It is used in Basque left-wing nationalist circles as a symbol of aspirations for a return to the Basque unity and sovereignty believed to have existed under his rule.

white-washed walls, green, red or blue-painted woodwork and red-tiled roofs. Originally the homes of fishermen and their families, these houses are mostly now divided into small apartments. Poplar trees line the street, along with a series of bars – *ostatuak* in Basque. There are also numerous fish restaurants, frequented by both locals and visitors. On a wall in one corner of the street, the Basque words "*Hemen Zabala hil zuten*", meaning "Here they killed Zabala", are scrawled in fading red paint, commemorating the shooting to death of a man from Irun by Spanish police in 1976 during a demonstration in favour of an amnesty for Basques imprisoned for political offences or involvement in ETA's violence. People walking up and down the street, partially closed to traffic, stop to chat to friends and relatives and, depending on the time of day, take a drink and a pintxo at the various bars. Children and teenagers hang out around the two sweet shops at either end of the street.

A few streets away, the jetty of the old fishing harbour provides a good view of Hendaia. Here, until 1997, fishing boats unloaded their catch for sale. A few fishing boats are still to be seen parked on the cement beside the harbour and close to the small early nineteenth century church dedicated to the fishermen. In 1998, the bulk of fishing activity, together with the offices of the local confraternity of fishermen, the *Hondarribiko Arrantzaleen Kofradia*, moved to a new site beyond the mouth of the estuary and the beach area at the other end of the marina. Since this date, the jetty of the old fishing harbour has been used by two small firms, one based in Hondarribia, and the other in Hendaia, that provide a ferry service across the estuary between the two towns.

Further along the estuary, smart cafés and bars lining the walkway to the beach advertise their wares only in Spanish and French. Two businesses in a street nearby, a veterinary clinic and a driving school, include the word Txingudi in their names. Close to the beach, a large residential area of villas and apartment blocks has grown steadily since the 1970s. Many of them, built in the late 1990s, have Basque names. This residential area is fast developing, encroaching upon the green fields that were once farmland. Amongst these houses are the two buildings housing the Basque-language school of Hondarribia. One of the roads leads into a range of hills called Jaizkibel, and on top of one of these hills is a chapel dedicated to the Virgin of Guadalupe, the patron of Hondarribia.

Going back in the direction of Irun, the lamp-posts are adorned with banners bearing the text "*Euskal Presoak Euskal Herrira*" and "*Euskal Presoak Etxera*",[15] calling for the return to the Basque Country of those people held in prisons in other parts of Spain on charges of involvement

---

[15]   In Basque this translates as 'Basque Prisoners back to the Basque Country', and 'Basque Prisoners back home'.

in Basque nationalist violence. The roundabout of San Kristobal, adorned with a small fountain and a flagpole bearing an ikurriña, leads into Arana Kalea, the main road along the estuary to Irun, named after Sabino Arana, founder of the Basque Nationalist Party, EAJ. Off it are the airport, sign-posted in both Spanish and Basque, and several industrial warehouses. A pet shop called Txingudi advertises its name in small green and black letters. Until 2001, much of the land to the right of the road was marshland interspersed with small vegetable patches, marking a break between Irun and Hondarribia. More recently, however, the area has been made over to the construction of a series of low-rent apartment blocks, as part of a social plan of the municipal council of Hondarribia in response to the Basque government's social legislation requirements. As a result, the delimitation between Hondarribia and Irun is becoming less and less clear.

As our quick tour of Bidasoa-Txingudi has shown, each of the three towns is marked both by expressions of Basque identity and by features relating to the state of which it is part. While Hendaia's French character is visually very evident, street names and road signs are often in Basque as well as French. In Irun and Hondarribia, the Basque influence is even stronger. Most roadsigns have been bilingual since the 1980s, reflecting the fact that both Basque and Spanish are official languages in Euskadi. While in Hendaia and elsewhere in Iparralde, the names of streets and public buildings continue to be named after French public figures, in Hegoalde many places once called after Spanish public figures have been rebaptised with Basque names.

Differences are also evident in other respects, from the opening and closing times of shops and bars to aesthetics, social behaviour and taste in food and drink. In the streets of Irun and Hondarribia, one's nose may be assailed by the scent of eau de cologne worn by many people, an unfamiliar smell in Hendaia. The smells in a Hendaian bakery differ from those in a bakery in Irun. Lunchtime smells in Irun and Hondarribia tend to be dominated by the odour of frying olive oil, while in Hendaia, the smell of *steak-frites*, or beef steak with chips, often fills the air. Sounds are also different. Hendaia is quiet for most of the day, with little noise other than the sound of traffic on the Avenue Charles de Gaulle. After 7.00 p.m., when most people are at home preparing for their evening meal, even this noise dies down. Irun and Hondarribia, by contrast, are alive all day long with the sound of people chatting in the streets and cars and motorbikes driving around, and the activity continues in the evening. People take pre-dinner drinks and, on the weekend, the bars carry on being lively till well into the early morning.

While French Basque cooking has its own specialities, I often heard people from both Iparralde and Hegoalde comment that if one wants a 'real' eating experience, one is better off in Hegoalde. Standing in bars drinking and eating pintxos is a ritual fundamental to the concept of eating in Hegoalde and unmatched in Iparralde. Hendaians, when thinking about a meal out, often think of Spanish Basque food, attracted by the experience of being in a lively Spanish Basque restaurant. Likewise, inhabitants of Hegoalde, rather than considering eating out in Iparralde, often prefer enjoying the liveliness of their own bars and restaurants. Indeed, something often remarked in the area is that if you want peace and quiet, you are best advised to go to Iparralde.

Differences are also evident in the way people dress and present themselves. In Hendaia, clothes shops focus on American-style sweaters, jeans and anoraks, while in Irun and Hondarribia they vary between a rather conservative homogenous style, with dark greens, brown, black, burgundy and purple, and funky surf wear. Fashion consciousness seems generally to be greater in Hegoalde. During the time that I was doing my fieldwork, the fashion among many young people in Hegoalde was large bell-bottomed trousers and tight surftops for girls and baggy surf trousers and sweatshirts with the label showing – either made in Hegoalde or in classic Australian or American styles – for boys. Amongst the slightly older generations, the darker and more sober dress stand out. To match these clothes, many women in Hegoalde wear plentiful make-up. Many also wear their hair long, and older women have it permed.

CHAPTER 2

Past and Present Boundaries
in the Basque Country

When Carles Pons i Altes, a teacher of classical guitar at the Conservatory of Irun, decided to organise a ceremony in honour of Lluis Companys, the former president of the Generalitat, the government of Catalonia, assassinated by the government of Spain's former dictator, General Francisco Franco, in 1940, he had little idea of the commotion his plan would cause. A Catalan by birth, resident in Irun since the mid 1990s, Mr. Pons i Altes wanted to take the opportunity of commemorating a historical incident that took place in the area to pay homage, not just to the Catalan politician, but to all Spaniards, including those from the Basque Country, many of whom had been forced into exile during the Civil War.

The specific event on which he wanted to focus took place on 29 August 1940. Companys had taken refuge in France along with the president of the Basque government, José Antonio Aguirre, but had been captured by the Gestapo. On 29 August 1940, he was handed over to the troops of Franco on Santiago Bridge between Hendaia and Irun. A few months later, he was taken to Barcelona, where he was tried by a military court, sentenced to death and shot. Mr. Pons i Altes planned to commemorate the sixtieth anniversary of the event, in a ceremony on the bridge linking Hendaia to Irun at 10.30 p.m. on 29 August 2000.

But few things are simple in the Basque Country, and least of all a ceremony with historical references and political overtones. What Mr. Pons i Altes had intended as a ceremony in favour of peace and reconciliation rapidly turned into a confrontation reflecting the conflict and symbolic struggle still taking place in the Basque Country. A few days before the ceremony was scheduled to take place, police defused a bomb connected to the car of the boyfriend of Cristina Laborda, a Socialist member of the Irun town council. At about the same time, Borja Semper, the senior representative of the Spanish conservative party, Partido Popular (PP),[1] in the Irun town council, announced that he would not attend the ceremony on the grounds that representatives of

---

[1] Meaning 'Popular Party'.

the left-wing Basque nationalist party Euskal Herritarrok (EH),[2] would also be present. "It is indecent", he declared in a letter to the Hegoalde-based newspaper Diario Vasco,[3] "that those who today give support to shooting someone in the back of the head for the mere fact of his having different ideological ideas, should be shameless enough to pay homage to a person who was killed for defending freedom".

Then, on the very day of the ceremony, Manuel Indiano, a PP councillor in the nearby town of Zumarraga, was assassinated by ETA. In spite of this, the organisers of the ceremony decided to go ahead. At 8.00 p.m., the mayor of Irun and most members of the town council – with the sole exception of the councillors representing EH – met outside the town hall. With them were the mayors of Hondarribia and Hendaia, as well as representatives of the Basque and Catalan parliaments and the mainstream Basque and Catalan nationalist parties. Instead of going straight in for a reception, as had been planned, they stood outside the building in silence for fifteen minutes as a sign of respect for Mr. Indiano and in protest against his assassination. In front of them, a small crowd of journalists and other onlookers stood watching.

Amongst them were a group of people who had come in buses from Catalonia for the event. While the politicians stood in silence, a man in a t-shirt and baggy trousers broke out of the crowd. Going up to the politicians and looking them in the face, he laid a Catalan flag on the ground in front of them. Throughout this performance, none of the politicians flinched and all remained looking straight ahead. Eventually, uniformed Basque policemen took him and his flag away.

The fifteen minutes of silence over, the politicians proceeded into the town hall where the EH representatives, who had refused to participate in the mourning ceremony, were waiting for the reception to begin. Meanwhile, on the bridge linking Irun to Hendaia, several hundred people were gathering to watch the ceremony. Graded benches had been set up, with reserved seats for local dignitaries to sit behind the politicians in the front row. Further away, in the old customs area, a bigger crowd gathered around a screen on which were projected the scenes taking place on the bridge. Amongst them were people carrying Basque and Catalan flags and others with banners bearing the legend "Euskal Presoak Etxera".

At 10.30 p.m., the ceremony began as planned with a series of speeches by political representatives. The Socialist mayor of Irun declared: "We are here today to give homage to Lluis Companys, a man

---

[2]   Euskal Herritarrok means 'We the Basque people'. Previously known as *Herri Batasuna*, or 'Popular Union', and subsequently renamed simply *Batasuna*, it is the only party which refuses to condemn ETA.

[3]   Edition of 26 August 2000.

who fought for freedom and who was killed in its name. And to our sorrow, we have to mention another death. Another person to whom they did exactly the same as to Companys, whose life was taken away by a group of fascists who are incapable of resolving their problems with dialogue". At this point, the sound of whistling and shouts of "Euskal Presoak Etxera" and "Amnistia"[4] rang out from a few people in the audience behind the politicians and in the crowd around the screen. The ceremony continued, but each time a politician made a reference to the recent attacks, the shouting and whistling resumed.

At one point, an argument broke out in the crowd by the big screen between a young woman holding a banner with the text "Euskal Presoak Etxera" and an old man who had been a refugee in France during the Civil War. Things calmed down when the speeches ended, giving way to a play in which actors dressed in 1930s clothes re-enacted scenes of people fleeing the war in Spain and trying to cross the bridge to safety in Hendaia. These scenes were a prelude to the re-enactment, by actors dressed up as Gestapo and Francoist officers, of the handing over of Companys. The main part of the performance ended with his shooting. His corpse was left lying on the ground on the bridge in a pool of blood.

As this anecdote shows, the past continues to condition attitudes and reactions among the inhabitants of Bidasoa-Txingudi today. The commemoration of an incident that took place in the early days of the Franco dictatorship at a time when France was under Nazi occupation is capable of re-igniting passions and antagonisms sixty years later almost as if it had happened yesterday. Violence and bloodshed exacerbate the tensions created by political rivalries, highlighting a struggle between opposing forces that dominates life in much of the Basque Country. In terms of boundary-drawing, political violence contributes to and becomes an integral part of a process of polarisation, forcing people to one side or the other and compelling them to reflect on their identity in relation to it. More than just a competition for political power, we witness here a contest between different intellectual constructions of reality conditioned by partisan interpretations of the past and the present.

The re-enactment of this event, although anchored in the history of the Spanish state, had particular local resonance. Among the participants and onlookers, a number were either former refugees themselves or the descendants of refugees from the Spanish Civil War, including José-

---

[4] In Basque this translates as 'Amnesty'. HB members demand that the Spanish government establish an amnesty, involving an end of police pursuit of ETA and freeing all the presoak, and subsequently set up a referendum in the Basque Country on the possibility of independence.

Luís 'Kotte' Ecenarro,[5] the deputy and subsequent successor of the mayor of Hendaia, whose parents had fled from Gipuzkoa to France during the Civil War. But there were other equally deep roots to the antagonisms played out in this incident. Central to them was the issue of who has the right to claim Basque identity, illustrated, for example, in the EH councillors' refusal to join the other politicians in their fifteen minutes of silence in protest against ETA. Despite the three towns' geographical proximity, differing attitudes to the state, differing individual ways of experiencing Basqueness, and strong local allegiances, all stood on this occasion in the way of a sense of common identity. Such oppositions are evident at other times too, not just in the context of public commemorations of historical events such as this one, but in the normal pattern of everyday life.

A Historical Overview of the Basque Country

If history is a source of controversy in a social context, it is not surprising that the incorporation of historical materials should be a difficult challenge for the anthropologist (Heiberg, 1989). Like any social phenomenon, history is a construct, often influenced by political interests. Furthermore, just as people fashion history, history fashions people, conditioning the development and maintenance of notions of the personal and collective self. Bearing in mind the inter-connection between the use of symbols and the exercise of political power, we must recognise that it is impossible to have any one 'true' version of history. Rather, all socially accepted versions have some degree of validity. There is no one objective historical basis from which contemporary anthropological research can proceed.

This is particularly evident in relation to attempts to understand and relate Basque history. Perceptions in the Basque Country are conditioned by political partisanship and propaganda. While the French and Spanish states have constructed their own versions of 'national' history, Basque nationalists accuse Spanish and French authorities of imposing their versions of history on 'the Basque people'. In demanding the right to interpret their own history themselves, they claim legitimacy for their attempts to construct and represent their view of the past (e.g. Eguren 1918:328; Haritschelar, 1983; 2001:8; Keating, 2001; Urla, 1987:50). Much Basque historical research has in fact been conducted with explicitly political aims in mind. This can make discussion of historical matters highly emotive, with participants frequently accusing each other of bias. For the purposes of this study, rather than getting embroiled in the

---

[5]   Kotte is a Basque equivalent of José-Luis, which Mr. Ecenarro prefers to use for himself.

politics of history, I shall endeavour to situate Bidasoa-Txingudi within a wider Basque, French and Spanish historical and socio-political context, while restricting my historical references to dates and events which cannot be denied by any partisan camp and have come to acquire popular importance (Foucault, 1977).

A defined notion of 'Basque identity' in a modern sense is a fairly recent phenomenon. But there is some evidence to suggest that the inhabitants of this region shared features setting them apart from other peoples around them. Anthropological research has produced evidence of commonalities among the inhabitants of the region in terms of cranial features and blood type. Traces of Basque roots have been found in place names across a much wider area than that covered by today's Basque Country.

If the Basque Country as a whole can be identified as a loosely defined cultural and geographic concept, the only time that it formed anything close to a united administrative entity was at the beginning of the eleventh century under the king of Nafarroa, Sancho the Great. What the seven provinces of the Basque Country did have in common until the late eighteenth century, however, was a particular set of codified privileges, known in Spanish as *fueros*, which their inhabitants enjoyed within the larger configuration of the French and Spanish kingdoms.

South of the Pyrenees, this system was particularly useful to the Spanish monarchy during the sixteenth century, when national energies were largely focused on overseas discoveries with little emphasis on nation-building at home (Alvarez-Junco, 1996). At a time when the Spanish monarchy was concerned with the preservation of Christian dominion over territories recently reclaimed from the Moors, the Basques were recognised as the best of Spanish subjects, due to their legendarily pure non-Moorish blood. The foral charters granted to the Basque provinces explicitly underlined the noble character conferred on them by the distinctive linguistic and racial characteristics of their inhabitants (Greenwood, 1977). In exchange for political and economic autonomy, the provinces owed allegiance to the monarchy in times of war, a relationship that helped to consolidate a sense of Spanish unity. Equally, however, the provinces retained their individuality and a sense of difference amongst themselves. Occasionally, this led to conflict as the shape of alliances with French and Spanish monarchs shifted. Provincial government ordinances made no mention of such a thing as a Basque identity, and the kingdom of Nafarroa never saw itself as a 'Basque' monarchy.

North of the Pyrenees, shifting feudal allegiances and dynastic changes brought Lapurdi, Siberoa and eventually Behe Nafarroa into the orbit of the French Crown during the sixteenth century. The consolidation of state borders nonetheless progressed slowly. The Edict of Pau, signed in 1629, was intended as a step towards the delineation of the border between Spain and France, but continued warfare between the two kingdoms made this ineffective. This situation was not resolved until 1659, when the Treaty of the Pyrenees was signed on the island now known as the Island of the Pheasants in the middle of the Bidasoa. Peace between the two states was sealed by the marriage of the French King Louis XIV to the Infanta Maria-Teresa, daughter of Philip IV of Spain, under a contract signed on the same island in 1660. However, actual demarcation of the frontier did not come about for another two centuries.

Following the French Revolution in 1789, French republican zeal for *égalité* did away with the historic privileges of the provinces of Siberoa, Lapurdi and Behe Nafarroa. Despite efforts by the brothers Dominique and Dominique-Joseph Garat, both lawyers and the latter a deputy in the local parliament of Lapurdi, to rally the local institutions of the three French Basque provinces in defence of their special privileges in a republican France, the French National Assembly went ahead with the administrative reorganisation of France into départements. In 1790, the National Assembly voted to set up a new département including Behe Nafarroa, Lapurdi, Siberoa and the linguistically and culturally distinct province of Béarn, stripped of their respective provincial privileges.

In the Spanish Basque provinces, other political developments led to the gradual erosion of the fueros. In 1832, the first Carlist war pitted rival factions against each other in a struggle for succession to the Spanish throne motivated in part by differing interpretations of the role of the fueros. Carlism took its name from Don Carlos, the brother of the late King Fernando VII, whose claim to the Spanish throne was championed by the inhabitants of the Basque provinces and Nafarroa. On the other side, the King's widow, Maria-Cristina of Naples, was defending the right to succession of her daughter Isabel. As a political movement, Carlism implied a conception of the state based on the divine right of the monarchy and Catholic supremacy, combined with the protection of traditional social order and local autonomies, in a manner totally opposed to Spanish liberalism influenced by the ideas of the French Revolution. While those close to the Spanish Crown viewed the fueros as concessions of privilege granted by the monarchy which could be modified or withdrawn, the supporters of Carlism viewed them as a written attestation confirming the ancient common-law bases of Basque society. When the first Carlist war ended in 1839 with victory for Queen Isabel, the Treaty of Vergara of that year providing for the minimal preservation of the fueros was accepted in Gipuzkoa and Bizkaia but rejected in Nafarroa and Araba.

A few decades later, chronic political instability and a resurgence of anti-clericalism under the First Spanish Republic between 1873 and 1874 gave Carlism a new opportunity to show its face. But the second Carlist war between partisans of Queen Isabel and the followers of Don Carlos was no more successful than the first, and the final defeat of Carlism in 1876 led to the abolition of the foral system in all of the Spanish Basque provinces except Nafarroa. In place of the fueros, the Spanish government agreed to a special fiscal and administrative régime – the *conciertos económicos* – for the Basque provinces, satisfying Basque urban liberals who were mainly concerned with fiscal autonomy. Among the nascent Basque nationalist movement, the fueros had begun to be seen as a symbol of the collective and historic rights of the Basques. Their abolition set the stage for the explicitly regional conflicts with the Spanish state which continue today.

Basque Nationalism

During the late nineteenth century, while the seat of political power in Spain remained in Madrid, industrial wealth developed in Catalonia and the Basque provinces of Bizkaia and Gipuzkoa. It was during this period that Basque nationalism emerged in the port city of Bilbao. Industrialisation, resulting in mass migration from the rest of Spain to these areas, accentuated local concerns about territorial and ethnic identity. These were translated into a perception that Basque traditional social values, equated with some primordially defined form of Basque identity, were under siege. Developing nationalist sentiments led in 1895 to the formation of the Basque nationalist party EAJ as a means of defending these values. Although EAJ initially attracted people of lower middle-class backgrounds and anti-industrial sentiment, it gradually expanded its reach and appeal to members of the grande bourgeoisie and liberal segments of Bizkaia society as a Christian Democrat party (Larronde, 1977).

Under the short-lived Spanish Republic, a left-wing government in Madrid promised the Basque provinces and Catalonia the status of autonomous regions. This plan, however, was thwarted by the outbreak of civil war in 1936. Republicanists and Basque nationalists were defeated by the right-wing forces of General Franco and the EAJ leadership went into exile to Paris. Franco's subsequent military dictatorship ruthlessly repressed regionalist sentiments. In the Basque provinces, the Basque language, already reduced to a low status as a language spoken only by a mainly rural and 'backward' section of society, suffered even more. Banned from use in public places, it remained confined to the family domain and gradually less and less taught to children. In reaction, the Basque language became a symbol of resistance amongst anti-Franco movements. It remains a rallying point for Basque nationalists today.

In 1953, a youth faction of EAJ seceded to create ETA, a left-wing movement committed to seeking Basque independence. Described by Collins (1986:12) as "a practically exclusively urban phenomenon", ETA reflected the situation in Bizkaia, where industrial development during the 1950s prompted soul-searching about what it meant to be Basque. Images of traditional country folk as the 'authentic' Basques provided an idealised model for youths who led urban industrial life-styles but who claimed to feel Basque too. Stressing the importance of language as a tool for recreating Basque identity, ETA set out to develop a broad-based working-class constituency, including the descendants of immigrant workers in industrial communities. Previously excluded from traditional conservative Basque nationalist aspirations, such people were now able, by learning Basque, even if only superficially, to gain entry into the less narrowly defined community of the left-wing Basque nationalists.

Zulaika (1989), in his anthropological research on the cultural context of political violence, notes how the traditional and religious values of rural parts of the Basque Country, such as honour, physical strength and Christian and pagan mysticism, played a central part in the birth of ETA and the support that it initially enjoyed. Cultural references to *Ama Birjina*, or the Virgin Mary, and *Ama Lur*, or Mother Earth, provided a basis for the constitution of a front against outsiders occupying the Basques' 'home-land', such as government officials and members of the paramilitary Guardia Civil with no cultural or kin relations to the community, catego-rised as "non Basques" (Heiberg, 1980:47). Watson, in an article on the way in which Basque nationalists draw on folk culture for political pur-poses, remarks how Basque folklore becomes a source of 'Basque truth', whose basis is "namely an essentialist difference from that which is Spanish" (1996a:29).

As a strongly Catholic area, the Basque Country traditionally produced many candidates for the priesthood. The association of religious piety with Basqueness was long one of the tenets of Basque society, summed up in the phrase *euskaldun fededun*, or 'Basque-speaker and believer'. During this period of political repression, it was not uncommon, in semi-naries across the Basque Country, for seminarists and their teachers to sympathise with strong feelings of Basqueness. Together with their theological training, students felt a strong attachment to their local com-munity, which it was their duty to guide. Many became involved with ETA in its early years.

In parallel, a clandestine movement in favour of Basque language edu-cation, provided by *ikastolak*, or Basque-language schools, emerged during the 1950s as an alternative to Spanish education with the aim of 'euskaldun-izing' children, or converting them into Basque speakers. The movement eventually became tolerated by the Franco régime and was able to operate within a legal framework applicable to private initiatives. In order to revive the use of Basque amongst the adult population, the association *AEK*, short for *Alfabetatze Euskalduntze Koordinakunde*[6] was set up in 1965. Financed by fund-raising activities, private benefactors and

---

[6]   This is Basque for 'Coordination for Basque Language and Literacy'.

on subsidies from local municipalities that sympathise with its endeavour, AEK extended its activities in 1980 to Iparralde.

After the death of Franco in 1975, Spain emerged from a period of political uncertainty to adopt a system of parliamentary democracy and constitutional monarchy. In 1978, the political party *Herri Batasuna* (HB)[7] was created in Hegoalde to represent the political interests of ETA in local and regional elections. One of its first concerns was to oppose a new Spanish constitution put to referendum that year. Proponents of the new constitution used the term 'nation' to refer both to the Spanish nation as a whole and to the 'historic nationalities' of its major non-Castilian populations in Catalonia, Euskadi and Galicia. However this did not satisfy many regional representatives, particularly in the Basque Country, where nationalists complained that it did not go far enough in terms of regional autonomy. For this reason and because the proposed constitution ignored their demand for the incorporation of Nafarroa, believed to be the cradle of the Basque people (Wastell, 1994), as part of an autonomous Basque Country,[8] the Basque nationalist parties encouraged voters to abstain.

In the event, the referendum won a majority of "yes" votes both in the Basque Country and in the rest of Spain. Under the new constitution, Spain became a State of Autonomous Regions, each with its own government, parliament and administrative system. In Euskadi, the Statute of Autonomy, voted by popular referendum in October 1979,[9] established the territory of the Autonomous Basque Community as the provinces of Araba, Bizkaia and Gipuzkoa, each with their own administrative system, called *diputación* in Spanish and *foraldia* in Basque. Basque and Spanish were declared its official languages. EAJ, as the leading party in the regional parliament, took on the leadership of the new regional government.

By this time, some ETA militants had put their arms aside and entered politics as members of a newly founded political party, *Euskadiko Eskerra* (EE), or 'Basque Left'.[10] With the creation of Euskadi, more militants left ETA, believing that it had lost its *raison d'être*. Nonetheless, because the electoral turnout for the referendum had been very low

---

[7]   In Basque, this translates as the 'Popular Union'.

[8]   The Constitution does in fact allow Nafarroa to join the Basque Autonomous Community should Nafarroa's citizens so wish.

[9]   41.14% of the population of Gipuzkoa, Araba and Bizkaia abstained, while 53.13% of voters of the population voted "yes" to the Statute of Gernika. All of the political parties, with the exception of HB participated in the negotiation of the Statute. HB recommended abstention during the referendum, considering the Statute to be flawed.

[10] This eventually merged with the Basque socialist party, the *Partido Socialista de Euskadi* (PSE), in 1993 to become the PSE-EE.

in the Basque Country,[11] some Basque nationalists claimed that the Basques had rejected the new constitution. Many of these took the view that ETA should continue its military strategy until full independence for Euskadi and the incorporation of Nafarroa and Iparralde were obtained. Thus began what Letamendia has called the "*front du refus*" (1997:57), a movement of 'counter-power' or anti-establishmentarianism embodied by a so-called Basque movement for national liberation, grouping a range of Basque social and cultural associations under the banner of left-wing Basque nationalism. In 1986, a schism occurred within EAJ, leading to the creation of *Eusko Alkartasuna* (EA).[12] This party distinguished itself from EAJ as being more determined in its quest for independence with its 'social-democratic' strategy, and from HB supporters by its condemnation of violent tactics. It went on, however, to run as an alliance with EAJ in many elections.

On the French side of the frontier, modern Basque nationalist sentiment emerged as a social and political force in the 1960s. Much of its inspiration came from Hegoalde, fuelled by the presence on French soil of Basque militants who had fled Franco's Spain to live in Iparralde. Under the protection of the French state as political refugees, these militants "continued with the lifestyle to which they were accustomed back home: socializing in bars, and so on", recalls José Itçaina, a Hendaian school teacher. "They brought life to our streets. Such a contrast to the way we live, with our French mentality..."

In contrast with Euskadi's predominantly industrial economy, Iparralde was more dependent on tourism and agriculture. Farming in Iparralde is mostly small scale and family-run, and heavily dependent on EU and French government subsidies. A lack of educational infrastructures,[13] combined with a relative paucity of job opportunities, meant that a significant proportion of young people had to go elsewhere in France to study and find employment. Reflecting on their situation in a culturally and linguistically distinct area marginalised from the rest of France and following a Marxist-Leninist discourse on the inequality of classes and economic oppression, some young people began to see the French government as deliberately keeping Iparralde in a state of "third worldishness" (Collins, 1986:212). The first organised group of modern Basque nationalists in Iparralde was created in 1960 under the name of

---

[11] 55.35% of the population of Euskadi abstained (http://www.elecciones.net).

[12] *Eusko Alkartasuna* means the Basque Gathering.

[13] The only tertiary education facility in Iparralde is a small pluridisciplinary faculty in Bayonne that is a satellite of the University of Pau, the main administrative centre of the département des Pyrénées Atlantiques. The next closest universities in France are in Bordeaux and Toulouse.

Enbata. Presenting themselves as a political group in the legislative elections of 1967, they received 4.63% of the votes.[14]

In 1969, following the model launched in Hegoalde over a decade earlier, a group of Basque nationalists and culturalists in Iparralde opened their first ikastola for small children in the village of Arangoitze. Parents formed an association called *Seaska* to provide funding and administrative support for the ikastola, since they received no support from the French government. In 1975, a group of Basque nationalist youths set up their own armed organisation modelled on ETA, which they called *Iparretarrak*.[15] This group claimed responsibility for a series of attacks on French government offices and "non-Basque sensitive" tourist trade initiatives, culminating in the early 1980s with a series of dramatic events, involving the death of both militants and police officials, as well as a few people mistaken as targets.

Some members of the local clergy supported movements for the re-assertion of the Basque language and Basque culture. At village level, younger people organised themselves into *herri taldeak*, or village groups which coordinated cultural activities promoting the "revival" of a "Basque nation" and maintained contact with Hegoalde. Mobilisation during the 1980s revolved around the idea of the 'internal colonialism of the French state'. As part of their drive to promote an indigenous economy, Basque nationalists attacked the tourist trade. In response, restaurant owners and others working in the tourist trade created an association to protect their interests. They called this "Turismoa bai" (Yes to Tourism) in Basque, in their own counterattack against what they saw as the Basque nationalists' control of Basque symbols. Tensions increased dramatically as a result of the activities of a secret Spanish right-wing paramilitary organisation called *GAL*[16] which engaged in clandestine operations, including shootings and assassinations of ETA activists hiding on Iparralde soil.

In 1986, a left-wing nationalist party linked to HB was set up in Iparralde under the name of *Euskal Batasuna* (EB)[17] as part of a drive for

---

[14] Enbata was disbanded in 1974, though its spirit remains alive in the weekly magazine of the same name widely read by Basque nationalists across Iparralde. In its place, another political grouping emerged, under the name *Euskal Herriko Alderdi Sozialista* meaning 'Socialist party of the Basque Country'. It did not, however, fare any better in the legislative elections of 1978 (3.4%).

[15] *Iparretarrak* means 'Those of the North'.

[16] GAL stands for *Grupo Antiterrorista de Liberación*, which is Spanish for 'Antiterrorist Liberation Group'. It was active during the 1980s, operating on the French side of the border thanks apparently to the tacit connivence of the French authorities. In the 1990s, several members of the Spain's former Socialist government were proven to have had links with this organisation.

[17] *Euskal Batasuna* means the 'Basque Union'.

closer coordination between the left-wing nationalist movements on both sides of the frontier. At the same time, a younger generation of Basque militants in Iparralde set up an alternative Basque nationalist organisation, under the name of *Patxa*. Viewing the older militants as too old-fashioned concerned only with the preservation of Basque culture and language in a traditional rural context, Patxa called for a focus on urban problems and the difficulties faced by young people. It also adopted a strategy that originated in Hegoalde, *Insumisoa* – or the refusal by young men to fulfill national conscription requirements. In 1988, the various left-wing nationalist factions in Iparralde merged under the name of *Abertzaleen Batasuna* (AB),[18] with the objective of presenting a united front in municipal elections. EA also established itself in Iparralde that year and EAJ followed suit in 1990. In the legislative elections of 1993, these Basque nationalist parties won a combined total of 6.65% of the votes.

During the 1990s, Basque nationalists in Iparralde shifted their strategy away from direct demands for independence to attempts at negotiation with regional and state authorities for special conventions in favour of linguistic, cultural and economic development in the area. Demands for the creation of a *"département du Pays basque"* became one of their main rallying points, based on the idea that a separate administrative structure would assist the economic and rural development of Iparralde. Graffiti and posters demanding *"independentzia"* gave way to slogans such as *"departamendua orain"*, or "département now". The French government responded by supporting the creation by the Regional Council of Aquitaine, the General Council of the département des Pyrénées Atlantiques and locally elected politicians of a special *Convention spécifique Pays basque 2010*, whose aim is to develop long-term cultural, linguistic and economic projects for Iparralde, with the collaboration of local Basque associations. However the French government has continued to reject demands for the creation of a new département, ostensibly because it does not consider this to be a feasible entity but in reality out of fear that this might foster ethnic separatism with negative consequences for the integrity of the French nation-state.[19]

Against this background of continued frustration for the Basque nationalist cause, collaboration between Basque nationalists on both sides of the frontier led in August 1998 to the signing of the Treaty of Lizarra-Garazi.[20] This confirmed the mutual recognition of the various nationalist

---

18 *Abertzaleen Batasuna* means the 'Union of Nationalists'.

19 In 1999, for instance, the then Interior Minister, Jean-Pierre Chevènement, declared that there was "nothing to gain from the setting up of ethnic relations in Europe, other than to Balkanize the whole of Europe" (*Le Monde*, 4 October 1999).

20 Signed in the towns of Lizarra (Estella in Spanish) in Nafarroa and Donibane Garazi (Saint Jean Pied de Port in French) in Behe Nafarroa.

parties as representatives of Euskal Herria and formalised an agreement to form a common front in negotiations with the Spanish and French governments. In this climate of consolidation, and in an attempt to draw a parallel with the Northern Ireland peace process, ETA proclaimed a ceasefire, declaring itself ready to negotiate with the Spanish government. Amid the resulting optimism and expressions of goodwill between Basque nationalist parties, some Basque nationalist groups explored new avenues of non-violent mobilisation. EH intensified its campaign for the transfer to the Basque Country of Basque militants in Spanish jails, under the slogan "Euskal Presoak Euskal Herrira", this time with the support of the moderate Basque nationalist parties.

The new wave of optimism was not to last long, however. In December 1999, ETA announced the end of its ceasefire, claiming that the Spanish government had made no effort to cooperate with EH or respond to its demands for the repatriation of Basque militants and that the other Basque nationalist parties had failed to commit to a genuinely united Basque nationalist project. ETA resumed its killings, targeting not only members of the Spanish army, the PP and the PSE, and businessmen, but also judges, journalists and members of the Basque regional police force. This return to violence shocked many people on both sides of the frontier. Even some left-wing Basque nationalists who had believed that violence was legitimate in the struggle for 'Basque liberation' now felt disillusionment and dared to express their disapproval of ETA. Suspicions that ETA had taken advantage of the ceasefire to re-arm led to a serious breach in relations between EH and the other Basque nationalist parties.

During my stay in Bidasoa-Txingudi, attacks were made on PP and PSE councillors in Irun and Hondarribia and on local bases of the Guardia Civil, as well as on some of the local media. Each time an incident clearly involving ETA occurred, members of the municipal councils, with the exception of the EH representatives, stood in silence for five minutes in front of their town halls in protest against the violence. In February 2001, police discovered in an industrial part of Irun the place where a kidnapped Basque empresario, José-María Aldaia, had been kept hidden by ETA five years earlier. At about the same time, left-wing Basque nationalist militants in Irun and Hondarribia were arrested for acts of sabotage. It was during these moments of tension that the municipal council of Irun hung out the banners "ETA no, ETA ez" from the balcony of the town hall in May 2001. Throughout this period, associations demanding the repatriation of imprisoned Basque militants continued to stage demonstrations in the locality, walking around with banners and photos of the prisoners to the sound of melancholy music. But while prior to the end of ETA's ceasefire such demonstrations had attracted relatively large numbers of supporters, the level of support now diminished, with most passers-by ignoring the demon-strators.

Turnout for parliamentary elections in May 2001 was a striking 79.8%, with EAJ-EA winning a clear majority. EH, by contrast, saw its electoral support drop from around 15% to 10.1%. Shortly afterwards, in an interview granted only to the Basque-language paper *Egunkaria* and the left-wing Basque nationalist paper *Gara*, ETA representatives rejected any responsibility for the electoral downfall of EH. This party, mean-while, engaged in a process of internal debate which led to its reformation in June 2001 under the name Batasuna. However, this was not sufficient to retain disillusioned EH supporters.

ETA's resumption of violence also prompted serious self-questioning among left-wing Basque nationalists in Iparralde. Supporters of AB who had never before criticised ETA became vociferous in their disapproval of its actions, seeing these as a hindrance to the Basque cause. Tensions came to a head in September 2001, when about one third of AB's mem-bers decided to join the newly formed Hegoalde party of Batasuna as part of an Euskal Herria-wide strategy. The majority that remained in AB issued a public condemnation of violence and declared themselves in favour of an Iparralde-centred nationalist campaign on the basis that the situations there required local left-wing Basque nationalists to adopt a different approach to that of their counterparts in Hegoalde.

In September 2002, Basque nationalists on both sides of the state fron-tier suffered a further jolt when a Spanish judge, Baltasar Garzón, with the support of the Spanish government, declared Batasuna illegal on the grounds of its alleged links with ETA. Soon afterwards, in September 2002, in an attempt to rally Basque nationalists of all political hues around a common cause, Juan Jose Ibarretxe, the EAJ president of the Basque government, put forward a proposal for a popular consultation to resolve the continuing dispute over the status of the Basque region. Predictably, this was rejected both by the PP government in Madrid, which claimed that it violated the Spanish constitution, and by the left-wing Basque nationalists, who maintained that it did not go far enough. In the months that followed, Judge Garzón launched further proceedings against Basque social and cultural associations, including the Basque language-teaching organisation AEK, the youth group *Segi* and the association supporting imprisoned Basque militants, Askatasuna, on similar grounds. In February 2003, he caused widespread outrage by shutting down the newspaper Egunkaria on charges of links with ETA. Shortly afterwards, on 22 Feb-ruary, some 80,000 people participated in a demonstration in San Sebas-tian to protest against what they saw as an attack on the Basque language and freedom of speech.

By March 2003, ETA had claimed a total of 815 lives. In addition to politicians, businessmen and members of the police force, artists, writers and academics have suffered intimidation, vandalism and assassination. Several Basque public figures have left Euskadi, in order to escape from what they perceive as its stifling political climate. As of the time of writing, while the mainstream Basque nationalist parties pursue a strategy of building bridges across the nationalist spectrum, the extreme left-wing nexus remains alive and active. Batasuna's successor representatives continue to claim that Euskal Herria is oppressed by the Spanish and French states. In consequence, they maintain their demands for amnesty and independence for Euskal Herria, insinuating that ETA's violence remains justified until these demands are met.

CHAPTER 3

Having Basque, Being Basque

Driving through Irun, Felipe Saragueta chats in Basque about his experience as director of the Partzuergo between January 2000 and October 2002. As I am more fluent in Spanish than in Basque, our conversation sometimes lapses into Spanish at my initiative. Felipe kindly obliges but repeatedly returns to Basque, the language he feels most comfortable with. A serious-looking young man in his mid twenties, with tidy short dark-brown hair, a plain light blue shirt, dark slacks and a pair of smart black shoes, Felipe is the image of youthful respectability. He is also a committed Basque nationalist, but one who prefers to set his own agenda rather than follow that of others.

Since leaving the Partzuergo, Felipe has been working as a legal consultant for a range of clients while taking evening classes for an advanced law degree. He is involved in projects with a number of local and regional institutions and organisations, giving them advice on how to set up cross-frontier partnerships. "I like this kind of work", he says. "You feel you are building things. And if you can contribute your bit to Basque projects, then so much the better."

Anxious to hear his views about issues of identity, I enquire upon an episode when I introduced him to some English friends of mine to whom, when they asked him where he was from, he first of all presented himself as Basque. Faced with incomprehension on their part, he had tried to explain but then had ended up by simply saying that he was Spanish. How did he feel in saying this, I ask. "Spanish is just my nationality", Felipe replies. "I am Basque. I speak Basque. I feel Basque."

The Basque word for someone who is Basque is euskaldun, which literally means someone who speaks Basque. And for many people in the Basque Country, the fact of speaking Basque in turn implies identification with Basque nationalism. This is the case for Felipe, although he doesn't identify with its more extreme forms. "If you are euskaldun", he continues, "it is practically inevitable that you should be nationalist too. Because you are more likely to feel attached to this language as a part of who you are. And so you want to defend it. I have moved away, though, from Batasuna and all those people, with their unclear position with regard to ETA".

In his nearby home town of Bera, in Nafarroa, Felipe says he knows many people involved in some way or other with ETA, whom he no longer sees as they have gone into hiding. "It's all so close to you. It's very difficult. And the fascist attitude of Spanish authorities... So it's hard not to get involved. I was invited recently to stand as a candidate in the local elections under the banner of Euskal Herritarrok. They see me as one of them, you see. I refused, however. I don't want to get that closely involved with these people either."

It is Sunday and a group of Batasuna supporters is returning from a demonstration demanding the relocation to the Basque Country of convicts held in gaols in other parts of Spain on charges of involvement with ETA. As we drive past some demonstrators sporting black and purple t-shirts, lycra leggings and mountain boots, earrings, Guatemalan and Peruvian bandanas, and ikurriñas, or Basque flags, Felipe mutters to me how ridiculous he finds them "altogether in a one-track-minded clique".

Suddenly, a girl in the group recognises Felipe behind the wheel of his car. Waving to us, she runs up, her loose dark hair bouncing up and down under her blue-and-black striped bandana. Felipe pulls off the road and the two of them chat together in Basque. But while the girl talks in an animated and friendly manner, Felipe says little and looks reserved, merely laughing politely from time to time.

As we resume our driving, he reflects on this encounter. "I just can't feel satisfaction in simply hanging out with these kinds of people, even though I may share many of their ideas about the situation here in the Basque Country. I need to do other things. Even their style of dress just isn't for me. I prefer to explore, to wear different things and have a style of my own, without these political signs all the time. I am Basque and I feel Basque and I don't have to demonstrate this in any way. For me, speaking Basque is important. And there is so much more to life than all this cliqueyness. Get on with things, meet different people, travel."

*

Basque music blares out from the stereo behind the rustic-looking wooden bar of Txirrimirri, near the beach area of Hendaia, where Nadine Oihanburu and I sit at a wooden table, chatting over cups of coffee. Born and raised in Hendaia, Nadine, a young woman in her mid-twenties with neatly combed brown hair, usually goes to the bar next door, Océanic, a bar with a modern, slightly clinical décor of white glass panels, game machines, and trophies behind the bar. There, her friends stand around, generally talking in French about rugby, football, fashion, American films or general gossip, or watching television. Today, I have suggested meeting her in Txirrimirri in order to be in a different context. As we chat, some youths come in, speaking a mixture of French and Basque. They are friends of the barman who plays in one of the Basque bands in Hendaia and Nadine knows them, but only greets them with a brief nod.

In her way of dressing, both at work and during her free time, Nadine has a conservative appearance which I have heard some people generally call 'Frenchy'. She wears her hair down to just above her shoulders and usually appears in a blouse and freshly ironed dark jeans with a lambswool sweater over her shoulders. Round her neck, however, she wears a prominent silver-plated lauburu, an old pagan symbol widely used as a token of Basque identity. In conversation, she occasionally inserts a few words and phrases in Basque into the otherwise French flow of talk.

Nadine does not speak Basque, although both her parents are descended from families that have lived in the region for generations and her father speaks some Basque. Her surname is Basque, and she says she would like eventually to learn the language. "But it isn't a priority at present", she adds. Her passion is rugby, a popular sport in the area, and she plays in the local women's team. She has no political opinions, she continues, and doesn't feel concerned by what she calls "le problème basque", a phrase often used by French-speakers to refer to the range of issues surrounding Basque nationalist demands.

She recently got her first job at Sokoa, the Hendaia-based company that makes office chairs, as an accountant. Sokoa, founded in the early 1970s by a group of Basque nationalist sympathisers, is well known locally as an initiative to give economic underpinning to the political cause of Basque nationalism. Because of a somewhat turbulent past, it is widely associated among non-nationalists with Basque nationalist extremism. When Nadine told her friends of her new job, their reactions in many cases confirmed this stereotype. "'Ah, the factory of the Basques!' they said. And they all assumed that we all spoke Basque there", Nadine recalls. Indeed, she adds, "there are quite a lot of Basque militant-minded people at Sokoa." But that doesn't prevent her from getting on well with her colleagues, she adds. "They are all nice and we are simply work colleagues really anyway."

Nadine's ambitions are mainly to be able to remain living in the area. In a region where unemployment is relatively high, Nadine considers herself lucky to have found a good employment. "For many of my friends, staying and living here is important", explains Nadine, "I am at home here and I like it. I don't want to go elsewhere". I ask her then what she means by 'here'. "I mean here, Hendaye, around... St Jean de Luz, Bayonne... Well... yes, the Basque Country, I suppose, in a way... And so, yes, I suppose... that's me being Basque. This definitely is my home, though of course I am French too."

Much has been written about the Basques as a centuries-old people with a singular blood type, distinctive physiognomy and a language supposedly unrelated to the other languages of Western Europe. They have even been claimed by some theorists of the late nineteenth century to be the descendants of Tubal, one of the sons of Noah in the Old Testament (Jauristi, 1986). Seen in such terms, the Basques could be regarded as an unusual pocket of separate racial/ethnic identity in an otherwise homogeneous Western European environment. Archaeological research has indeed produced some evidence of commonalities among the inhabitants of the region in terms of cranial features and blood type.

In the late nineteenth century, the Basque nationalist party EAJ explicitly emphasised a concept of Basque ethnic distinctiveness as a response to the increasing numbers of immigrants arriving in the Basque Country, who not only did not speak Basque but also looked physically different and led different lifestyles. Sabino Arana, the party's founder, regarded Basques and Spaniards as members of different races and regarded this distinction as something that needed to be preserved. On the other hand, he placed little emphasis on the Basque language, which at the time was regarded by the bourgeoisie as a language of the lower orders and was in decline in many urban areas.

Reflecting such concerns, nascent Basque nationalism focused on ethnic attributes, such as Basque surnames, in its search for a distinguishing feature of identity for the Basque people. The Basque nationalist movement drew on and encouraged archaeological, anthropological and linguistic studies which might shed light on the origins of the Basque people. The early twentieth century saw the emergence of anthropological and archaeological research in the rural areas of the Basque Country, and the veneration of figures such as the archaeologists and anthropologists José-Miguel Barandiarán, Telesforo Aranzadi and José-María Basabe Prado. Basque nationalism has also relied heavily on folklore and symbols, such as the ikurriña flag.

While the initial emphasis of EAJ on explicitly racial criteria became attenuated in the following decades, archaeological and anthropological interest in the Basques' supposedly unique origins has persisted. Despite the emergence of other approaches to the definition of identity, the image of the Basque people, with their fiery, independent character, strange tongue and distinctive physical features, remains strong. The status of the Basque language as one of the few non-Indo-European languages spoken in Europe, along with Finnish and Hungarian, and the scientific evidence of distinctive blood types among the region's inhabitants are often taken as proof of the supposed antiquity of the 'Basque people'. By drawing on this myth-ridden traditionalism as a partial explanation for the political conflict that persists in the region, the media and external commentators have helped to sustain this image. The

Basques continue to be popularly presented as a racially distinct people with ancient roots in the Western Pyrenean soil.

And yet, a study of issues of identity in the Basque Country cannot focus solely on the physiological, ethnic or linguistic characteristics of the region's inhabitants, any more than it can focus exclusively on political claims regarding the existence and defence of a Basque nation or on manifestations of so-called traditional Basque folklore. That would entail a neglect of actual experience, marginalising those individuals who either fail to fit into one category or another or who reject or are excluded by others from such categories. As I observed in Bidasoa-Txingudi, varying and sometimes conflicting ways of expressing the 'self' can be found within the Basque, French and Spanish contexts that coexist in the locality, giving the border area a particular 'multilocal' and 'multivocal' quality (Douglass, 1998; 1999). Different political factions claim to represent 'Basque identity', while often virulently opposing each other. None of the representations of 'Basque identity' proposed by these factions adequately covers all the various notions of self actually felt by the inhabitants of the Basque Country, however.

Rather than supporting or criticising notions of Basque uniqueness and difference, my objective is to look beyond them in order to discover how such notions are used in the context of social interaction. In Felipe and Nadine, for example, we have two contrasting examples of individuals who feel Basque and attached to their locality, but in very different ways. Both Felipe and Nadine have Basque family names and are descended from Basque families who have been long established in the area. But they each have different perceptions of their sense of self in relation to their Basque origins, and each expresses his or her identity differently.

Felipe, as he himself proclaims, feels he is first and foremost Basque. Born in Bera, a frontier town not far from Irun in the mountains of Nafarroa, he grew up speaking Basque and developing a strong attachment to his surroundings. Aside from his dark hair and clean-cut features, however, he bears few visible markers of his Basque identity, which is only clearly indicated by his preference for speaking in Basque. Nadine, on the other hand, while acknowledging that she is Basque and that she likes to live in the area, feels more Hendaian and French. Her identification with 'Basqueness' is expressed simply by her occasionally using a few Basque words in conversation and by the lauburu that she wears round her neck. In this way, these two people each create their identity by drawing selectively on certain markers and boundaries while ignoring others. While Nadine and Felipe construct and express their identity in these particular ways, other people do so in yet other ways.

The concept of identity has a long history in Western philosophy. While ancient Greek philosophers were among the first to address the dilemmas of permanence amidst manifest change and of unity amidst diversity, the word identity has its origins in the Latin *idemtitas*, an abstract concept which conveyed the notion of 'being the same thing'. By the eighteenth century, the concept had acquired a sense of 'something permanent', referring to individual sameness and yet distinctiveness within the collectivity. Such a view enabled the categorisation of people within a social context, in which they were held to fit specific roles.

At the turn of the twentieth century, Freud defined identity in a psychoanalytical context, as the sum of a particular person's psychological development. Identity was seen as the resulting product of the identification processes of the narcissistic 'I'. Building on Freud, the anthropologist-cum-psychoanalyst Erikson pinpointed three features that he regarded as being central to 'identity': unity, distinctiveness and continuity (1972:14). Identity, in its sense of sameness, was used by Erikson to refer to commonalities associated with the group. In a social and cultural world which he held to be composed of different segments, he accorded significant cognitive content to groups and viewed individuals' identities as emergent properties of their memberships of group categories.

Building on this, Devereux, another anthropologist with a psychoanalytical approach, insisted further on the importance of the influence of reified culture on the individual's sense of self (1970). By shifting academic focus onto 'culture', this approach paved the way for the emergence of a more reflexive type of anthropology. Goffman (1967) especially contributed to the conceptualisation of the notion of the representation of the self on the basis of social role-playing in interactionist theory. His work is particularly significant in putting stress on how and why people behave the way they do in the company of others and what that means for the understanding of their identity.

The interest of anthropologists in identity grew stronger with the emergence of modern concerns with ethnicity and social movements in the 1960s. But the concept continued to be widely used in a largely socio-historical way to refer to qualities of sameness in relation to a person's connection to others and to a particular group of people. An innovative approach, in this context, was provided by Barth in his analysis of ethnic identity (1969). This approach to identity, which I call subjective, interprets the concept as deriving from a sense of self formed out of an awareness of distinctiveness, of difference to 'Others'. By introducing the concept of ethnic boundaries as an analytical tool for looking at ethnicity, Barth helped to de-essentialise ethnicity and ethnic identity and to challenge their *a priori* existence or continuity. He drew attention to the ethnic group as a socially constructed phenomenon. Analyses of ethnic groups, he suggested, should focus on their use of symbolic boundaries to mark the limits of group belonging. Ethnic groups were thus seen to be active creators of their groupness, a process which he described as involving three stages: self-ascription, mutual recognition and mutual ascription.

Over the following decades, identity came to be seen as an object of personal struggle in social and political studies. Scholars saw new social movements and minority nationalism as attempts by small social groups to regain control of their destinies. Identity came to be understood as a potential ideological construct for political mobilisation, thereby causing the concept to be brought alongside that of ethnicity and nationalism. While this approach helps us to understand how some groups manage to construct and maintain a sense of identity particular to the group as a whole, it fails to recognise the possibility of different interpretations of this identity amongst the group's members. Indeed, this approach has perversely led some scholars to assume that nationalist movements are the main representatives of the ethnic group and as a result to concentrate their studies solely on such movements. Such an approach, as demonstrated by the examples of Felipe and Nadine, is clearly not tenable. Nonetheless, it raises the question for the anthropologist of how to characterise the identity of people who feel that they belong to an ethnic group while not sharing any political commitment to it.

Barth himself, by treating the ethnic group as a social organisation maintained thanks to the drawing up of boundaries between it and other groups, denied the individual interpretive power of the ethnic group's members (A.P. Cohen 1994a; 1994b; 1998). Since Barth, by contrast, other scholars (e.g. Calhoun, 1994; Douglass, Lyman and Zulaika, 1994) have pressed the point that members of the ethnic group have their own ways of defining their membership and understanding of their ethnic group, which they express through their own use of symbolic boundaries. While they may share many common characteristics of a prototypical ethnic identity, in other words, they do not share all of these characteristics. Ethnicity thus becomes a construct conditioned not only by inclusive/exclusive external boundaries, but also, I argue, by the existence of internal boundaries drawn up by members of the ethnic group in relation to each other. In this way, ethnicity can be perpetuated by the different visions and experiences both of members and of outsiders, regardless of whether there is agreement between these different actors or not. This is precisely what we witness in the cases of Felipe and Nadine.

Ethnic identification, however, is only one aspect of identity. In an age of 'globalisation', 'mass culture' and electronic communications that span the world, individuals increasingly define themselves in terms of multiple attachments and feel at ease with different subjectivities. In an attempt to grapple with the analytical challenges posed by such multiple identifications, scholars have come up with new qualifiers for the concept of identity, such as 'hybridised identity' (Pieterse, 1995), 'hyphenated identity' (Caglar, 1997), 'creolised identity' (Hannerz, 1987), 'diasporic identity' and 'transnational identity', in a bid to capture the complexity of the practices, cultural configurations, and identity formations of trans-local and culturally 'nomadic' people. Identity formations are understood as "products of cultures and histories in collision and dialogue" (Clifford, 1994:319).

Others have put forward the idea of 'multiple identity', whereby an individual builds up and expresses a range of identities based on personal experience. Based on the idea that a person can have more than one group allegiance at the same time, some scholars have discussed the ability of members of regional populations in any country to feel a sense of 'national identity' in some cases and allegiance to more narrow collective identities in other cases (Moreno, 1997; Sangrador, 1996).

While demonstrating the potential for individuals to identify with a range of social, cultural and political attachments at the same time, however, such approaches shed no light on the formation and everyday expression of identity. On the contrary, concepts such as 'hyphenated identity' or 'multiple identity' continue to assume that 'identity' is a root base and that the various identifications are fixed and uniform in their nature rather than fluid and eclectic. In this way, they merely serve as covers for an understanding of identity as a mish-mash of different fixed identities. They also fail to distinguish between how a person is viewed by others in contrast to how the person views himself.

This exploration of different approaches to the concept of 'identity' demonstrates how difficult it is to pin down. Since identity is a virtual thing, it is impossible to define it empirically. As an alternative, some analysts have sought to capture the dynamic and fluid qualities of human social self-expression by treating identity as a process, so as to take account of the reality of diverse and ever-changing social experience (e.g. Hall, 1992; 1996). Others have put forward the idea of identification (e.g. Cuche, 1996; Guibernau and Rex, 1997; Passerini, 1998; 2000), whereby identity is perceived as made up of different components that are 'identified' and interpreted by individuals. Under this approach, the construction of an individual sense of self is perceived as being achieved as a result of personal choices regarding who and what to associate with.

Such approaches represent an advance in their recognition of the role of the individual in social interaction and the construction of identity. Nonetheless, despite growing acknowledgement that individuals can differ in their interpretations and experiences of their identity, whether 'ethnic' or otherwise, there have been few empirical studies of how this occurs. It is to the bridging of this gap that I wish to contribute, by showing how markers and boundaries are brought into play by individu-

als as elements of identification in a constant process of identity formation and affirmation.

A Key Figure in Basque Society – The *Abertzale*, or Basque Patriot

*Seated behind his desk in an emerald-green high-backed office chair
with dark wooden armrests, Patxi Noblia gives some instructions over
the telephone in French to one of his employees. His large 1970s style
desk is neatly stacked with papers and folders, and the dull grey plastic
partition-walls and plain dark carpeting on the floor add to the air of
austerity. As the co-founder and director of office-chair manufacturer
Sokoa, Mr. Noblia is a well-known public figure in Hendaia and a
prominent member of the Basque nationalist cause. Serious to the point
of brusqueness in manner, he gives the impression of a person who is
hard-working and deeply committed to his company and his Basque
nationalist ideals.*

*From the windows behind him, the view is of the main road linking
Pausu and Hendaia close to the frontier with Irun. Two paintings on the
wall, showing impressionistic views of the Bay of Txingudi, form the
only decorative elements in the office. The chair on which he sits is a
product of his factory, and his conversation with a visitor, once he
finishes his telephone call, is dominated by references to the importance
of economic development for the self-assertion of the Basque people.
His purpose, he says, is to develop the economic infrastructure of the
Basque Country, "north and south", in order to "provide employment
and share the riches that are reaped".*

*Now in his late fifties, wearing a checked shirt and plain dark trou-
sers, Mr. Noblia looks little different today, with his ruffled dark hair
and close-trimmed beard, from his appearance in photographs dating
from thirty years ago when he first launched Sokoa with a group of
friends. Fluent in Basque, he nonetheless chooses to continue talking
French to me, unlike his wife, who works in the administration of the
firm and shares his office, and who, knowing that I am learning Basque,
often talks to me in Basque.*

*In today's relatively precarious economic climate, Sokoa stands out
as one of only a few local companies that continue to enjoy steady
growth. That is a considerable achievement for Mr. Noblia, who
explains his objective as one of "contributing to the economic development of the Basque Country for the Basque Country". True to his
philosophy, Mr. Noblia is active in a series of Basque Country-wide
economic initiatives geared to encouraging the emergence of new businesses and promoting a favourable climate for their growth. Amongst
other initiatives, Sokoa invested in the creation of the Hegoalde-based*

*Basque language newspaper Egunkaria in 1981. It also gives financial
assistance to local Basque cultural initiatives, such as the ikastola, or
Basque language school, and AEK, the association teaching Basque to
adults. Mr. Noblia is a permanently active member of a development
council created in Iparralde in 1994 to advise and inform local politicians on economic issues. "Local increased prosperity will help Basque
culture and the Basque language to thrive", he affirms with unremitting
earnestness.*

*Apart from his beard, there is little about his physical appearance to
indicate his identification with Basque nationalist ideals. He does not
even attempt to speak Basque at every possible opportunity in order to
indicate his Basqueness. He responds modestly to references to his
success in fostering economic development in the region. Yet he is much
admired in Basque nationalist circles as the archetype of an abertzale,
or Basque patriot, and though declining suggestions that he is in some
way an exemplary figure in this respect he readily accepts the identification as "someone who feels he belongs to the Basque people and who
tries to work for them".*

The figure of the 'abertzale', or Basque patriot, is of key importance
in Basque society. Within the complex interplay of social, cultural and
political forces in modern Basque society, the abertzale occupies a crucial
position as a creator and promoter of modern expressions of Basque
culture and, at the same time, as a possessor and controller of symbolic
power. Reflecting the struggles for power underlying abertzalism, use of
the term is controversial. Essentially, the term signifies someone who
defines himself or herself clearly within the spectrum of local politics as a
Basque nationalist. But how it is used and to whom it is applied are the
subject of constant contest. In many ways, debate surrounding its use and
meaning mirrors the political, cultural and social tensions that condition
many aspects of interpersonal relations in the Basque Country.

The neologism 'abertzale' was first used in the late nineteenth century
in Hegoalde by EAJ supporters who drew their motivations from their
view of a golden age of the Basques as a racially distinct group with their
own unique traditions, rather than from aspirations for an independent
nation-state. More recently, reviewing the situation in the Basque Country
from the late 1950s onwards following the emergence of the left-wing
Basque nationalist movement in Hegoalde, the anthropologist MacClancy
defined the abertzale as "one who actively participates in the political
struggle for an independent Basque nation with its own distinctive culture" (1993b:86; 1996:213).

Among left-wing Basque nationalist militants, the term abertzale is
used as a positive term of self-identification. Rather than birth, aspiration
to an independent Basque nation becomes the criterion for recognition
as a Basque. The most radical nationalists define 'true Basques' in exclu-

sive terms of their commitment to the Basque cause, politically and linguistically, consigning all others to the category of "anti-Basque" (Heiberg, 1980:58).

In both Hegoalde and Iparralde, left-wing abertzaleak advocate so-called grass-roots action and self-sufficient economic initiatives such as the setting up of businesses, cooperatives, unions and associations representing farmers and workers of different specialisations. Linked to this is a concern with education, for the development of Basque awareness based on a specific view of Basque history and attachment to certain Basque cultural references.

The abertzale typically claims a commitment to bringing Basque identity out of the 'ghetto', for example by participating in the modernisation of the Basque language and its raising from the status of a 'minority language' to that of an everyday language used in both the public and private domains, thanks both to its 'normalisation' and the 'euskaldunisation' of the local population. As such, the abertzale is often an enthusiastic speaker of the Basque language and an active organiser of and participant in a wide array of Basque cultural activities. As a self-declared abertzale explained to me, to be an abertzale "is, in a way, to embody the modern Basque identity... that is not simply given, but must be acquired and worked on. Being an abertzale doesn't just mean living the Basque way. You have to be committed". People who organise their lives in this way end up forming their own distinctive cultural grouping. They know each other, if not through direct contact, then by hearing about each other through the information channels of the abertzale network.

Sokoa is an archetypal example of an abertzale initiative. In its early years, it employed many people who had come to Iparralde fleeing repression in Hegoalde. As it grew, its example encouraged the emergence of other businesses in Iparralde. Today, it is a beacon of cross-frontier business cooperation, with partnerships with businesses in Hegoalde and employees who cross the frontier daily from Irun, Hondarribia and other towns in Hegoalde to come to work in its factory. French, Basque and Spanish are all to be heard within the firm, which brings together people from different cultural and political backgrounds. Some employees from Hegoalde know little French, despite working on French territory, as they can communicate in Spanish or in Basque with their colleagues. Many employees from Iparralde, by contrast, have a good understanding of Spanish, some actually learning it at work by talking with their Spanish-speaking colleagues.

Inevitably, Sokoa's history has been marked by the political tensions that dominate the Basque Country. Late in 1986, the French police discovered a cache of arms in the basement of its office building. Sokoa's business operations were brought to an abrupt stop, as more than a third of its personnel were arrested on the grounds of dealings with terrorist organisations. The company's managers denied any involvement in the affair, claiming that the arms had been hidden without their knowledge. Mr. Noblia underwent trial and, though he was eventually cleared in 1989, the episode dealt a temporary blow to Sokoa's business, causing it to lose a significant number of clients and business partners, particularly in France. Nonetheless, Sokoa managed to recover and even to increase its business on the international market. It recruited more employees from a range of social and political backgrounds, fulfilling its objective of providing more local employment. Now employing just over 200 people, Sokoa, says its head of communications and personnel, Gilles Chaudière, "seeks to be appreciated first and foremost as a company like any other".

Even so, while primarily focusing on economic success, Sokoa stands out amongst local businesses for its concern with Basque nationalist issues, its financial donations to a selection of Basque associations and its openness to employing so-called Basque political refugees. Over the 1990s, there was a new wave of these people coming to Iparralde. Many were people who had previously left the Basque Country during a spate of violent anti-Basque nationalist attacks by the GAL in the early 1980s in order to take refuge in Latin America, either of their own accord or at the orders of the French government. Sokoa provided employment to a few of these. Although fluency in Basque has never been one of Sokoa's criteria for employment, in 1998 the company recruited a new receptionist from Irun who could speak Basque, in addition to Spanish, French and English. "It was an extra advantage", explained Mr. Chaudière, "so that people calling Sokoa from either side of the frontier could speak Basque if they so wished".

A factory employee at Sokoa, with whom I became friends during my period of fieldwork, mentioned to me the distinct cliqueyness that he felt in his work environment. As a person with no interest in Basque politics, yet feeling Basque nonetheless, he noted that, in the factory, "whether you are an abertzale or not makes a serious difference in your relationship with others... you are a bit left out if you're not. You can feel it, just this particular kind of camaraderie... which you are excluded from". On another occasion, he complained about pressures that he sometimes felt from this 'clique'. When one of the factory managers was put in prison for alleged collaboration with ETA in March 2000, some employees collected funds to help his son pay for the cost of travel to visit his father in prison. Fellow employees were asked to donate a minimum of 7.50 euros every month. At the beginning, my friend held back from participating, but after a month he realised that he was the only one in the factory who had not yet given his 'share' and so paid up. In this particular incident, the manager who had been arrested had not been particularly liked in the factory. However, as an abertzale in trouble with the state authorities, he benefited from the solidarity of his abertzale colleagues, demonstrating the inclusive quality of the abertzale boundary.

Links between Sokoa employees and left-wing Basque nationalist extremism, whether real or imagined, still continue to influence perceptions of the firm's identity, as we have seen from the comments by Nadine. In April 2000, another factory employee was arrested by French police on the grounds of not having his identity documents in order and on suspicion of having taken part in a kidnapping plot in Brittany during the mid-1980s. Such occurrences have helped to maintain a view among some people of Sokoa as a haven for Basque nationalists.

Although abertzaleak[1] form the core of the Basque nationalist movement in Hegoalde, there is tension between those who support the left-wing Basque nationalist creed of HB and its successor parties and those who support the Basque nationalist party EAJ and its splinter party EA. Such tensions flare up, for example, in relation to campaigns for the repatriation of Basque convicts and in relation to self-sufficient development projects as opposed to Basque government-led initiatives. However, despite the claims of abertzaleak to represent the essence of Basqueness, it would be unfair to accept their assertion that they are and should be identified as the 'only true Basques'. In Iparralde, there are many people who are Basque-speaking and of Basque descent but who have no interest in Basque nationalism or participate in associations concerned with so-called Basque initiatives. There are also people active in local development in the Basque Country who are Basque-speaking and of Basque descent but not involved in Basque nationalist politics. Even for a non-Basque speaker, as we have seen in the case of Nadine, it is possible to feel Basque in one's own way without adhering to nationalist discourse.

Culture Yes, Politics No: The Role of the *Euskaltzale*

In the complex web of identifications in the Basque Country, a category with some parallels to the abertzale is that of the *euskaltzale*, a term used to refer to someone who appreciates and makes an effort to identify with Basque cultural and linguistic markers without necessarily making these into the most important feature of their identity, in contrast with the abertzaleak. Typically, such people are active in Basque cultural contexts such as Basque dancing and the organisation of art exhibitions, send their children to receive their primary education at the ikastola and themselves attend classes to learn Basque. Many abertzaleak use the term euskaltzale in a negative way. Because of the eukaltzale's less-than-total political commitment to the cause of Basque independ-

---

[1]   The suffix '-k' is used to form the plural in Basque.

ence, some self-declared abertzaleak to whom I spoke dismissed such people as being simply interested in Basque identity "in the folkloristic way" as "something simple and inoffensive" and "ethnologically interesting". In Iparralde, some abertzaleak cited the fact that such people would send their children to the ikastola for kindergarten and maybe also primary education, but not for secondary education. "That shows how they see Basque just as this pretty language, nice to keep for local traditions, but then for serious matters it's back to French", one person commented.

It is ironical to note, in this context, that while some abertzaleak to whom I spoke rejoiced at the growing popularity and acceptance of the ikastola, they also expressed regrets about the decreasingly militant character of the ikastola. In the same vein, others complained about how certain Basque symbols were increasingly being used by people who had no nationalist consciousness. One young man, a self-proclaimed supporter of EH in Irun, described these people as "having no idea about what it is really all about. All these ikurriñak you see hanging from car rear mirrors – and all these lauburu pendants and bracelets, it doesn't mean anything to them... just a fashion". Such comments illustrate the abertzaleak's desire to exert control over certain symbols and impose their own particular understanding of how these symbols should be perceived and used.

Despite the disparaging manner in which many abertzaleak use the term euskaltzale, it is a positive form of self-identification for some non-abertzaleak. Serge Lonca, a teacher at the Hendaia ikastola who is also an environmental campaigner and who learnt Basque in order to integrate better into the local community, describes being an euskaltzale, in distinction to abertzale, as simply signifying non-acceptance of a nationalist project. This, in his view, does not entail taking Basque culture and language any less seriously. Indeed, I have observed him very much involved in many Basque initiatives concerned with the development of the Basque language and promotion of Basque culture, which he describes as "not just folklore but an important part of what living here is all about, that needs to be taken seriously". He adds: "That is why I often get criticised by abertzaleak. Because I am very involved in Basque language and cultural issues but I don't identify with them".

Other self-defined euskaltzaleak to whom I spoke concurred that the term signifies someone who defends the Basque language and culture. These were Basque people concerned with the development of the Basque language and interested in Basque cultural expressions, but who did not support any particular political stance. They said they preferred to call themselves euskaltzaleak rather than abertzaleak, so as to avoid radical political connotations. When asked to distinguish between the two terms, all defined euskaltzale as 'the non-political one'. Many, however, then added that it was inevitable that politics should come into issues relating to support for the Basque language and culture. The result is a degree of ambiguity that at times can provide a convenient leeway in defining self-identification but which also gives rise to uncertainty. An example of the latter is Elisa, a young woman who lives in Irun and works at Sokoa and is learning Basque, but who, in a long conversation, explained to me her hesitation in defining herself by either of the terms, abertzale or euskaltzale. As she portrayed it, her reluctance to accept either term reflected the often "extremist connotations" of the word abertzale and the "too dull" image of the euskaltzale. Likewise with political allegiances: "I don't support EH, but neither do I feel close to the other nationalist parties… which are really quite conservative. So I don't know".

Such is the ambiguity of boundaries that many people with no links to the Basque nationalist world often consider parents who send their children to the ikastola as abertzaleak on the grounds that "they are taking part in the construction of a Basque identity in their children", as one French-speaking woman in Hendaia said to me. Many such people see no difference between the terms abertzale and euskaltzale and some even regard euskaltzale as a 'disguise' for the abertzale.[2] When some people in my grandmother's village in the rural hinterland of Iparralde heard in 1996 that I was taking Basque lessons, they assumed that I had 'become abertzale'. Likewise, an old woman recalled to me how a decade earlier the fact that she had hung a lauburu, a traditional Basque symbol, above her fireplace had caused gossip in the neighbourhood about her being an abertzale.

In Iparralde, many people not involved in the Basque nationalist movement told me that they associate the term abertzale with anybody who condones violence as a means of backing political demands in a Basque context. A retired teacher in the French state school system living in Hendaia described abertzaleak as "those who fight for independence and are disposed to use violence to attain it". Another person in Iparralde referred to abertzaleak as "extremists" while yet another described them as "big mouths, bigots, who sully the image of real Basques". In Spain, the national political parties, and the PP in particular, tend to identify Basque nationalism with extremism, radicalism and terrorism. Much emphasis is also placed on the importance of condemning ETA violence

---

[2]   In Spanish, a person active in the promotion of Basque language and culture is called a *Vasquista*. In French, such a person is called a *Basquisant*. During the 1970s, 1980s and 1990s, basquisants were also referred to as *Enbatistes* from the name of the first Basque nationalist organisation in Iparralde, Enbata. This term continues to be used by some older people, demonstrating the continuing political connotations of cultural militancy.

and the fact that Batasuna does not condemn it, often without considering the possibility of violence on the part of the state authorities.

Even within the world of those who call themselves abertzaleak, there are disagreements over who is and is not entitled to this designation. In Hegoalde, differences began to emerge in the abertzale movement in the new socio-political climate of post-Franco Spain. Those who disagreed with the way in which events unfolded following the constitutional referendum sought to continue their resistance and protest in social and cultural movements . The result was a loosely structured conglomeration of associations and organisations supporting left-wing abertzale ideas, identified by their organisers as the Basque national liberation movement. These continuing social and cultural projects are kept distinct from the violence of ETA, with any links between the two being a matter of individual initiative. The main characteristics of this movement are its flexible and diffuse organisational structure, its rejection of any compartmentalisation of political activity as separate from day-to-day social, economic and cultural activities and its refusal to recognise the existing institutions of the Basque Country. Through it, a series of associations and foundations provide alternative initiatives to those of the Basque government. So, for instance, AEK works alongside *HABE*,[3] the Basque government's service for teaching Basque to adults set up in 1982. Other expressions of this alternative fringe include associations supporting Basque militants incarcerated for alleged links with ETA and their families, associations dedicated to fighting against drug addiction, feminist and gay groups and anti-nuclear and environmental groups. In March 2000, *Gazteriak*, a group of young Iparralde abertzaleak, merged with *Jarrai*, a group of young Hegoalde abertzaleak, under the name of *Haika*. This organisation was outlawed in February 2001, following allegations by the Spanish state of links with ETA. Since then, radically inclined left-wing abertzale youths have re-formed under the banner of a new group called Segi.

Members of EAJ or EA are frequently denied recognition as abertzaleak by their left-wing counterparts, both for their different ideological stance and their alleged insincerity in claiming to want Basque independence. In some cases, they are even accused of being "traitors" to the Basque cause.

On one occasion, I witnessed over dinner with some friends how an EAJ partisan was greeted by a snigger from a left-wing Basque nationalist when he referred to himself as an abertzale.

---

[3]   Abbreviation for *Helduen Alfabetatze Euskalduntza*, meaning 'Adults' Literalisation and Basquisation'.

Also in this vein, Marije Zapirain, a Batasuna councillor in Hondarribia, told me that she did not regard the mayor of Hondarribia, Borja Jáuregui, who is a member of EAJ, as an abertzale but as "an *españolista*". By this she meant he was pro-Spanish. Another Batasuna councillor in Hondarribia, Jaime Anduaga, drew a distinction in Spanish between *'nacionalista'* and 'abertzale', telling me that Mr. Jáuregui "would not call himself an abertzale but simply a nacionalista". For Mr. Anduaga, Mr. Jáuregui used the discourse of Basque nationalism, but was 'not really Basque' in the sense of putting a commitment to Basque independence into practice in his daily life, and so not a genuine abertzale. When I asked Mr. Anduaga to tell me what would, for him, be the Basque translation of nacionalista, he said *"jeltzale"*. Jeltzale is the name for an EAJ supporter,[4] quite distinct, Mr. Anduaga insisted, from an abertzale.

However, when I asked Mr. Jáuregui himself how he responded to such criticism, he described himself as being an abertzale, adding that the "only difference between me and these HB people is that I support democracy, whereas they are exclusive, authoritarian and intolerant". In a similar vein, other supporters of EAJ and EA insisted to me that they, and not the "left-wing radicals", are best able to improve the popular image of the abertzale, by avoiding connotations of violence. Beñat Oteiza, a representative of EAJ in Iparralde, explained that "EAJ enables people to disassociate abertzalism from terrorism".

Harmony, however, is also lacking within the camp of the left-wing abertzaleak. As was pointed out earlier, differences have become particularly prominent since the the the end of ETA's 'truce' in 1999. In Hegoalde, *Aralar*, a new political party officially running since 2002, stands as an alternative to Batasuna, while in Iparralde, there are tensions between AB loyalists and those who sided with Batasuna. AB members say they are often criticised by the Batasuna group as not being real "left-wing abertzaleak". One 27-year-old AB member noted to me, "of course, a lot of it has to do with these fancy ideals. You know, revolutionary ideas, anti-colonialist discourses, etc. And well, us, with our strategy of going 'little by little', asking first for the creation of a département du Pays basque, that is not so romantic and revolutionary and appealing to young people as is the idea of outright Basque independence..."

Basque nationalists in general like to associate themselves with parties representing national minorities in other parts of the world, such as Plaid Cymru in Wales, Sinn Fein and the Scottish National Party, calling them

---

[4]   Jeltzale has its origins in EAJ's dictum *Jangoikoa Eta Lega Zaharra* which translates as 'God and Ancient Laws'.

"fellow abertzaleak".[5] Often, to specify their ideological distinction from others who claim to be abertzaleak, the left-wing Basque nationalists will add the adjective eskerra, or "left-wing", to the term abertzale. This does not go uncontested, however, as for example by a supporter of the grouping EE, now merged with the PSE, who wrote a letter to the Diario Vasco newspaper protesting at attempts by HB supporters to monopolise this label. He complained that "when HB and their torch bearers talk about the left-wing abertzale, they are usurping an option which others in our work attempt to develop…We are still waiting to find out what is the economic and social model of this political formation…"[6] While being aware of this monopolisation, which again is an example of symbolic control, I have decided for purposes of simplification in this book to use the term 'left-wing abertzaleak' to refer specifically to members of AB, Batasuna and Aralar, and their sympathisers. My justification for doing so lies in the fact that, in general talk in the Basque Country, these abertzaleak are practically always referred to as "left-wing" and that EE is now aligned with the Spanish Basque Socialist political strategy.

So abertzalism covers a range of sentiment, from strong attachment to the idea of a Basque cultural community to demands for new policies and priorities in the field of local culture, language and grass-roots development, and full-blown separatism. Some people have even come to adopt the term abertzale for themselves, without necessarily being active within the conventional abertzale groups, such as the mayor of Hendaia, Mr. Ecenarro. He specifically rejected the alternative term of euskaltzale, seeing it as referring to someone with only a "passive identification with Basque culture, someone who says Basque culture is all nice and everything, but does little for it".

Nonetheless, there's no doubt that the militantism of left-wing Basque nationalists can be credited as having encouraged a change in local perceptions of Basque culture and language, from something old-fashioned and traditional to something that can form part of a modern and dynamic sense of self. Many people taking part in Basque civil associations of one sort or another commented to me that the left-wing abertzaleak are the most committed participants. "Whether we like it or not", remarked a resident in Hendaia of New Zealand nationality who sends his children to the ikastola in Irun, "it is HB people, who are the most active and dynamic when it comes to cultural activities for our children. With puppet shows, clowns, imaginative children's stories in Basque, etc." Because it is difficult to act in any of these spheres without the involvement of left-wing abertzale militants, civil society remains largely dominated by this movement, restricting space for other actors of

---

5 *Enbata*, 13 May, 1999.

6 *Diario Vasco*, "ETA y su izquierda", 22 December, 2000.

different ideologies. The network of Basque cultural and political initiatives linked by left-wing abertzale ideology has become in effect a culture of its own whose representatives wield symbolic power in environmental, social and cultural movements throughout the Basque Country.

The way in which the left-wing abertzaleak's exercise of symbolic power has enabled them to take the lead in both civic issues and the use of the Basque language is exemplified in a comment made to me by a young Hendaian member of an ecological association covering the Bidasoa-Txingudi area. When I asked what language its members from the three towns used to communicate with each other, I received what appeared to my interlocutor as a logical response: "In Basque. And that's not surprising: a young ecologist is also very likely to be a Basque militant". A man from Irun who supports a controversial campaign to have women parade in a traditionally male-dominated parade in the annual town fiestas of Irun and Hondarribia also illustrated how closely the idea of civic action and Basque left-wing nationalist identity have become linked. As we discussed the political profile of this movement, he remarked that "it is only normal that it should be mainly left-wing abertzaleak who are active in it: they are the most open-minded people here".

Inevitably, this domination also causes frustration among some people. According to Ion Elizalde, a representative of EA in the municipal council of Hondarribia in charge of the promotion of the Basque language, "working in the area of Basque culture is difficult because of this domination of these causes by those people from HB... As a member of the other nationalist camp, you are made to feel pretty small... criticising you, as if they are the only ones who know best and really care about Basque culture and language". Similarly, Marina Grijalba, a sixty-year-old Spanish-speaking woman from Irun who chose to run in the *Korrika*, the annual rally held by AEK in support of the Basque language, told me how dismayed she was to see how many participants were carrying placards with left-wing Basque political slogans on them, asking for the return of Basque prisoners: "It makes me angry. Because I am not running for them, I am running for the Basque language. It is so frustrating because everything gets mixed up, language, politics. Before, yes, it was necessary, in order to officialise Basque. But not any more. Always these HB people there, infiltrating... imposing themselves". Another example is the experience of a woman from Iparralde who, feeling personally concerned by a government plan to construct a motorway going through the Basque Country, attended a street protest against the project and received cynical looks from some representatives of Batasuna she knew leading the demonstration. Frustrated by this, she exclaimed to me, "they know I am not one of them, and that is why they gave me these ironic looks, as if to say 'what is she doing here?' As if it is necessary to be abertzale to mobilise against such things as the motorway. But no, why should it be always them? It shouldn't have to be this way. In fact, they give these causes a bad name. Always them. It puts off other kinds of people from mobilising too".

CHAPTER 4

Not France, not Spain…

Hau ez da Frantzia, hau ez da España: Euskal Herria da.
(Basque for "This is not France, this is not Spain, this is Euskal Herria")
Chorus of a song by the popular rock band Skunk from Hendaia

A burly man aged about sixty walks into the town hall of Hendaia. Looking both confused and amused, he goes up to the desk of the "état civil", or civil register, where he addresses Claude Urrutia, an employee who is standing behind the desk. "Tell me", the man exclaims in Spanish, "What in God's name do I do with this?" He brandishes a French identity card and, then, still laughing, pulls out another identity card, which is Spanish. Mr. Urrutia, visibly accustomed to this kind of situation, patiently explains to the man his rights as a holder of French nationality.

"We get a lot of cases like this", Mr. Urrutia explains once the man has left. "People who for one reason or other, for example marriage, or because they were born in one country or another and so on, have dual nationality. Some just get completely confused over it. Others, of course, know it is an advantage. I remember a cousin of mine who has both and lives in Hendaye… About twenty years ago, when we would cross the frontier to go out in the bars, on the way there and on the way back, the Spanish police and then the French police would stop us to check our papers, and my cousin, to avoid complications, would always show his French I.D. And they would just let us pass. Easy. Showing your Spanish I.D. would cause an endless list of problems, what with checks for terrorists and so on."

In a frontier area like this one, there is plenty of scope for taking advantage of such situations. As a result of recent electoral reforms, people from other European Union countries who have official residence permits to live in France or Spain, even if they do not have the nationality of that country, can vote in municipal elections and elections for the European Parliament. "Some people, although normally it is illegal, have two residence cards", says Mr. Urrutia, "because they live here and also across the frontier… things like that. And they vote twice in the elections. Which is illegal, of course!" Launching into the subject,

Mr. Urrutia proceeds to describe other advantages of living in a frontier area as far as taxation and social service benefits are concerned. Depending on a person's income and assets and number of children, if any, he explains, it may be more beneficial to obtain residence by buying or renting a home on one side of the frontier or the other so as to be taxed less or benefit from cheaper and better social services. Indeed, it is not uncommon to find people living in Irun or Hondarribia and paying taxes there but holding an extra bank account in Hendaia or having a car with a French number plate.

The *Muga*

The notion of the frontier, or *muga* in Basque, plays an important role in local consciousness in a number of ways. On the one hand, as we have just seen, the existence of the state frontier provides an opportunity for individuals to engage in strategies of various sorts designed to take maximum advantage of the environments in which they live. On the other hand, it is a constant reminder of the political and administrative reality of a divided Basque Country or Euskal Herria. By dividing the Basque Country between two states, the frontier is the ultimate obstacle to the Basque nationalists' goal of a united Euskal Herria. Its existence is evoked in many Basque songs and poems of the last two centuries harking back to a romantic and legendary past when the Basques were a 'free' people, in contrast with their alleged subservience to two alien states in modern times.

From the point of view of the centralizing state, the areas on either side of state frontiers are peripheral to the centre due to their location on the limits of state territories. This, however, overlooks the perspective of the people who inhabit such border areas, for whom these places are the centre of their world. According to Felipe Saragueta, the lawyer whom we met earlier, the frontier isn't an obstacle to social communication. "All my life I have known a lot of Basque people on either side of the frontier", he says. "Even with the frontier closed, we still continued to live with our own sense of identity. It goes well beyond the frontier. Together, as Basques, we make our own space. You make your natural space, in which you live, have your friends, your social circle, with people, and that's it."

Indeed, for Basque nationalists, the frontier is not a dividing line between two countries, but a meeting point between the two parts of the Basque Country known by many people locally, either for nationalist reasons or merely as a matter of 'political correctness' in the local environment, as Iparralde and Hegoalde. In this alternative definition of geopolitical space, the muga fulfils a function in the delimitation of the provinces, here marking the boundaries between Lapurdi and Gipuzkoa and further to the east between Behe Nafarroa and Nafarroa. So for example, the left-wing nationalist newspaper Gara makes a distinction in its articles between the frontier, as a boundary imposed by the two states, and Euskal Herria's 'natural boundaries', those of the provinces. In Bidasoa-Txingudi, the frontier is the muga between the provinces of Lapurdi and Gipuzkoa. A few kilometres further to the east, it becomes the muga between Behe Nafarroa and Nafarroa.

Traditionally, the Basque word muga is also used to refer to boundaries negotiated and agreed upon by local populations. Indeed, before the establishment of the frontier between French and Spanish territory, the word muga was used to refer to demarcation lines marked by landmarks or by natural frontiers such as rivers that defined the areas in which local inhabitants enjoyed rights to pasture, fishing and hunting (Descheemaeker 1950; Fairén-Guillén, 1955; Gomez-Ibáñez, 1975; Zubiaur Carreño, 1977; Fernández de Casadevante, 1989). Such boundaries were known in Spanish as *facerías*, contracts between neighbouring villages sharing land and various natural resources. One such accepted frontier was formed by the river Bidasoa, long before it was identified in 1659 as part of the state frontier between French and Spanish territory. In such a context, the muga can have positive connotations of centrality and tradition for Basque nationalists. The Bidasoa, explains Robert Arrambide, one of the leaders of Hendaia's left-wing Basque nationalist group *Biharko Hendaia*,[1] "for us is not a frontier. Rather, it is a place that unites two sides".

Such ambiguities are nothing new. Throughout history, the muga has simultaneously united and divided the inhabitants of neighbouring Basque areas. Despite a common language, shared traditions and the fact that many families had close relatives living on the other side of the muga, a sense of difference between the two communities on either side was formed well before any demarcation of Spanish and French territory. Disputes were rife at a local level over resources, notably between the fishermen of Hondarribia and Hendaia for control of fishing rights in the Bidasoa. Records of quarrels between the two camps date back to the fifteenth century, and in 1793, Hendaia was reduced to ruins by the Spanish army in a battle with the French revolutionary army.

It was only with the Treaty of Limits in 1856, followed by the Treaty of Bayonne 10 years later, that a formal demarcation line was agreed between the two states. Based on the work of a commission made up of officials appointed by the French and Spanish states, these treaties traced out the frontier "from the estuary of the Bidasoa to the point where the département des Basses-Pyrénées, Aragon and Nafarroa converge" (Michelena, 1997:184). In the area now known as Bidasoa-Txingudi, they

---

[1] This literally means 'the Hendaia of tomorrow' in Basque.

fixed the position of the border in the middle of the Bidasoa's current at low tide, simultaneously demarcating the fishing zones on either side and rights to control passage up and down the river. The treaties delimiting the frontier also brought with them an innovation in the form of border guards. From 1861, it became illegal to take goods across the frontier without paying a tax and smuggling began to thrive among the border population. Thus began a tradition whereby not merely goods but arms and people are smuggled back and forth across the muga even today.

In the late nineteenth century local feuding led to the installation of French and Spanish garrisons in Hendaia and Hondarribia. Hendaia's population did not begin to grow again till the mid nineteenth century, boosted a few years later with the establishment of the railway line from Paris to the frontier. During the First World War, men with French nationality crossed into Spain from Iparralde to avoid military conscription. The municipality of Irun, meanwhile, proclaimed its support for France and gave assistance to Hendaians. Following the armistice, Irunians took part in the celebrations in Hendaia. During and after the Spanish Civil War, thousands of people fled from Spain to France, many settling just beyond the frontier in Iparralde. In the opposite direction, many people crossed into Spain during the Second World War, either fleeing Nazi persecution or to join the Free French Forces.

Hendaia, during this period, provided temporary shelter for numerous refugees from Spain, including many Basques. But while many were welcomed and assisted by the municipality of Hendaia and its population, there was also suspicion towards them as politically engaged people. At the time of writing, there are still people alive in Hendaia who remember how as refugees they were regarded with mistrust by the local population as poor, politically dubious and undesirable newcomers. In October 1940, the train station of Hendaia was the venue for a meeting between Franco and Hitler at which one of the main issues on the table was the possible presence of Nazi forces in Spain. Franco, however, refused to allow this, instead simply agreeing to a policy of mutual non-intervention (Puche, 2000). During the Nazi occupation of France, a few local people were involved in helping refugees to cross the border into Spain. However, the municipality of Hendaia declared its official support for the Vichy government, and many Spanish refugees were denounced and sent to a prison camp in Gurs, in the nearby province of Béarn, originally set up to house refugees fleeing Spain during the Civil War. During the years immediately after Second World War, relations between France and Spain were minimal. Although the frontier was re-opened in 1948, movement across it remained restricted and the towns on either side of it developed independently of each other. In the 1950s, while Hendaia and Irun expanded their industrial and railway facilities, an airport was built in Hondarribia, with no regard for the disturbances it caused to the people of Hendaia by flying very closely over the town.

In the mid 1950s, a partial relaxation in border crossing regulations brought about closer links between the two sides. People from Irun and Hondarribia crossed the frontier to Hendaia to purchase and smuggle home goods unavailable in Spain. Hendaians crossed to Hegoalde to buy cheaper alcohol, cigarettes and petrol, and to go to bars that stayed open later. With further alleviation of border controls in the 1960s, many Irunians and Hondarribians also sought work in Hendaia in order to earn higher salaries. During the 1970s and 1980s, over half the local population was employed in some frontier-related activity such as customs, police or transport services.[2] In Irun and Hondarribia, customs and transport represented approximately a quarter of all jobs, with 80% of these employees Irunians and 20% Hondarribians (Puche, 2001:179). In Irun, shops selling tobacco and alcohol and Spanish products were set up specially to cater for the population of Iparralde, who called them "ventas", or "Bentak" in Basque. From the early 1980s onwards, numerous children from Hondarribia and Irun went to school in Hendaia, to benefit from the supposedly higher quality of the French national educational system. Likewise, a few parents in Hendaia who wished their children to follow Basque education began sending their children to the Basque high school in Hondarribia. Every day, they would be stopped at the frontier for routine controls. Through such contacts, many local inhabitants got to know the national language of their neighbours.

Throughout this period, the frontier formed a dividing line between two very different socioeconomic contexts. On one side was France, developed and democratically emancipated and a founding member of NATO and the European Community. On the other side was Spain, economically backward and still ruled by a right-wing military dictator. At the same time, the frontier also provided a shield for Basque nationalists from Hegoalde seeking political refuge in Iparralde. Among them were militant members of ETA who, during the régime of General Francisco Franco, were commonly granted refugee status by the French state, which defended them as victims of a dictatorial régime. Their arrival continued a tradition whereby, throughout the twentieth century, numerous people crossed from the Spanish side of the frontier into France seeking refuge from repression or better economic prospects, making Hendaia a "ville d'accueil",[3] as many Hendaian informants put it to me. Many so-called political refugees from Hegoalde now live in

---

[2] *La Lettre d'Activités en Pays Basque*, March, 1991, No. 403, p. 6-8.
[3] This could more or less be translated as 'town of welcome' or 'place of refuge', open to inhabitants from other areas.

and around Hendaia and other parts of Iparralde, unable to return home still for fear of arrest.

Following Spain's return to democracy in the late 1970s, official French attitudes to ETA militants began to change. From the early 1980s, onwards cooperation between the French and Spanish states in combating ETA resulted in the tracking down and arrest of numerous militants and the extradition of some of these to Spain. In response to ETA's violence, meanwhile, the secret Spanish right-wing paramilitary organisation GAL engaged in clandestine operations, including shootings and assassinations, on French soil.

Spain's entry into the European Community in 1986 marked another major turning point. Higher standards of living and lower real estate prices in Iparralde prompted many Irunians and Hondarribians to purchase land in Hendaia and establish their residence there. Although border controls still continued, these new residents went back and forth across the frontier, many continuing to work in Hegoalde. In 1993, members of the growing Spanish-national community in Hendaia formed the asociación de trabajadores transfronterizos, an association for "Cross-Border Workers", to represent them in their administrative relations with the municipality of Hendaia. In 1997, a survey by the municipality of Hendaia carried out "in order to better know our Spanish Hendaians", as Hendaia councillor Jean-Baptiste Etcheverry explained to me, found that 20% of the town's resident population was of Spanish nationality. In December 1999, electoral records showed that 18.6% of people registered to vote were of Spanish nationality. An even larger proportion of Hendaian residents have ancestral links to Hegoalde or other parts of Spain. Various Hendaians to whom I spoke estimated that 70% or more of the population might have a parent, grandparent or great grandparent that came from the other side of the frontier. "We are all Spanish somewhere", fifty-year-old Jacques Artola, the owner of two photography shops in Hendaia, declared to me.

In parallel, the depreciation of the Spanish peseta over the 1990s led many Hendaians to do their shopping on the other side of the frontier. Increased local mobility back and forth across the frontier led for some people to the emergence on a local scale of what in effect can be seen as a "transnational" lifestyle. Until the introduction of the euro in January 2002, many of these people carried two purses, one for francs and the other for pesetas. Reflecting the close family, professional and Basque political relations entertained by many local people in Irun and Hondarribia with people in Hendaia and further up the Iparralde coast, Elena Etxegoien, an EAJ councillor in Irun, people in Irun and Hondarribia "have always spoken in an affectionate way of *el otro côté*", a term combining Spanish and French to refer to 'the other side' of the frontier. The town hall employee Claude Urrutia, who does not speak Basque despite having a Basque name, noted that "for many of us, Spanish is our second language".

Over recent years, the meaning of the word muga has been extended in line with political and socioeconomic change. Its use in the context of the official name of the cross-frontier consortium grouping the three towns of Bidasoa-Txingudi takes the word far from the world of Basque tradition and Basque nationalism, raising it to the level of inter-state relations in the context of the EU. Here too there is scope for ambiguity and disagreement. While Basque nationalists are happy with the projection of Euskal Herria on the European scene and the rapprochement between Iparralde and Hegoalde that the Partzuergo entails, they criticise the use of the word as part of the name of the cooperation agreement, arguing that it is a contradiction in terms. The Consortium's name in Basque, Mugaz Gaindiko Partzuergo, literally means 'cross-frontier cooperation agreement'. Just when the Partzuergo is supposed to be talking about union, complain the nationalists, it maintains the existence of a frontier through the use of the word in its name.

Indeed, for many people, the frontier remains a dividing line between two worlds even today, with different political and social conditions on either side helping to sustain support for its continued existence among many people. During the 1980s, the violent confrontations between ETA and the Spanish state spilled over into Iparralde and incidents took place in Hendaia, many inhabitants of Iparralde saw the frontier as reifying the dichotomy between the peaceful "French Basques" and the troublesome "Spanish Basques", complementing other cultural stereotypes contrasting the populations of either side. Even some Basque nationalists in Iparralde integrate the frontier into their analysis of local politics when they complain about what they perceive as a lack of sensitivity on the part of their Hegoalde counterparts to the "historical and cultural differences" conditioning nationalist politics on the French side of the muga. In October 2000, the destructive street violence, or *kale borroka* in Basque, of some young Basque nationalist militants from Hegoalde during demonstrations against a European Council summit meeting in Biarritz sparked concern among Iparralde nationalists that this could prove harmful to their cause and complaints that their Hegoalde counterparts were treating Iparralde as part of "their territory".[4]

More generally, many people in Iparralde continue to regard people in Hegoalde and further afield in Spain as the "raucous" and "brutish" Spanish. Such perceptions are in line with the once widespread French view of Spain as an archaic, politically and economically weak and isolated place, reflecting its outflow of immigrants into France during the 1960s. In Hendaia, long-time residents complain about the way in

---

[4]   See editorial "Nous sommes sinistrés" in *Enbata*, 19 October, 2000, No. 1648, p. 2.

which recently established 'Spanish' newcomers treat the town as an extension of their territory on the other side of the frontier. By continuing to observe codes of behaviour typical of Hegoalde rather than Iparralde and by failing to make any effort to speak French, many of these new arrivals from Hegoalde display a refusal, whether deliberate or unconscious, to acknowledge that they have crossed not only a state border but a socio-cultural one.

In everyday discourse, I heard many Hendaians express suspicion of neighbours in Hegoalde, commenting that the loud and extrovert "Spanish" are "eating us up" economically and culturally. Equally, many people who have settled recently in Hendaia from Hegoalde voice stereotypical attitudes about their French-national neighbours. Some told me they found "the French" boring because of their habits of eating lunch at midday and going to bed at 9.30 p.m., in contrast with the much later hours observed in Hegoalde. The same people characterised Hendaia as "a comfortable suburb of Irun and Hondarribia" where they were at home enjoying peace and quiet when not socialising on the other side of the frontier. Consequently many did not even install French telephone lines in their homes, relying instead on their Spanish mobile phones, with which they still managed to connect to the local Spanish network.[5] Most admitted to knowing little more of their adopted hometown than the way to the beach and to the doctor and the supermarket.

In Irun and Hondarribia, meanwhile, I heard many people speak dismissively of Hendaians as "the French", or refer to them in a derogatory manner using the word *gabacho*, even in some cases if both they themselves and the people they were talking of were Basque-speakers. It is common on the Spanish side of the frontier to hear people complain about the failure of 'French' people to respect local etiquette when they come onto "our side". I was able to witness instances myself, for example in the case of a group of French-speaking middle-aged men and women in a popular bar in Irun behaving in a noisy manner which made them stand out from the rest of the crowd. The act of crossing the frontier can be taken by some as an opportunity to behave in a different manner than normal. Influenced by a popular image of romantic, hot-blooded Spain, many French people may also think this is the way to behave, or to feel more liberated, when on the other side of the frontier and separated from their habitual sociocultural references.

In another example, I witnessed a surprising change of behaviour in relation to myself and some friends on the part of some left-wing nationalist youths from Hegoalde when we encountered them in Iparralde. After having taken no notice of us in the bars of Hondarribia and Irun, where we

---

[5]   Conversely, my mobile phone with a French network worked in Irun and Hondarribia as if I were still on French territory.

had seen them on numerous occasions, they suddenly adopted an attitude of friendly familiarity with us on seeing us in similar bars in Iparralde. As one of my friends remarked with some cynicism, "they completely ignore us when they see us in Hondarribia, and now that we find ourselves across the border, they suddenly think we are the best of friends". In spite of these youths' fervent Basque nationalist discourse and their insistence on treating either side of Euskal Herria as their home, crossing the border evidently produced a particular effect on them. Their lack of identification with Iparralde and their perception of it as a different space were revealed by the alteration in their behaviour. This is also revealed in other instances by the ignorance and clichéd attitudes concerning Iparralde of some Hegoalde nationalists. Despite frequent comments about how "sweet" and "pretty" and "simple" Iparralde is their knowledge of the area often goes no further than the main coastal towns. This in spite of their commitment to knowing all that is 'necessary' about the history of Euskal Herria.

Such incidents explain why, despite the ending of frontier controls, the frontier retains its symbolic status in Basque nationalist discourse. Indeed, the ending of border controls has given rise to new opportunities for using the frontier as a focus for protest. This was exemplified in July 2000 when an association advocating the liberation of imprisoned Basque nationalist militants organised an impressive silent demonstration spanning the border. For an entire afternoon, supporters of the association stood at approximately fifteen metre intervals from each other along the road from Hendaia across the frontier to Irun and Hondarribia, wearing white masks and holding up flags with the slogan "Euskal Presoak Etxera". On another occasion, in the context of two days of 'civil disobedience' organised by several left-wing Basque nationalist groups from Iparralde and Hegoalde in October 2001, demonstrators crossed the Bidasoa and occupied the Island of the Pheasants for an afternoon. The aim, according to one of the participants, was to "show that Euskal Herria well and truly does exist. We occupy this island as Basques and, in this process, reject the denial of the existence of Euskal Herria by the French and Spanish states which claim to be its owners".[6]

As a focus for symbolic acts of various sorts, the frontier plays an important part in the political rhetoric of the Basque nationalist movement. Road signs by the border marking French and Spanish territory are often painted out or, as in the case of signs on the bridge between Irun and Hendaia, 'corrected' to inform the reader that he or she is entering Gipuzkoa or Lapurdi. In early 2001, the restoration by the Irun town council of a stone sculpture by the Basque sculptor Jorge Oteiza on Santiago Bridge

---

[6] Interview with Gorka Torre, representative of the Iparralde non-violent resistance group *Demos*, and organiser of the event, 17 October 2001.

leading to Hendaia caused much polemic because of the words 'España' and 'France' engraved on it. The annual day of the Basque homeland, *Aberri Eguna*, involving a big gathering of Basque nationalist supporters from both Hegoalde and Iparralde, has often deliberately been held close to the border. In April 1996, this celebration began in Hendaia and ended across the muga in Irun, where participants were able to end their day eating and drinking in the bars of the town centre. In October 2000, EAJ organised a gathering for its supporters in Hendaia to coincide with the EU summit in Biarritz. By holding this meeting in Iparralde, the president of EAJ, Xabier Arzallus, was making a symbolic statement regarding the right of the Basque people as a nation to be represented at such a European summit, and of presumed support for this objective in both Iparralde and Hegoalde.

While free circulation is now permitted across the frontier, members of the French police force and the regional police force of Euskadi, *ertzaintza*, are often seen patrolling their respective sides of the frontier on the bridge between Irun and Hendaia. In addition, state authorities on either side retain the power to close the frontier in an 'emergency'. In March 2000, the French authorities closed the frontier in order to prevent a large group of Basque nationalist organisations from Hegoalde from crossing it in order to join a demonstration in Bayonne. French police squads were deployed along the frontier crossings to block passage into Iparralde. Representatives of the demonstrators subsequently made an official complaint, stating that the French authorities had violated the rights of EU citizens to freely cross the frontiers, as provided for under the Schengen agreement.[7] In October 2000, on the occasion of the EU summit in Biarritz, the French state briefly contemplated closing the frontier to keep out demonstrators from Hegoalde, largely made up of a large contingent of members of the Basque left-wing youth movement Haika. In the end, the frontier was kept open, though heavily patrolled by both Spanish and French police.

Other events provide similarly explicit reminders of the frontier's existence. In September 2000, for example, a sharp rise in French petrol prices temporarily reinforced the role of the border as a social and economic boundary between the local populations. Lower petrol prices in Spain became even more attractive than usual for inhabitants of Iparralde, creating queues at petrol stations in Irun as car owners from the French side of the frontier nipped across the border to fill their tanks. For inhabitants of Irun and Hondarribia, this prompted much criticism of the "French" coming "to nick our petrol". In the spring of 2001, when foot-and-mouth disease was rife in France, disrupting the movement of livestock, mats doused with disinfectants on the roads leading across to

---

[7]   *Enbata*, 23 March, 2000, No. 1620, p. 7.

the Spanish side of the frontier provided a further reminder of the frontier's continued existence. Traffic rules on either side of the frontier also prevent lorries from crossing the frontier on public holidays. As these are often different in Spain and France, they regularly result in long lines of waiting trucks in Irun and Hendaia along the roads connecting to the motorway. Smuggling also continues, though now on a more international level, involving precious stones, drugs and arms. So French and Spanish customs officers continue to keep watch on the motorway going through Irun and Biriatu, occasionally stopping vehicles, especially those with Dutch or non-EU number plates. In April 2002, when French customs officers went on strike in support of demands in relation to working conditions, they blocked the motorway at the frontier for a whole day, creating major traffic jams.

The frontier in the Basque Country is thus a focus of much contestation. It remains a fundamental barrier for state administration: the powers of the Spanish and French administrations extend to the frontier but no further. Despite talk of 'a Europe without frontiers', it is understood as a fixed limit both by those who value its role in defining the territory of the nation-state and those who regard it as the major obstacle for Basque national unity. Traffic back and forth across the frontier has increased to such an extent since Spain joined the Schengen area in 1995 that many people now view the areas on either side of it as one space. Nonetheless they remain faced with repeated reminders of the complexities of negotiating that space, as will be seen in the following vignette.

The Korrika – A Cross-Border Rally

Today, 6 April 2001, is an exciting day for Basque nationalists and those concerned with maintaining and developing use of the Basque language: at around 11.00 a.m., the Korrika will pass through Bidasoa-Txingudi. The Korrika, which means the run or race in Basque, is a special marathon organised by AEK to raise funds for the promotion of Basque. A baton symbolizing the Basque language is carried by a runner and passed on as in a relay after laps of one kilometre. The Korrika is mainly funded by associations, businesses and other organisations which 'buy' a lap and then designate someone, usually a key figure in efforts to develop the Basque language, to carry the baton. Behind him or her run people of all ages, all motivated by their support for the Basque language. Some identify themselves as abertzaleak, though they do not all share the same political affiliation, while others prefer the label of euskaltzaleak. The Korrika is a rare event in which all of them can come together in relative harmony. As Del Valle remarked in her anthropological analysis of the Korrika (1988), it is a ritual bringing together people who identify with the Basque language.

The Korrika follows an itinerary traced by the AEK organisers through the seven provinces of the Basque Country. Weaving its way through both Hegoalde and Iparralde, it mobilises crowds of supporters. Crossing the state frontier is a moment of great excitement, expressing a defiance of state division and a sign of Basque communication and unity as the baton is passed to the next relay runner waiting on the other side of the frontier. The event is particularly emotive for some Basque militants originally from Hegoalde but living in Iparralde, as they risk arrest by the Spanish police if they cross the frontier: as they approach the muga, they abandon the Korrika, unable to go any further.

This year's event began several days ago in Bilbao. After already crossing over once into Iparralde it is now heading back towards Bidasoa-Txingudi and Hegoalde. It will enter Hendaia from the east, run through the town centre and across the border again into Irun, and then pass through Hondarribia before going back a third time across the frontier in order to finish in Bayonne two days later.

With Elisa, a friend from Irun who works at Sokoa and studies Basque with me at AEK, I walk up to one of the roundabouts in Hendaia where the Korrika will pass. Here we plan to join in the run, together with other students of AEK. When we arrive, most of the other participants are already waiting, wearing tracksuit trousers and a vest bought from AEK as a contribution to the event. On the vest is this year's Korrika logo, a cartoon-style drawing of an astronaut holding the Korrika baton and flying in space with the planet Earth far below. Sharing our excitement, we greet each other and chat in Basque. Other people present include children and teachers from the ikastola and French schools in Hendaia, as well as a few local inhabitants, members of Basque cultural associations. Amongst them is Serge Lonca, who teaches at the ikastola and represents the local Green party on the town council.

Soon, we hear the sound of the Korrika jingle "Mundu bat bildu" [8] *approaching up the hill. Behind a van with the AEK logo leading the Korrika is a large group of people running. Most of them are factory employees at Sokoa, which has paid to run one of the laps. Despite the cheering from onlookers on the side of the road, the Sokoa team members look very serious, intent on their task of running. At the roundabout, the baton is handed over to one of the ikastola children and the Korrika carries on towards the town hall of Hendaia. There, amidst*

---

[8]   Meaning 'Bring together one world' in Basque. This evokes not only the building of
a world of Basque speakers but also a world against 'globalisation' – the second part
of the jingle sings about 'Big Beñat' which is meant as a humorous local alternative
to McDonald's Big Mac hamburger. Beñat, meaning Bernard, is a common Basque
name for a man.

another crowd of children, regional journalists and television cameras are waiting to see the mayor, Kotte Ecenarro, take the baton.

Also wearing a tracksuit and the Korrika vest, the mayor leads us through the main square and down the hill towards the station. One of the organisers sitting in the van at the head of the Korrika shouts through the loudspeaker in Basque "Ttipi ttapa, ttipi ttapa!"[9] *Everyone running responds with the jingle to the rhythm of the music. Gorka, a factory employee at Sokoa and the boyfriend of Katia, a teacher at AEK in Hendaia, is running along looking very serious. He has been running since the start of Sokoa's lap where the neighbourhood of Pausu ends. So has Imanol, an older man with a big bushy moustache, also a Sokoa factory employee, now running beside Elisa and me. Directly behind the van leading the way runs Helia, another Sokoa employee in his mid twenties whose parents left Hegoalde during the last years of the Franco dictatorship to live in Hendaia. A few years ago, he spent time in prison for allegedly vandalising a French bank in Hendaia. With a group of friends, he holds on to a big AEK banner. One of them wears a beret, his long curly hair bouncing out and up and down to the rhythm of his steps. They all concentrate on their running, their faces growing redder and redder. As we accidentally bump against each other, we smile and nod friendly greetings in Basque. The feeling of complicity is strong as the music from the van keeps us going, up and down, up and down, at a steady pace.*

Just before the station, a few policemen are standing beside the road, supposedly to keep order, along with several onlookers. As they approach, Gorka, Helia and a few others raise their voices and chant "Euskal Herrian Euskaraz!"[11] *and "Mugarik ez!".*[12] *Gorka raises his fist at them and cries "Askatu!"*[13] *in their face. The policemen, with their arms crossed, look back with expressionless faces.*

Not far away, Hendaia councillors Jean-Baptiste Etcheverry and Benito Zubeldia stand watching the passing throng. At this point, the mayor's lap ends. He hands over the baton to an AEK organiser and stops running to join his fellow councillors by the side of the road.

As we approach the frontier, a French police van with flashing lights drives up in front of the AEK van to lead us along the bridge. In my eyes, this formalises the event about to take place. A mixture of appre-

---

[9]   Meaning 'Step by step, little by little' in Basque. This was another slogan of the Korrika, which draws the analogy between running in the Korrika and the progress made by the Basque language.

[11]   'The Basque language in the Basque Country!'

[12]   'No frontier!'

[13]   'Freedom!'

*hension and excitement is visible on the smiling faces of my fellow
runners. As we reach the frontier, in the middle of the bridge, Imanol,
who is running beside me, mutters to me, "I'm leaving you here. I can't
go on". He and another couple who fled Hegoalde a few years ago for
fear of reprisals from the Spanish police to take refuge in Iparralde, do
not want to risk stepping on Spanish soil again. They stop running just
before the Spanish flag marks the end of French territory, and rest on
the edge of the bridge.*

*The rest of us carry on running and, as we get closer to the middle of
the bridge, it is now the turn of the ertzaintza to control us. This year,
fear of the foot-and-mouth epidemic already existing in France has led
the Spanish authorities to take measures to avoid its spreading onto
their territory. One of them is the placing of mats doused with disinfectants on the frontier lines. As we approach these mats spread across the
bridge, the ertzaintza asks us to slow down so we can effectively wipe
our feet. A strange and rather occurrence, it reminds us even more of
the existence of the state dividing line.*

*A crowd of people are waiting for us a little further on, beyond the
recently made derelict former Spanish customs buildings. Most are
teachers and students of AEK in Irun. Over their tracksuit trousers,
some are wearing purple or blue shirts with horizontal white stripes.
Many of the girls wear their hair tied up in Guatemala-made bandanas,
while some of the men have their hair short in the front and long in the
back. The baton is handed over to one of them and we carry on running
up the Iparraldeko Ibilbidea towards Irun.*

*Just before we reach the centre of Irun, a famous Basque rock star
from Irun called Fermin Muguruza waits, surrounded by journalists and
fans. All smiles, he takes the baton and runs on, amidst much cheering
from the crowd following on behind him. As he runs up the street, he
looks back at us from time to time, still with a big smile, showing that he
is running with us, not just leading the race, in contrast to the mayor of
Hendaia who looked straight ahead as he ran on his own.*

*At the top of the avenue, a much bigger crowd is waiting. People of
all ages, including children and old people, are standing on the side
watching the Korrika go past, while others join the running. Amongst
them, Marina Grijalba, a Spanish-speaking sixty-year-old woman living
in Irun, prepares to join the race. At this point, a large of group of
people carrying banners and billboards with black and white pictures of
Basque 'political' prisoners dominate the Korrika. They represent
associations demanding the return of these convicts to Euskal Herria. In
front of them, others are carrying banners announcing a general strike
called by EH in all of Euskal Herria on 15 April.*

The Korrika passes through Irun to the roundabout from which the road leads to Hondarribia. Here, a smaller group of people, many of whom I recognise from Muara, a bar patronised by supporters of the Basque left-wing movement in Hondarribia. Some of them, including friends Aitor, Ibai and Aritz, dressed as usual in sneakers, tracksuit trousers and t-shirts with Basque slogans, are carrying similar banners and placards to the ones in Irun. Also amongst them is Marije Zapirain, the representative of EH in the municipal council of Hendaia. The baton is handed over to an old man, whom I have also often seen in Muara. He begins running and the rest of the group follows behind him. Running along the road to Hondarribia, we pass the airport on the right, where teachers from HABE, the alternative organisation to AEK set up by the Basque government, are standing waiting to join the Korrika.

We reach the city walls of Hondarribia and, still running at a steady pace, enter the medieval gates and go up the cobbled street that leads to the town hall. There, in front of the town hall, employees of the municipality are standing waiting with Ion Elizalde, EA councillor of Hondarribia in charge of the development of the Basque language. He is waiting to take on the baton. The mayor is nowhere to be seen. I wonder whether he has chosen to stay away after an incident two years ago when he took the baton and was booed by Aitor and his friends for his failure to make an effort to learn Basque.

Up comes the Korrika and Mr. Elizalde takes the baton amidst cheering from the municipal employees. Aitor, Ibai, Aritz and their friends run behind him, still holding their placards and banners. Mr. Elizalde runs through the narrow streets of the old part of town and down and out again towards the marina. There, a crowd of children from the various schools of Hondarribia join in behind Mr. Elizalde and the Korrika proceeds round the marina area, up one street and down the main avenue before exiting Hondarribia again. At that point, I bump into Aitor who, exhausted by all the running, sits down by the side of the street to catch his breath. All red and hot and tired out, we sit in silence watching the commotion around us. Aitor, finally getting his breath back, searches for words and blurts out "so moving".

CHAPTER 5

Language as Uniter and Divider

One day, in the supermarket where I am working in Hendaia, I en-counter Maialen doing her shopping. A native of Hendaia, Maialen lives and works at the smart spa hotel of Serge Blanco in the Sokoburu marina area of Hendaia. Three times a week, we meet at AEK's branch in Hendaia, where we take Basque lessons together. A tall woman in her mid thirties, with delicate clear skin and short hair cut in the neat style common among many women of Iparralde, she appears happy to see me. We chat together in Basque, which she speaks fairly fluently as a result of her diligent attendance at AEK over the past two years.

Basket in hand, a woman in her sixties wearing a brown raincoat approaches. Seeing her, Maialen switches to French and introduces her to me as her mother. Knowing that her mother speaks Basque and wishing to carry on speaking in this language, I address her mother in Basque. She looks astonished and then, with slight irony, remarks in Basque, "It seems that it really is a fashion amongst young people now to learn Basque. I suppose it is good... I don't know. Not very useful though... Not like English or German or... And you all learn this Span-ish Basque don't you? Batua?" Next to me, Maialen blushes, clearly ill at ease. While I carry on talking to her in Basque, her replies to me are no longer so fluent.

In this brief encounter, we witness some of the tensions and contra-dictions surrounding the Basque language as a vehicle of daily commu-nication in the Basque Country. Maialen and I are *euskaldun berriak*, or 'new Basque-speakers', learning Basque as part of our commitment to Basque culture and a 'Basque identity'. Maialen's mother is an *euskal-dun zahar*, or 'old Basque-speaker', who learnt the language as a child in a family context but who now sees little use or value in the language as a means of communication in the 'modern' world of globalisation and consumerism. Not only did she not transmit the language to her daugh-ter as a child but she sees little purpose in learning it today, dismissing our enthusiasm as a fad and providing no encouragement to her daughter in her endeavour. What might have been an inclusive element in our relationship becomes an obstacle to mutual understanding. Instead, Maialen's mother imposes an exclusive boundary between those who, like herself, grew up speaking Basque and others, like Maialen and myself, have made the effort to learn the language.

The negative force of such contradictions becomes clear when we consider that the Basque term to define 'a Basque person', euskaldun, means 'somebody who has the Basque language', or in other words someone who can speak Basque. While the terms vasco and vascongado in Spanish and Basque in French are more inclusive, referring to someone who has Basque origins, regardless of his or her fluency in the Basque language, there is no word in Basque to describe a person who is of Basque ancestry but does not speak the language. Furthermore, not all those who support the Basque nationalist cause are necessarily Basque-speaking, or even of Basque origin. Indeed, only a minority of the population in the whole of the Basque Country actually speaks Basque. Equally, someone who speaks Basque may not have Basque origins or be a Basque nationalist. Such is the case, for example, of Serge Lonca, the French teacher at the Hendaia ikastola who learnt it as part of his endeavour to participate more effectively in Basque society.

In France, one of the goals of the territorial re-organisation that followed the Revolution was to combat the persistence of provincial loyalties and localism (Weber, 1977). French citizenship was founded on the 'belonging to the territorial community', or "ius solis". The state preceded the nation, in the sense that nation-building largely depended on state effort. Language was a key element in this process of French-nation building. During Robespierre's reign of terror, the revolutionary Abbé Grégoire produced a survey of language use in France, with the ultimate objective of setting up a homogeneous 'French' nation. He considered that a plurilingual France would mean "a tower of Babel" (Gazier in Jacob, 1985:32), and preached instead the universalism of French. At about the same time, an official of Jacobin persuasion expressed his prejudice against Basque people with the words "fanaticism speaks Basque".

Even as late as 1863, official estimates recorded only about a quarter of the population of France actually speaking French. Under the Third Republic, improved communications and governmental subsidies gradually helped to generate a sense of belonging to the centralised state among local populations. During the twentieth century, a national educational system, supplanting the Catholic Church in the provision of basic literacy, military conscription and centralised social services underpinned a state in which citizens were expected to speak French and see themselves as members of a common nation. The French Basque region was no different from anywhere else in this respect. The combination of French centralizing policies and rural economic decline led to declining use of the Basque language in Iparralde, in favor of French and what was perceived by many people as the more prestigious French identity. Modernity was associated with a French-speaking elite, while Basque was largely confined to the rural and traditional world and the private sphere. For most of the twentieth century, there was no concept of Basque modernity under which Basque could compete with French as a modern means of communication. Figures such as the village priest and the local notary, who typically spoke both French and Basque, acted as intermediaries between the two worlds. Following the decision of Vatican II to end the use of Latin in church services in favour of vernacular languages, the Catholic Church's promotion of Basque helped to preserve the language in written texts but simultaneously accentuated the schism between the category of 'French/modernity/laicity/universal reason', on one side, and that of 'Basque/tradition/Catholicism/communitarian morality' on the other (Jaureguiberry, 1993). The Basque language came to be seen not only by many French people but by Basque people too as a 'patois',[1] lacking the status of a proper language, an attitude that continues today particularly amongst the older generations.

Negative attitudes towards ethnic cultures in France continue to be widespread today, both at a political level and among many ordinary French people. This is demonstrated by the negative reactions of some French people when they are informed that some people with French nationality actually feel more attached to an identity such as Basque or Breton or Corsican and continue to speak these languages. Attempts to explain away these 'anomalies' within the French Republican model are apparent, for instance, in a description I have often heard of "les Basques" as "spéciaux" – 'special' in the sense of 'peculiar', in that they are rather different and so excessive and fiery in character, to the point sometimes of 'extremism'.

Along with Greece, France is the only country in the EU not to have ratified the European Charter for Regional and Minority Languages. In May 1999, having acknowledged that "regional languages do not pose a threat to the integration and cohesion of the French Republic", 39 of the 98 clauses were signed. While this was still unsatisfactory for cultural activists and nationalists, it was already a step too far for 'Jacobins', or supporters of a centralising state government. The Charter was referred to the Constitutional Court which ruled it unconstitutional, on the grounds that it went against article 2 of the French constitution which states that French is the only language of the French nation. President Jacques Chirac then refused to support Prime Minister Lionel Jospin's proposal for a Constitutional amendment, causing the government to go back on its decision of ratification.

---

[1]   This is a French term to refer to a way of speaking that is not conventionally viewed as the standard, 'national' language. As such, the term connotes the inferior status of this language or form of communication.

As for the Convention Pays basque 2010, this was successively re-negotiated in 2000 to create the Convention Spécifique Pays basque 2001-2006, with a total budget of 400,230,000 euros provided by the French government, the region of Aquitaine and the département des Pyrénées Atlantiques. A special section relevant to the development of the Basque language was put into practice with a total budget of 7,165,103 euros. In order to ensure the smooth running of this scheme, a Basque language council was also created bringing together Basque associations, local councillors and delegates of the region of Aquitaine and the département des Pyrénées Atlantiques.

This convention is significant in that it involves an official recognition on the part of the French government of the specific needs of the Basque Country in socio-economic, cultural and linguistic matters. However, as the then Secretary-General of the Basque language council, Eguzki Urteaga, stated to me in an interview, there is still a great need for diplomacy and careful treading in relations with government authorities.[2] For example, rather than talk of 'normalisation' of the Basque language, which they still see as threatening, government authorities prefer to talk of *aménagement* – or 'organisation' of the Basque language.

South of the Pyrenees, the environment was until recently even more negative for the Basque language. From the twelfth century onwards, the presence in the Basque region of a Castilian-speaking elite deprived the Basque language early on of support from an established upper social stratum. Differences between the various Basque dialects were so marked that, in some cases, speakers had great difficulty in understanding each other. The development of overseas trade during the Middle Ages brought increased urbanisation and a stronger Spanish presence, increasing the differences between cities, inhabited by a predominantly Spanish-speaking population, and Basque-speaking rural areas. A distinction was made between those who were speakers of some kind of Basque dialect, known as *euskara*[3] or euskaldun, and those who spoke a foreign tongue, *erdara*, and who were known as *erdaldun* (Peillen, 1998:96). Castilian was made the official language of the Kingdom of Spain in 1716. This coincided with a period during which Spain began to look inwards again, in an attempt to consolidate a Spanish national identity. From then on, the existence of other languages than Castilian, such as Basque, Catalan and Galician, and

---

[2]   At the time of writing, while the Basque government had expressed willingness to give financial assistance, this offer had not been taken up for fear of jeopardising relations with the French authorities. It has been possible nonetheless to include a delegate from the Basque government in the working group on language issues.

[3]   Today the word *euskara* is used in the Batua version of Basque to signify the Basque language. However, according to Peillen (1998:96) until the late Middle Ages, the word *euskara* or *uskara* was also used to refer in Basque to a Basque person.

the maintenance of the foral system, began to be seen by Spanish central-ists as obstacles to the forging of a Spanish national identity. Further decrees in the eighteenth century established Castilian as the language of education, trade and business transactions.

By the early twentieth century, the Basque language was in serious decline, restricted to the most isolated rural areas. Under Franco, prohi-bition of its use in public places assisted in its marginalisation. Many parents during this time ceased to speak Basque to their children in order to avoid trouble with the authorities. For Basque militants, the Basque language came to be considered a crucial feature of Basque identification. From the 1960s onwards, the language was actively promoted, particularly in left-wing nationalist circles. In their search for a broad-based constituency, the fact that people of non-Basque descent could learn Basque, even if only superficially, provided an opportunity for expanding membership of the Basque community. Someone who had learned Basque could be identified as Basque within the left-wing nationalist movement, even if he or she was not of Basque descent. Knowledge of the Basque language provided a new inclusive boundary for group belonging.

Today, in Euskadi, Basque has equal status with Spanish in the public domain and is increasingly used by young people, particularly those with Basque nationalist sensitivies, for personal communication in preference to Spanish. Following the creation of the Autonomous Basque Commu-nity, efforts to support the Basque language were among the first priorities of the territory's new political leaders. The Basque government also led an effort to promote the use of Basque place-names, in preference to Spanish. Thus, Hondarribia, previously known by Spanish-speakers as Fuenterrabía, became known by the Basque form of its name, with the Spanish form less frequently used. Knowledge of Basque is strongest among young people and those over 65. Use of this knowledge however, is another matter. According to the same 1996 survey, 42% of the population of Euskadi claimed to know Basque. However, only 33% of the 70% of the population between the ages of 16 and 25 claimed to use Basque in their daily life.

In Iparralde, Basque remains a non-politicised medium of linguistic communication for many native Basque-speakers in a rural context. In parallel, it is the symbolic language of choice for people of Basque na-tionalist sentiment, while its value as a marker for the expression of Basque identity is increasingly appreciated among the general public. Only a minority of people use it in daily business transactions however, even among those who grew up speaking it. According to a survey carried out in 1996,[4] 26% of the population Iparralde claimed to be ac-

---

[4]   *Enquête sociolinguistique au Pays basque,* 1996.

tively bilingual in Basque and French, while 64.2% of the population did not know Basque at all. The majority of Basque speakers are old people: 43% of the population over 65 could speak Basque, in contrast to 24% between the ages of 16 and 24.

Generally, a person actively committed to Basque identity will attempt to use Basque where possible as his or her main mode of communication. In many nationalist fiestas, speaking Basque, however badly, is *de rigueur*, as a way of expressing solidarity between like-minded people and demonstrating identification and acceptance. In an effort to broaden the meaning of euskaldun, and so address the challenge of including non-Basque-speakers who identify themselves as Basque into the 'Basque category' while allowing for differentiation between those who speak Basque and those who don't, I have sometimes heard the term *euskaradun* used for Basque-speakers. This neologism, which also signifies 'someone who has the Basque language', is intended by its proponents to make a clear distinction between the Basque-speaker and the euskaldun, whom they present simply as 'someone who has Euskal (Herria) in his or her heart'. In practice, however, it does little to resolve the ambiguities surrounding the use of language.

One of the factors limiting the effectiveness of Basque as a means of communication has been its lack of homogeneity. Dialectal variations are strong between regions, and even from one mountain valley to the next, and there is no socially or culturally recognised 'correct' way of speaking Basque. Even within communities, there are differences in the way in which Basque is spoken. In Hondarribia for example, members of the fishing community speak in a way that differs markedly from that of the rest of the town's inhabitants. In response to these variations, the unified form of Basque known as Batua was developed from the 1960s as a synthesis of mainly the Nafarroan-Lapurdian and Gipuzkoan dialects. Batua was initially promoted by a group of enthusiasts acting under the aegis of *Euskaltzaindia*, or Basque Academy, formed in the 1920s by Basque intellectuals from both Iparralde and Hegoalde.

Thanks to the standardisation provided by Batua, the public use of Basque has grown to the point where it is no longer narrowly associated with traditionalism and the rural hinterland. Within the complex network of social imperatives that characterises the Basque Country, however, it is difficult other than in an isolated rural context for an individual to speak Basque without any additional connotations of a political or social nature. Many euskaldun zaharrak continue to lament that Batua is not the 'real' Basque, undermining the efforts of the abertzaleak to bring people together through a common language. In an attempt to show sensitivity to dialectal variations, AEK and the ikastolak teach the local way of speaking Basque. Despite their efforts, the discomfort felt by many non-nationalists with the 'radical' politics of the abertzale movement, perceived by many non-nationalists as a threat to the status quo of Basque society, often leads people who use the language in a rural context to be wary of its political connotations in a more urban context.

As for non-Basque speakers, they effectively have to choose between ignoring Basque or getting caught up in the social construction that results from the transmutation of a traditional means of communication into a highly charged social symbol. Depending on the social context, individuals' attitudes to the Basque language are thus conditioned by the pervasive impact of Basque nationalism on local society. Whether a person speaks French, Spanish or Basque becomes a marker of identification with a certain idea of a political and cultural group and a boundary including other fellow speakers and excluding non-speakers.

In both Hegoalde and Iparralde, the extent to which Basque is used in daily life varies considerably, depending both on the composition of the local population and the degree of commitment of individuals to Basque culture. While Batua now largely dominates the way Basque is spoken and written in Hegoalde, Basque speakers in Iparralde continue to use local dialectal forms, with different vocabulary and pronunciation. Differences are clearly noticeable between the Basque spoken by people from Hendaia and that spoken by people from Irun and Hondarribia. Many Hendaians speak Basque with a French sounding accent, pronouncing Rs as uvular trills and Js as palatal approximants, while Basque speakers in Hegoalde will pronounce Rs as apical flaps, and their J's as harder uvular trills. The vocabulary and grammar also change in accordance with Spanish and French grammar. Basque words in Hendaia continue to remain both French and local-dialect specific. Ways of writing place names and personal names in Basque also differ on either side of the frontier as French and Spanish have had an influence on how Basque is written as well as spoken. Maps of Hendaia for example continue to feature "the bay of Chingoudy", despite the currency given to the Batua form, Txingudi, by the Partzuergo and its proponents.

A high level of Basque fluency and literacy is now required to obtain a post in the regional administration of Euskadi. While not obligatory elsewhere, fluency in Basque is similarly becoming a significant criterion for employability in private businesses. Municipalities in Euskadi have Basque translation and interpretation services. However, the decision whether or not to introduce simultaneous Spanish-Basque interpretation services remains a matter of choice for individual municipal councils, depending on their willingness to devote a substantial part of the municipal budget to such services, and many left-wing nationalists still criticise the Basque government for not doing enough to promote the use of Basque.

On both sides of the frontier, learning – or, in many cases, re-learning – the Basque language is an increasingly popular activity no longer necessarily reflecting political engagement. AEK classes, formerly dominated by young abertzaleak, nowadays include people of different ages and backgrounds. These vary from young men and women, whose parents chose not to speak it to them, as in the case of Maialen, to older people who heard Basque as children but stopped speaking it as they grew up and who are now anxious to establish their right to a Basque linguistic heritage, and people who come from totally different backgrounds but wish to integrate into Basque society.

In 1999, the municipality of Hendaia, in an effort to show its concern with the state of the Basque language, produced a survey on attitudes to and use of the Basque language among the local population. It found that only 18.9% of the population of Irun were fluent Basque speakers (SIADECO, 1999a), in contrast to 30% and 65% in Hondarribia (EUSTAT, 1996). Accompanying the results of the survey was a list of suggestions for the development of the Basque language in Hendaia, such as providing more signs and information in Basque, more Basque cultural activities and encouraging municipal employees to learn the language (SIADECO, 1999a:14). In order to implement these measures, SIADECO recommended that some of the municipal councillors of Hendaia form together a Basque language commission (SIADECO, 1999a:15). At the time of writing, only two municipal employees had taken the initiative of learning Basque with AEK in Hendaia. The former mayor, Raphaël Lassallette, is also taking lessons. However, the other suggestions made by the survey remain to be followed up. The Hendaia council's website for example is available only in French. Efforts to put bilingual street signs remain half accomplished.

In the public domain, Basque names and words are often used for decorative and local identificatory purposes. Many shopkeepers in Hendaia who do not speak Basque nonetheless employ Basque names for their shops. So, for example, a café by the leisure port named Sokoburu is called Bi Ur Arte, meaning Between Two Waters (referring to the fact that it is close to both the sea and the river) but the owner speaks no Basque. The state subsidised social centre in a marginal neighbourhood of Hendaia is called Centre Social Denentzat, Denentzat meaning 'for everyone' in Basque. When it comes to more 'serious' notices in shops and businesses, however, the state national language tends to be favoured. For example, at the Banque Inchauspé located by the station which belongs to an Iparralde family of the same name, while adorned by its logo saying "herriko bankoa" or local bank in Basque, a sign by the door advertises "Change, Cambio, Wechsel" only in French, Spanish and German.

In Hegoalde, a similar phenomenon can be observed in the public use of Basque names as markers of cultural identity alongside a general concern with political correctness. Many businesses, for example, even though in some cases run by people who are not Basque-speaking, have a Basque name in addition to a Spanish one. In this way, accusations of discrimination against Basque are avoided. So can be understood for instance the decision to change the name of Irun and Hondarribia's development agency from Adebisa, an abbreviation for the Spanish *Agencia de Desarollo del Bidasoa*, meaning Development Agency of the Bidasoa area, to *Bidasoa Bizirik/Bidasoa Activa*.[5] Most inhabitants of Hegoalde, even if they do not speak Basque, also use key words in Basque, such as *Agur*, for goodbye, *Kaixo* for hello, *Egun On* for good morning and so on. These can be used to begin a conversation before lapsing into Spanish again. For a non-Basque speaker, such a tactic involves acknowledging the Basque language as a boundary and making an attempt to overcome it. While such a person does not actually speak the language, he can make his own claim to it and thus make it part of his identity.

Whether, under what circumstances, and to whom a person speaks the local Basque dialect, the standardised Basque language, Spanish, or French, form an important part of the expression of that person's identity and of his or her presumptions with regard to the other person's identity. This is illustrated, for example, in local telephone etiquette: an urban Basque nationalist sympathiser with only rudimentary knowledge of the Basque language may answer the telephone in Basque but then switch to French or Spanish to conduct a conversation. Conversely, a local farmer may answer the telephone in French but then hold a conversation in her local Basque dialect if the caller is someone she knows.

In some cases, use of Basque can serve as a deliberately exclusive boundary. So, for example, a friend in Hendaia who had taken Basque lessons but still did not speak it well and so continued to speak French to his friends, commented that he was discouraged from going to *Gaztetxeak* – militant Basque youth centres where music concerts take place – because he felt ill at ease in the presence of others who heard him chat in French to his friends. Another friend complained about the attitude of an old acquaintance during an AB meeting where the threat of schism due to the prospective creation of Batasuna was being discussed. This person chose to address the meeting entirely in Basque despite knowing that my friend and a fair number of other AB members in the audience could not understand Basque. This person had learnt Basque from zero only three or four years ago and, according to my friend, "just because he now speaks Basque, he thinks he is part of some great exclusive club,

---

5   This means 'Active Bidasoa' in Basque and Spanish.

and thinks he can be so much more Basque than the rest of us non-Basque speakers here... That really gets on my nerves. I completely agree about the importance of using Basque in meetings and all that. But his particular attitude then was so full of arrogance and evoked a pretty exclusive stance."

The choice of personal names and how to spell one's surname have also become a focus of this symbolic struggle. In Hegoalde, where Basque first names were prohibited under Franco, giving one's children Basque names such as Gaizka, Iker, Arkaitz, Garazi and Nekane is now very common. In Iparralde, where French names like Marie-Jeanne, Yvette, Jean-Marie and Bernard were once mainstream, Basque names have regained popularity. It is not rare either to find adults altering their names to fit Basque pronunciation and spelling. In this way, a person whose birth certificate bears the name Michel in French, or Miguel in Spanish might present himself in Basque social circles as Mixel in Iparralde, or Mikel in Hegoalde.

Place-names can also be referred to in a particular language so as to mark identification with speakers of that language, and a corresponding rejection of other languages and association with other people. For instance, Robert Arrambide, the leader of Biharko Hendaia, sometimes refers in conversation to Hondarribia as "Ondyarbi", using the affection-ate appellation given by inhabitants of Hondarribia to their town. In doing so, Mr. Arrambide can be seen as seeking to apply the local dialect in order to emphasise his association with this feeling of locality. This also marks him off from people who use the officially approved name Hondarribia or who continue to refer to the town by its Spanish name, Fuenterrabía, or its French name, Fontarabie. Most of the people I heard using Fuenterrabía were non-Basque-speaking inhabitants of Irun, though there were also some Basque speakers who, when they spoke in Spanish, used the Spanish term. A similar tendency can be observed in Hendaia, as we saw earlier, whereby a proud Basque-speaker from Hendaia but with family origins in Hondarribia and Irun, insists, when speaking in French, on pronouncing Irun as if it were a French word, sounding something like 'Eerungh' and talking about Hondarribia the French way, as 'Fontarabie'. This serves to mark the speaker's identifi-cation with 'French culture' in spite of his strong commitment to the Basque language and 'Basque culture' and personal links to Hegoalde.

Similarly, despite the great effort made by Basque nationalists to avoid using state references when talking of the part of the Basque Country on the other side of the frontier, referring instead to Iparralde and Hegoalde or to *bestaldea*, 'the other side', it is not uncommon to note some of them getting their terms mixed up and talking of going "to France" or "to Spain" instead, before quickly correcting themselves. Such lexical dilemmas and slips of the tongue demonstrate that the border remains very much present within personal consciousness, whether desired or not. Similarly, people not identifying with Basque nationalism but conscious of the importance of political correctness for smooth social relations often take care about how they refer to the various parts of the Basque Country.

The different situations of the language in Iparralde and Hegoalde have also had consequences for the significance of the Basque language as an element in the sense of self (Tejerina Montana, 1994). In Iparralde, its non-official status and effective marginalisation from public life means that for many, learning Basque is very much a personal motivation, linked to the emancipation of one's sense of self. In Euskadi, meanwhile, the motivation to learn Basque is increasingly linked to professional necessity. Many in Euskadi learn Basque as an obligation and regard the language as having little or no significance for their sense of self, other than in potentially compromising situations when it can serve as a marker or boundary of their identity or to signal their belonging to the Basque-speaking community. So for example, a teacher in Irun who had to learn Basque late in his life in order to keep his job, said he did not identify with it in the least. By contrast, the enthusiasm of those who want to learn confirms a certain set of values that sets them apart from local French and Spanish people who do not speak Basque and from those euskaldun zaharrak who have chosen to forsake the language in favour of French or Spanish, as we saw in the case of Maialen's mother.

In the same year that Hendaia's town council set about making a survey of local use of Basque, the local branch of AEK launched a campaign to provide Basque-speaking shopkeepers with stickers saying that they could speak Basque – "euskara badakigu". Thanks to these stickers in shop windows, it was hoped, customers would know that they could speak Basque to the shopkeepers rather than French. Volunteers from AEK went around all the shops of Hendaia, offering these stickers to Basque-speaking shopkeepers. While some took to the initiative well, others reacted negatively. A few complained that the sticker was like a brand mark, thereby reflecting the fears and taboos felt in relation to Basque identity and the Basque language by many of the older generation. Such reactions illustrate the ambiguous relationship of many inhabitants of Iparralde to the Basque language. Similarly ambiguous attitudes can be observed in Irun and Hondarribia.

Within such parameters it can be difficult for people to adapt to new boundaries, even when they may wish to do so. The complex pluricultural context of Bidasoa-Txingudi means that language can be used as a symbolic boundary in a rich diversity of ways. The potential for misunderstanding in a plurilingual context is greater than in a monolingual one, as can be illustrated by my observation of social interaction in

Bidasoa-Txingudi with Dominique, a man in his mid-twenties from Hendaia who declares himself to be an abertzale and attempts to form part of what he understands to be the abertzale world. The way he does so, however, is sometimes the source of misunderstandings:

Unable to find interesting work in Iparralde, Dominique works in Bordeaux, the capital of the region of Aquitaine some 270 kilometres north of Hendaia. As often as he can, however, he returns to the Basque Country at weekends. Concerned with what he sees as a lack of Basque political, cultural and economic dynamism in Iparralde, Dominique is a member of AB.

Dominique did not grow up speaking Basque. Because of his new job in Bordeaux, he says, he has too little time to start taking Basque lessons, although he says this will eventually be one of his priorities. Together, we communicate in French but, as I soon find out, Dominique very much enjoys speaking Spanish, which he learnt at school and over the years from much partying in Hegoalde. He compares the inhabitants of Iparralde unfavourably to those of Hegoalde, whom he praises at length. "They are so much more lively and friendly", he said on one occasion when we met in Irun. "So much more active and open than us pathetic people in Iparralde with our Frenchy mentality. It is practically impossible to motivate people there. We abertzales are such a minority there." His dream, he tells me, "is to eventually come and live here in Hegoalde. Or at least have a house here. Forget Hendaia and its lousy practically non-existent night life, and just come and hang out here. Be in a real Basque atmosphere".

The first time that I arrange to meet Dominique in Bidasoa-Txingudi, he suggests that we have lunch in Hondarribia. Knowing that lunch in Hegoalde will be later than in Iparralde, I suggest we meet at half past two in the afternoon. When he arrives, he is not enthusiastic about my suggestion to eat in one of the fish restaurants in the area of the old port, where many French tourists, he says, tend to gather. Instead, he insists we have a drink in Muara, one of the main meeting places of the Basque left-wing nationalists in Hondarribia. Although I know the place, Dominique seems keen to lead the way. So I follow him up to the medieval part of town and through the entrance of Muara. Beyond the threshold, before one reaches the bar area, one has to proceed across a small empty space, through another door, and along a narrow corridor, like an antechamber, preparing the intimidated initiated for the spectacle of posters, stickers and other paraphernalia donning Basque left-wing nationalist symbols decorating the bar at the end. There, Dominique confronts the barman, cheerfully addressing him in Spanish and orders us drinks. He then turns back to me and addresses me in French. We begin to talk about how life in Iparralde compares to that in Hegoalde and Dominique describes the people of Hegoalde as so much more open-minded and warm-hearted than those of Iparralde. Feeling hungry, I eventually ask Dominique if he would like to eat. Surprised, he replies that he has already had lunch. He had not understood why I had suggested we meet at 2.30 p.m. and, considering it, according to Iparralde custom, far too late for lunch, had already had his lunch at home before meeting up with me. So while I was working up an appetite, he had assumed we were meeting just for a drink.

Apart from demonstrating the romantic and rather superficial image that is sometimes held by non-Hegoalde people in relation to Hegoalde and the rest of Spain, this anecdote shows the extent to which certain boundaries can be engrained in the construction of the self. While Dominique may wish to associate himself with certain cultural boundaries, it remains difficult for him to assimilate them. Because we had not 'checked' each other's symbolic boundaries and observed how they were used in different contexts, I had mistakenly presumed that, from the laudatory way he talked about Hegoalde and the strong identification he professed to have with it, he could adapt himself to its symbolic boundaries. The differences between what he said about himself and how he actually behaved reveal significant aspects of his identity construction.

One evening, Dominique joins me on a night out in Irun with some girlfriends of mine from Hondarribia. As self-proclaimed left-wing abertzaleak, Aurkene, Miren, Maite and Izaskun, choose to begin the evening in Hazia, a bar similar to Muara in Irun.

On this occasion, we are sitting at the bar chatting away in Basque when Dominique walks in with another friend from Iparralde. Both are wearing t-shirts. Dominique's sports the AEK logo and his friend's t-shirt is made by the Basque fashion company 'Kukuxumusu', based in Pamplona, the capital of Nafarroa known in Basque as Iruña. I invite them to join us and, speaking in Basque, introduce them to my friends. Wishing to be sociable and friendly, Dominique chats to them cheerfully in Spanish. However, in response, Aurkene and her friends only nod and smile briefly. Evidently not wanting to speak in Spanish, they resume chatting with each other in Basque. Undeterred by their reserve, Dominique talks to me in French, throwing in a few Spanish words. Apparently impressed by my Basque friends, he takes me aside and asks me how I got to know them.

We continue to stand by the bar drinking together, Aurkene, Maite, Miren and Izaskun chatting amongst themselves in Basque, and I standing between them and Dominique and his friend, who are chatting to me in French. I feel I am in an awkward position, unable to get everyone to talk to each other in a consensual way. Aurkene does speak some French, having spent a couple of years studying in France. But, in this situation, she does not appear to wish to use this language. Dominique,

still eager to get to know my friends, continues to chat to them in Span-
ish, asking them questions and cracking jokes. This, however, does not
have much effect, as Aurkene and her friends continue to seem unwilling
to speak Spanish. As this scene continues, I feel increasingly embar-
rassed by Dominique's carefree insistence.

Eventually, Aurkene, Miren, Maite and Izaskun decide to move on to
another bar. As Dominique and his friend plan to return home early, I
remain with them in the same bar for a last drink before joining Aurkene
and her friends elsewhere for the rest of the night. We resume chatting
in French, I more at ease now that there is no more language miscom-
munication.

This anecdote briefly illustrates the difficulty of communicating between supposedly like-minded people even when there is a mutually
understood language. Dominique is keen to mix with people of the left-
wing abertzale circle in Hegoalde. But his entrance into that world is
marred by his failure to recognise and observe the necessary symbolic
boundaries. While his style of dress as well as his choice of bar clearly
signal his identification with left-wing Basque nationalists and facilitate
his integration with them, his inappropriate choice of language creates
an obstacle that makes his respect for these other boundaries ineffective.

The unsatisfactory situation in which Dominique finds himself is not
due to the fact that he does not know Basque but to the fact that he does
not adequately compensate for this lack of knowledge. Many non-
Basque speakers who identify with left-wing abertzale culture, conscious of the importance of speaking the language for being fully included in the social group, try and learn it. Those unable to take lessons,
for whatever reason, make up for their lack of fluency by peppering
their speech with Basque words and phrases. They will often begin a
conversation with a brief cordiality in Basque, before resorting to Spanish or French. Others excuse themselves by explaining that "unfortunately they do not speak Basque" before proceeding to talk in French or
Spanish. Yet others may choose simply to remain unusually quiet,
unwilling to 'impose the majority language'.

Surprisingly, Dominique, although a self-proclaimed abertzale, does
not engage in any of these strategies. Although well-informed about the
political and cultural situation in Hegoalde, he continues to associate the
Hegoalde lifestyle with the Spanish language, which he takes pleasure in
speaking instead of French. Perhaps, in his pleasure at speaking Spanish,
the language of a culture which he admires for its mythical warmth and
liveliness, he is unaware of the complexities of local identity formation.
Practically all inhabitants of Hegoalde are quite capable of speaking
Spanish, and their way of living and expressing themselves in social
relations is very much linked to the general culture of the Iberian peninsula. Indeed, from time to time, in order to explain a point, Aurkene and

her friends use Spanish. When they do so, however, it signifies a deliberate acceptance of a symbolic boundary marker in a specific situation, and they do so by choice. At times in my conversations with them, since my Basque is not fully fluent, I would have liked to use Spanish to express myself better. However, on the few occasions when I did contribute to the conversation in Spanish, I did not sense an enthusiastic response on their part and their replies continued to be in Basque. As an honorary member of the group, I was required to fit in with their boundaries. So when I was sometimes slow to construct my sentences in Basque, they were patient and helpful.

As this example shows, since these boundaries were set by them, they could decide whether to comply with them or not, breaking into Spanish from time to time if they so desired. The difference between speaking Spanish among themselves and speaking Spanish with Dominique is that in the latter situation the boundary marker would be imposed on them by someone they do not know. Were Dominique to have made a few preliminary excuses about his inability to speak Basque, or to have used some Basque words, the reaction of Aurkene and her friends might well have been different. In fact, however, their coldness was already evident before Dominique even began talking to them, as he chatted to me in French. On another occasion, I recall, when I was talking about some friends of mine in Hendaia, Aurkene had asked me whether they were euskaldunak. When I said "no, frantsesak", her face showed a little smirk. It seemed to me that she was thinking "frantsesa=gabatxo",[6] ignoring the fact that in Iparralde, it is not because one is French-speaking that one is necessarily gabacho and, one may, like Dominique, be a supporter of left-wing Basque nationalism. Aurkene could have spoke to Dominique in French to avoid the Spanish boundary. She may have preferred not to do so for lack of confidence in her own fluency in French. But my interpretation is that French was also simply not one of the boundary markers that she wished to employ in that particular situation, on a night out with her Basque-speaking friends in a bar surrounded by fellow left-wing Basque nationalist sympathisers.

In other situations, while communication takes place in French or Spanish, occasionally saying something in Basque serves as a reminder of the inclusive boundary that bonds the speakers together. For example, in a meeting I once had with a representative of the former party Euskal Herritarrok in the municipal council of Irun, after initiating the conversation in Basque, I asked if we could switch to Spanish, so I could be sure to capture all he wanted to say in the interview. He kindly obliged. Once the interview over however, he returned to Basque to chat more informally and bid me goodbye. Similarly, with two friends from Irun,

---

[6]   'Gabatxo' is the Basque version of the Spanish derogatory term 'gabacho'.

most of our face-to-face conversations were carried out in Spanish for the sake of spontaneity, but then, when it came to writing to each other, Basque was the language we used. This indicates what our ideal way of communicating together would be if I was fluent enough: always in Basque, a shared boundary marking the more intimate quality of our relationship.

The boundary quality of the Basque language in this case is also well illustrated in a meeting I attended in Hendaia, organised by the left-wing Basque nationalist group, Biharko Hendaia. When I arrived, the meeting had already started, and about a dozen people were already sitting around a blackboard in discussion with Robert Arrambide, the leader of the group. When I walked in, they all turned round to look at me. I was the only person present who was not a member of the group. But, as Mr. Arrambide and I were already acquainted, he introduced me to the rest of the group. This he did in French, at which point, a woman in the audience whom I had also once talked to in Basque a few months before, added in Basque: "And she knows Basque!" At that moment, I understood I was welcome into the group. Mr. Arrambide proceeded with the debate and, although his notes on the black board were in Basque and he referred to the town by its Basque name, "Hendaia", rather than the French "Hendaye", all the discussion was carried out in French. The reason for this was that some people in the audience did not know Basque and, in such a small meeting where practically everyone knew each other quite well, having the discussion in Basque and then translating it to French would have been too cumbersome. So, differently to the case of Aurkene and her friends, what bound the people together in this situation was the agreement that Basque is important – which allows me in – and yet their acknowledgement of the need to make an exception in the case of this meeting for practical reasons. The inclusive quality of the boundary of Basque was maintained by continuing to use Basque for references to place-names and Mr. Arrambide still writing words in Basque on the black board.

Lack of knowledge of the Basque language, on the other hand, can be a source of voluntary self-exclusion. For example, Martine, a middle-aged woman living in Hendaia, says she has no interest in learning Basque, in spite of her claims to feeling Basque and her Basque roots on her father's side. Her reason, she says, is that she feels a constant pressure from people around her to speak it, especially at Sokoa where she works. "It is all a brain-washing enterprise, making everybody feel they have to learn it. It would just be a service to the militants. I won't succumb to this", she explains. One time, she recalls, a work colleague had commented on the fact that a new member of staff had taken Basque lessons and had concluded in jest: "Now you know what you have to do, hey, Martine? Learn Basque". At this, Martine got angry and categorically replied: "No, I shan't" and then stormed off. So Martine engages in the symbolic struggle over the Basque language by refusing to learn it, in effect rejecting the Basque language outright.

At the same time however, it must be considered that Martine engages in a dialectic which involves justifying her disinterest with the Basque language by putting the blame on the political situation in the Basque Country. When I asked her whether she didn't feel the urge to learn Basque simply for her own satisfaction, following her own terms of identification, she replied that this would not be possible. "Not with this pressure I feel around me. It provides no choice." However, later on in the conversation, she adds: "Anyhow, I don't need to learn Basque to feel Basque. I would prefer to spend my free time doing other things". So Martine justifies her lack of interest in the Basque language as an aspect of her identity repertoire by accusing Basque militants of exerting pressure and a bad image on the language. In this way, she is able to use the Basque language as a way of setting up her own boundary between herself and Basque militants.

Even native Basque speakers sometimes avoid speaking Basque in public, so as to disassociate themselves from possible political connotations. The preference for Spanish rather than Basque in the presentation of news programmes on the local Irun-based television station Txingudi Telebista can also be understood in this way. Txingudi Telebista is a member of *Bai Euskarari*, a Basque Country-wide initiative to promote the Basque language in the workplace. If it were truly to aspire to being a 'Txingudi' television station, it should in theory use Basque and French as well as Spanish. Since most of the station's audience are elderly non-Basque-speakers living in Irun, however, the television team chooses to broadcast most of its programmes in Spanish. Only a few programmes and news items are presented in Basque and even fewer in French. The team manager, although a fluent Basque speaker, preferred the news to be presented in Spanish or French rather than in Basque. I could not find any reason to explain this choice other than her lack of appreciation of the Basque language as a possible alternative mode of communication in the professional context and maybe even a desire to avoid Basque out of fear that it might be associated with militancy. The argument that too few television viewers understood Basque was invalid, since very few could understand French either.

Felipe Saragueta, the former director of the Partzuergo, once remarked to me how great a difference it made for him to be able to communicate in Basque with the people he had to deal with in municipal offices and on the town councils. Negotiations and trust became easier on both sides, giving him an advantage over those who could not speak Basque. The language boundary marked an increased closeness between those within it compared to those outside it. However, in the context of his job, he also avoided overdoing his use of Basque, especially in the presence of non-Basque speakers, in order to avoid giving the impression of setting up a boundary between himself and non-Basque speakers that would prevent any bonding within or across other symbolic boundaries, such as support for one or another political party. In my own personal experience, it also happened that, in some situations, it was best for me to downplay my knowledge of the Basque language with local inhabitants who did not know it. This helped to avoid misunderstandings on their part about my possible nationalist sympathies or making them uncomfortable about their lack of knowledge despite being more 'Basque' than me.

CHAPTER 6

Hitting the Town:
Symbolic Boundaries at Play

It is past 2.00 a.m. on a Saturday night in Calle de la Mierda,[1] *literally meaning 'Shit Street', a street in Irun more conventionally known as Cipriano Larranaga Kalea but popularly known for the drug addicts who used to frequent the area a few years ago. Today, the street has been cleared of such people and a row of night bars has opened. At weekends, these bars, with flashy modern façades and in some cases with catchy English or Irish names, attract numerous young revellers from Irun and its environs, including Hondarribia and Hendaia. As the bars fill up, the street becomes a noisy hangout, littered with glasses and empty cigarette packets.*

One of these bars, No. 10, is packed with people dancing to chart music, practically elbow to elbow. The average age is about 25, and most of these people are clustered in same-sex groups of four or five men or women, sharing drinks and cigarettes. The interior is dimly lit, with the walls painted in dark colours, highlighting the varnished wood trimmings with jagged and curved edges on the walls, the ceiling and the bar. As part of the gaudy décor, cocktail recipes in Spanish are painted on the walls all around. The music blaring out from the small hi-tech stereos makes verbal communication difficult other than by shouting in other people's ears. Instead, social communication consists of squeals of laughter, smiles and a general shuffling and singing along to the lyrics, as the revellers sip from their large plastic glasses of spirits mixed with soft drinks.

Not far from the bar, four women are standing together. As they dance self-consciously to the music, they look around at the rest of the crowd. Nora, Ana and Vanesa are wearing close-cut black trousers and skimpy tops, while Laura wears a glittery red a-line skirt with high-heel boots, a silk cream shirt and a fuchsia neckerchief. Nora and Ana both have the Basque lauburu hanging from their necks. They are all wearing makeup, consisting of foundation, red lipstick and eye shadow. Above

---

[1] I use Spanish since this is how I have always heard this street referred to, even by Basque speakers.

the noise, they try to hold a conversation in Spanish. The Spanish sum-
mer hit 'Bomba' comes on. Shrieking, the four jump about and dance
with increased vigour, singing in unison to the chorus.

Elsewhere in the crowd, another group of friends, this time made up
of five boys – Antton, Iker, Eduardo, Iñaki and Urbil – are also dancing
to the summer hit, though less wildly, and singing along to the lyrics.
Edging closer to the bar, they order another round of cola mixed with
rum and a second packet of American cigarettes. Eduardo and Iñaki
wear dark checked shirts and new-looking jeans and their hair is short
and gelled back. Eñaut, Iker and Urbil are wearing dark jeans, plain
t-shirts and lambswool sweaters, with their hair newly washed but
without gel. Eñaut stands out from his friends with his ears pierced with
small silver rings. As they get jostled around by the crowd, they manage
to hold a brief chat in Basque, above the sound of 'Bomba'.

Grasping his wallet decorated with an ikurrina, Eñaut tries to get the
attention of the barman. As he does so, he accidentally jostles another
man next to him busy in conversation with a woman with permed blonde
hair and a pink skimpy top. This man, similarly dressed in freshly ironed
jeans and a dark checked shirt, but with his hair slicked back with gel,
angrily pushes Eñaut back, swearing in Spanish. Thus begins a little
scuffle, as Eñaut answers back, also in Spanish. Neighbouring groups of
people, including Nora and her friends back off from the bar to a safer
place. Luckily, the confrontation dies down as both men refuse to ac-
knowledge each other's existence any further. Everything falls back into
the familiar rhythm of dancing to the music and passing drinks and
cigarettes round.

A short distance away in an older part of town, more young people
are partying. A dozen bars surround or stand just off Plaza Moscú, –
Moscow Square – or Mosku in Basque for short, a rectangular space
lined with poplar trees, officially known as Urdanibia Plaza. It is un-
clear where the popular name originates, though many reckon it is
related to the left-wing Basque nationalist and anarchist character of
those who have frequented this area over the last forty years or so.
These bars are older looking, occupying the ground floor of the many
eighteenth and late nineteenth century buildings that surround the
square.

Mikel is one of these bars, located in a street giving onto the square.
A wooden sign hangs above the door with the name of the bar carved
out in pseudo-traditional Basque style letters. On the front door, a
poster advertises bertsolari, an improvised singing contest, in a bar in
Pausu, on the other side of the Bidasoa near Hendaia. Past this door, a
medium-sized room with dark rugged stone walls is illuminated by the
lamps above the bar. Like many of the bars on this square, the interior
has a rustic atmosphere due to the low wooden beams on the ceiling, the

window sill and the bar that fills the left side. In the middle of the bar, by the beer taps, a collection box gathers funds in support of Basque convicts and their families. Behind the bar is a collection of handmade objects: an African mask, some witch dolls made of wood, straw and clay and a leather mask of the kind often found in arts and crafts fairs in different countries.

Mikel is similarly crowded, mostly with small single-sex groups of friends in their late teens to late twenties. Amongst them is Aurkene, with her women friends Estitxu, Ainara, Nerea and Maite. They are more simply dressed than Nora and her group, in dark close-fitting shirts and sweaters and dark, loose-fitting jeans. The music they dance to, as they pass around glasses of cola and rum, and kalimotxo, a mixture of red wine and cola, has more of a hard rock flavour, with Basque lyrics. At one point, it changes quite radically to the familiar 'Bomba' song. The reaction is less euphoric than at No. 10, but Aurkene and her friends nonetheless appear to enjoy the music as they dance animatedly.

A group of four boys enters. Josu, wearing a simple checked shirt and combat trousers, with scruffy hair and several silver rings in his ears, leads the way. His friends, Eneko, Garicoitz and Gorka are all wearing t-shirts with Basque slogans on the front, one produced by AEK promoting the use of the Basque language, and another calling for independence. On seeing Aurkene and her friends, they exchange greetings in Basque: they know each other from hanging out in Muara, the bar in Hondarribia with links to the left-wing Basque nationalist movement. But after acknowledging each other's presence, the two groups resume partying on their own.

Not far away is another group of four friends, this time men and women together. Elsa, dressed in a black long-sleeved shirt and matching black trousers, wears a badge with the logo calling for Basque convicts to be transferred back to Euskal Herria above her left breast and a golden lauburu hanging from a chain around her neck. Alongside her, Antoine, Xabi and Marise are also wearing t-shirts with the AEK logo. They have come together from Hendaia. They order beers and stand close to the door, away from the crowd and the music, chatting in a mixture of French and Basque.

At this moment, Nora comes in with her friends. Just as they were leaving Calle de la Mierda to go home to bed, Nora realised that she had forgotten her jumper in Mikel, where they had begun their night out. As she heads towards the bar, Nora runs into Aurkene. They greet each other briefly in Basque, as they know each other from having been in the local equivalent of the Girl Guides together when they were children.

*Having retrieved her jumper, Nora and her friends leave Mikel
again. On their way home, they walk through San Juan Plaza, another
part of the old centre of Irun lined with bars, where things are also in
full swing. On the way, Nora's friend Vanesa bumps into Stéphane, a
young man from Hendaia whom she knows because they both work in
the same company in Hendaia. Breaking into French, she greets him
and his mixed-sex group of friends, who have also come from Hendaia
on a night out. They are dressed in smart jeans, surf t-shirts, and thin
woolly sweaters loosely tied around their shoulders, and the women are
wearing makeup and some of them lauburus from chains around their
necks. Amongst them, I recognise Nadine with two of her friends from
the Océanic bar in Hendaia, the principal meeting place of rugby fans.
Clutching big plastic glasses of rum and cola which they have bought in
one bar, they are heading for Kutxa, a bar around the corner from San
Juan Plaza, which is their habitual haunt, decorated in a similar way to
No. 10 in Calle de la Mierda, with a flashy glass façade and dark, mir-
rored interior, before eventually ending their evening in Zona, a discothèque nearby.*

Here we have briefly met six groups of friends in their mid to late
twenties during a typical night out in Irun: Nora with her group of
women friends, and Aurkene with hers; Eñaut with his group of men
friends and Josu with his; and Elsa and Stéphane, each with their group
of men and women friends. Generally, they all seem to enjoy themselves
more or less in the same way, going from bar to bar, ordering drinks and
passing them around, dancing in clustered groups to very loud music
which includes a mixture of Spanish summer hits, and smoking American cigarettes.

However, subtle differences can be noted in their style of dress and
taste in drinks and music, and further details would give more clues
about how each of these characters uses boundaries affecting language,
dress and behaviour to construct his or her personal identity. Here, I
have chosen to hint only superficially at these, so as not to distract from
our specific interest in the use of space.

There are many ways of describing 'going for a night out' or 'hitting
the town' in Bidasoa-Txingudi. This reflects both the choice of phrases
available in Basque, French and Spanish in the area and the cultural and
political implications of using one or other of these languages. Few
people speak all three, and those who do often prefer to use one rather
than another for a variety of personal, cultural and socio-political reasons. At the same time, words from each language are used in conversation by people speaking in one or other of all three languages.

Generally, Basque speakers in Hegoalde talk about *farra egin* or *parranda egin*. Farra or its dialectical variation parra means to laugh or to
have fun in Basque. A Spanish speaker might hispanicise the noun and

say *ir de parranda* or *ir de farra*. He or she might also say in Spanish *ir de juerga* or *ir de copas* or, more rarely, *ir de potes*. 'Juerga' is a Spanish colloquial term meaning partying, while a 'pote' is a Spanish colloquial term meaning a drink. This last word has been adopted by the French-speaking inhabitants of Iparralde to talk about *faire le poteo*. Some Basque-speakers in Iparralde use the expression "*poteo egin*" but more often they simply talk about *besta egin*,[2] which literally means to 'make fiesta'.

Irun provides the main nightlife location for young people in the area. With a larger population than either Hendaia or Hondarribia, it has a markedly wider choice of bars. On occasion, young people from Hegoalde who identify with left-wing Basque nationalism may go for a night out in Iparralde, for example to attend a celebration organised by a Basque association or in favour of a Basque cause. This has become possible thanks to the ending of frontier controls in a way that it never was during the Franco years and the transition years that followed. Sometimes, for example, young people from Irun and Hondarribia go out to listen to a bertsolari in Pausu, at a bar called Xaia, or to a dinner evening in support of Basque prisoners, or, more rarely, to the annual cider day, *Sagarno Eguna*, in the main square of Hendaia. Further afield, some also attend the annual *Herri Urrats*[3] held in support of Basque-language schools in Iparralde outside the town of Sempere, or the *AEK Eguna*,[4] which rotates its venue among local villages every year. Following current fashion in Iparralde, the most popular alcoholic drinks at such events are beer, cider, *patxaran* (a typical Basque liqueur usually made in Nafarroa), and kalimotxo.

For the most part, however, nightlife in Iparralde is dismissed by young people in Hegoalde as a dull affair. Indeed, in Iparralde, there is no tradition of 'poteo' other than, most often, on the occasion of the annual fêtes, or fiestas that take place in every town and village at some point during the year, when bars set up in the streets by the local fiesta committee and associations contribute to the general festive atmosphere. On these occasions, young people tend to drink mixtures of soft drink and spirits, such as BabyBanga, made of orange squash and whisky, and GinKas, made of gin and lemonade. Around eight bars offer some sort

---

[2]   Or "pesta egin", a dialectical variation more commonly found in the rural interior of Iparralde.

[3]   This literally means the 'Step of the People'. It is an event organised to raise funds for *Seaska*, the coordinator of Basque language schools – *ikastolak* – in Iparralde.

[4]   In addition to the Korrika, AEK organises many fund-raising events. One of these is the AEK eguna, which means the day of AEK. It usually involves a whole day of festivities, with shows, cultural activities, friendly competitions, concerts with Basque groups and a dinner.

of social nightlife in Hendaia on a year-round basis. However, it is rare to find these full, other than during the annual fiestas in August.

In general, young people in Hendaia prefer to cross over to Hegoalde – nowadays with greater ease thanks to the ending of frontier controls – to enjoy its lively atmosphere and cheaper prices in bars. In Hegoalde, too, the most common drinks are spirits mixed with soft drinks, but the ingredients are different: cola and orangeade, for instance, mixed with rum or whisky in big glasses which are often shared between friends. In summer, once the annual fiestas of Irun in late June are past, Hondarribia, with its picturesque fishing harbour and its seaside resort and historic centre, becomes an active place for nightlife. Following the annual fiestas of Hondarribia in early September, however, Irun comes back into its own.

Whether in Irun, Hondarribia or Hendaia, in choosing which bars to frequent and which bars to avoid, individuals impose their own symbolic boundaries, adapting these as necessary in order to fit their personal sense of self. At bars in Hegoalde, young people from Hendaia often stand out from their local counterparts because of their use of French and their different manners and behaviour. What is more, they tend to favour a few specific bars and discothèques in Irun. Locals sometimes comment that the French, or gabachos, set themselves apart by their boisterous behaviour and excessive consumption of alcohol, getting extremely drunk before the evening is over and often ending up in brawls. While young people from Hegoalde generally go out in groups, or *cuadrillas* as they are called in Spain, those from Hendaia tend to go out in mixed-sex groups.

In the scenes in Irun that we have just witnessed, four bar areas stand out. First, Calle de la Mierda, in a central part of Irun which has been restored over the past forty years with the construction of blocks of flats and, over the past decade, following the removal of drug dealers and addicts, bars on the ground floor. These bars are modern in style, with flashy façades. The young people who come here mostly dress according to mainstream fashion, and the music is mainly Spanish pop music. Spanish predominates as the language of communication. On this street, we observed interaction in the bar called No. 10.

Secondly, Mosku Plaza, in another central part of Irun where the streets have retained their eighteenth and nineteenth century architecture. The bars on the ground floor of many of these buildings have a more traditional style than those in Calle de la Mierda. This style is deliberately maintained, for example in the Basque names of the bars written in pseudo-traditional Basque letters. Inside, many of these bars cultivate an 'ethnic' style, with craft objects as decorations. Their explicitly Basque character is demonstrated by stickers and posters stuck on the walls and windows displaying traditional Basque symbols, advertisements for Basque cultural events and slogans promoting the use of Basque. Some of these bars have in addition an overtly left-wing Basque nationalist tone, with posters calling for the independence of Euskal Herria, portraits of Basque convicts and collection boxes in support of the convicts and their families. The young people who come here tend to dress down, often wearing clothes that convey explicitly left-wing Basque nationalist messages. In this area, we observed partying in the bar called Mikel.

Thirdly, the area around San Juan Plaza, another old part of Irun with bars with a correspondingly traditional appearance. Compared with the bars in Mosku Plaza, however, they have fewer Basque symbols, particularly political ones. They are also more spacious and more brightly lit.

Finally, near the area around Plaza San Juan is a street called Joaquín Gamón Kalea which, like Calle de la Mierda, has been redeveloped with blocks of modern flats. On the ground floor, there are a number of bars similar to those in Calle de la Mierda, one of which is Kutxa and another, more in discothèque style, is Zona. Many of the same young people from Irun and Hondarribia who go to San Juan Plaza and Calle de la Mierda also frequent this area. In addition, it is popular among young people from Iparralde, many of whom speak little Spanish and often no Basque.

While there are more bars in other parts of Irun, these four areas are the main points of reference for young people going out in Irun. Each has specific connotations for the people that frequent them. Eñaut, for example, whom we saw partying with his male friends in No. 10, in Calle de la Mierda, makes a clear distinction between each of the four areas. For him, Mosku Plaza is "an area quite linked with the abertzale left, I mean the HB people. And well, I don't really like going there. It's not my kind of... I just don't enjoy the aura of the place". By contrast, he sees Calle de la Mierda as "more a place *de copas* – for drinks – basically a place for *pijos*[5] – people with gelled hair, more money, and more conservative. Whether they identify themselves as Basque or not, it makes no difference. Of course, it is a place which you would associate more with the Spanish, the PP, if you really had to generalise". As for the other two areas, he adds, "you have the French area, two discothèques where the French go: the Jennifer, this big discothèque on the road to Hondarribia, and, more central, a few bars, like Zona, Kutxa etc... Next to these, you have the area of San Juan Plaza, which is more

---

[5] This is a Spanish expression to refer to people who are quite snobbish and fashion conscious. At the same time, pijos are also known to have a distinctive dress code which, while consisting of all the most trendy labels, is rather sombre and conservative.

of an atmosphere *de toda la vida*,[6] the old Irun. Which I would say is more nationalistic – in a different way to those in Mosku. You can definitely see a difference, in the décor and the style of people."

Nora defines the four areas in a similar way, although her boundaries are slightly different. On this occasion, we see her and her friends starting out in Calle de la Mierda and ending up at Mikel in Mosku Plaza. On other occasions, I have seen her enjoying a drink in the area of San Juan Plaza. At Mikel, Nora is well aware of the presence of symbols in support of the Basque left-wing nationalist movement, such as the collection box "in support of amnesty and the return of Basque prisoners and all that and... no, I don't support that, when it comes down to it but... I just don't pay attention. I enjoy coming to this bar because I like the general atmosphere, the mixture of people and the music". Nonetheless, she draws a line between Mikel and some of the other bars in Mosku Plaza, stating that she does not go to all of them. Some like Hazia, are really left-wing abertzale, and it's just too much. Others like Eskina, because they are too *macarra* – too grungy, all these druggies and punks. And then, the other one, Kabegorri... too 'alternative'".

By contrast, Aurkene, the daughter of a councillor representing the left-wing Basque nationalist political party EH in Hondarribia, and Josu, a young man currently unemployed but involved in voluntary activities with AEK and also on the local committee of the abertzale youth group Haika, enjoy going not only to Mikel but to the other bars in Mosku Plaza as well. Both say they like these bars "because they are much more Basque-speaking". Josu explains that he attaches great importance to being able to speak Basque rather than Spanish in the bars that he frequents. "I am from Hondarribia. But once, when I was small, my family had to live in Irun for a while. I really didn't like that. So few people here are Basque-speaking that you always have to use Spanish. I remember... at one point, I became conscious of the fact that I was always having to use Spanish, in the streets, in the shops, with Spanish television and I realised how difficult it actually is to live in Basque. And that is what I like about Hondarribia: the fact that it is possible to just speak Basque, go into a shop and just speak. In Irun, you still get these disagreeable comments sometimes. You walk into a shop and when you speak Basque, some people just say nicely, "I'm sorry, I don't understand", and so at that point I'm happy to speak in Spanish. But then you get the occasional fool who tells you: "Talk to me in *cris-*

---

6   This Spanish expression evokes the idea of a 'real' or 'genuine' Irunian atmosphere – of always.

tiano.[7] So basically, when I do go out in Irun, well, Mosku is the place where I like to go." In a similar vein, Aurkene emphasises her attachment to speaking Basque and adds, "Mosku is more abertzale".

Nonetheless Aurkene and Josu also go to the bars in Calle de la Mierda. "OK, they are not so explicitly abertzale, but so what?" says Aurkene to me in Basque. "I am not interested in following political lines the whole time. These bars I really like for having fun, their atmosphere, the music and all that." As for Elsa, who lives in Hendaia, when she wants a big night out, "basically, to do the poteo", she practically only goes to Mosku Plaza. "Sometimes I will start the evening around San Juan. I like to go there too because it is part of the old Irun and Basque-speaking. But I will always end up in Mosku. I like Mosku because it is my kind of atmosphere. It's friendly... most bars have Basque music..." When I asked her about Calle de la Mierda, however, she said she was not aware of its existence. "But anyway", she adds, "I am not interested in hanging out with the Spanish and the *franchouillards*.[8] When I am here in Hegoalde, what I like is to be in abertzale places, which are not easy to find in Iparralde, or basically just really limited." As a self-defined left-wing abertzale, Elsa has a firm idea of where she wants to go: "the places where the abertzaleak are, where I can get a Basque atmosphere".

Clearly, then, there is more to the 'atmosphere' of bars in Irun than just music and friendly jostling together in a small crowded space. Asier, the bar tender in Mikel, explains the appeal of his particular bar: "You have a mixture of different people who come here. Before coming here, I worked in a bar by the train station, and there it was more just old men coming in for their daily glass of wine, the *txikiteo*, you know. And many of them just spoke Spanish the whole time. That was another generation and another cultural environment-Irunians, but many with Spanish origins. Here, on the other hand, I can speak Basque. And for me this is important. There, there was no way I could speak it. And at the same time, this place is not political. You can come in dressed as you want. We don't mix things up. I think that's important too. OK, we have the collection box in support of Basque prisoners. But this is just a support of general principles, you know, Human Rights. There is no pushing politics down people's throats here".

---

[7]   This is used by some sections of the Spanish-speaking population to express the idea that Spanish is the 'proper' – Christian – language, as opposed to the 'pagan and prosaic' Basque language.

[8]   This is a derogatory term used to label those 'typically' French people of 'French mentality' who have no interest in Basque culture and no consciousness of Iparralde as different to the rest of France.

Mikel attracts a range of different clients by having sufficient Basque cultural and political markers for people like Aurkene, Josu and Elsa who identify strongly with Basque left-wing nationalist culture, but not so many as to antagonise people like Nora, who speaks only Spanish and whose style of dress is considered by many as "Spanish" in general cultural and political terms. The atmosphere can include popular modern Basque music as well as Spanish chart music. Asier, Aurkene, Josu and Elsa all attach importance to the fact of being able to speak Basque in Mikel, while Nora is not prevented by language boundaries from enjoying Mikel like everyone else.

Nonetheless, some other people who also identify themselves as Basque feel less comfortable in Mikel. One such is Eñaut, an active member of the Basque nationalist party EAJ who speaks Basque and Spanish fluently and identifies himself "firstly as Basque". He says, "I used to go down to Mosku. Especially Mikel... Now I don't really enjoy going there. I can't explain, I just don't feel at ease... It's not necessarily the political thing. I don't have a problem going somewhere run by an HB person. It's not that I think these bars are more radical or anything, or that there is a risk of getting attacked or whatever, no. It's just the atmosphere, with the decorations, the music, and... yes, the posters saying things with which I don't agree... When I go out, I want to have fun. I don't want to have to deal with all this business".

Dislike of Mosku Plaza is much more forcefully expressed by Iulene, a 27-year-old woman with Spanish parents who grew up in Irun and who is a friend of Eñaut. Despite having done all her schooling in Basque, she seldom uses Basque in her own social circle and she dresses in a way similar to that of Nora. "I really don't like this environment of hard-line nationalism. It really gets on my nerves, with their labels and slogans and their spliffs. It's all the same all the time. And you are made to feel completely out of it." Instead, like Eñaut, she enjoys going out in the area of San Juan and ending her night in Calle de la Mierda.

Eñaut denies that his dislike for Mosku Plaza is politically based, but he talks about being in disagreement with the markers of an inherently political kind that he sees in the décor and atmosphere of the bars there. These include Basque cultural symbols that promote political ideas of Basqueness in a particular way, which Eñaut and his party do not support. As for the possibility of speaking Basque in the bars of Mosku Plaza, even this is not sufficient to attract him to the area. The Basque language is an important feature of Eñaut's sense of self: he took the initiative of learning the language when he was a teenager, by attending evening classes. But he is also comfortable in a Spanish-speaking environment. "I am very committed to the Basque language – in fact, I take part in a local initiative which deals with the promotion of the language. I practically always speak Basque with my friends and other people. But

I won't oblige people around me to speak it. I have no problem speaking Spanish too; it is also my language after all. Of course, it would be great if everyone could speak Basque all the time."

As for Calle de la Mierda, which he describes as a place frequented by people "of a more conservative sort, people wearing clothes with labels, guys with gelled-back hair etc. – basically more people who support the PP", Eñaut says he likes it as a good place for having fun. "All I want is to have fun. It's not because I am in a place where there is no typically Basque décor that I cannot be Basque. I am just on a night out. The problem is that HB people very much dominate Basque kind of stuff. And anyway what is so 'Basque' about the way they are? I don't have to be like them in order to feel Basque, you know. I like American music and going to an Irish pub too… Anyway, on a less big night out, I actually do prefer to go to San Juan Plaza, which is more Basque and Irunian de toda la vida, which is my kind of place."

So Eñaut's personal sense of self as Basque is something that he can maintain as a private affair in the context of partying. Despite the importance that he attaches to the Basque language and Basque symbols of the sort that decorate the bars of Mosku, he insists that they are not indispensable for his sense of self. On the other hand, he objects to the way in which members of a particular sociopolitical group can dominate perceptions and the use of these symbols. For this reason, Eñaut avoids Mosku in favour of Calle de la Mierda, where these particular symbolic struggles are not felt and where, despite his critical view of the Spanish conservative types that he finds there, he can enjoy a night out. Partying beside people who may be "supporters of the PP" does not necessarily make him and his friend Iñaki PP supporters too – even if Iñaki also dresses in a similar way, with his hair slicked back with gel, after-shave and creased trousers. Eñaut and Iñaki may share some boundaries with these people but they manage the symbolic markers present to make them fit with their own sense of self. Were they to feel the need to demonstrate their Basqueness in a more decisive manner, they could resort to other symbolic boundaries. This is already shown by the ikurriña sticker on Eñaut's wallet, for example, or his chatting to his friends in Basque above the noise of No. 10.

Among those who go to San Juan Plaza and the area around it, Stéphane and his friends are the sort of people that Elsa describes as 'franchouillards' and many young people in Hegoalde refer to as 'gabachos'. Although he was born in the Basque Country and both his parents are Basque, Stéphane does not speak Basque. He explains that he does not like to go to Mosku Plaza because it is too "*bascoille*.[9] It's always just the same kind of people. You know, these people who think they are so

---

9   French derogative word to refer to Basque nationalist militants.

Basque. I mean, for example, they all dress the same. With their t-shirts which say *Presoak*[10] or Independence... or... AEK... And..., *l'habit ne fait pas le moine*,[11] you know, it's not because you dress Basque that you are Basque. And they are all the same, like sheep. That's not me. I might wear a t-shirt that says something, but it would be discreet. An ikurriña? ... Maybe. I did once have a big one hanging from the window of my van, but after a while I took it off... Firstly because I didn't want to have problems with the police, and secondly because it is also a bit too 'bascoille'. I am Basque simply because my mother, my father, my grandparents were all from around here. So what? I could have been born elsewhere. You know that a lot of the people who dress like Basques... some of them are not even from here, or they don't even know how to speak Basque. So... anyway, these bars in Place Moscou are just full of these people, and... it just gets on my nerves. Where I like to go is completely different. There, you can really have fun: the Kutxa, the Zona, in Calle de la Mierda. The Jennifer? That's more when I was 16, 17 years old or so, where you get your first real *cuite*,[12] you know, get completely drunk. That discothèque is really French, I must say. You even have busloads of kids who sometimes come down from as far as Bordeaux."

Unlike Eñaut, who learnt Basque as an adolescent, Stéphane expresses no interest in learning the language. "Do I wish I could speak Basque? ... Not really, no... I don't have the time... Anyway, it's not my thing, all this Basque business." And yet, Stéphane will often pepper his speech with Basque words like *goazen*, meaning "let's go", or *harritua*, meaning "amazed". In this way, he can appropriate for his own use certain Basque symbols without having to associate himself with people of more pronounced Basque nationalist views that he does not support. He is able to maintain a sense of self close to that of a 'French identity', without losing the sense of difference that he draws from his personal association to a Basque identity. In the company of people from other parts of France, he is proud to say he comes from the Basque Country. But the same subtle juggling with symbolic boundaries for the construction and expression of his sense of self sees him choosing to go out to bars in Irun associated more with 'the French' crowd.

In the same way, Aurkene and Josu set firm boundaries between themselves and people like Eñaut, for all his Basque attachments, whom they regard as more Spanish than Basque "with their pijo look". While they occasionally go out in Calle de la Mierda, they draw the line at

---

[10]   Meaning 'Prisoners', alluding to the left-wing campaigns calling for the repatriation of so-called Basque political prisoners.

[11]   This French expression is similar to the English "do not judge a book by its cover".

[12]   *Avoir une cuite* is a French expression meaning 'to be in a serious drunken state'.

Plaza San Juan. Aurkene dismisses the area as "stuffy, too traditionalist and with quite conservative people". Josu explains: "I am OK finishing a big night in Calle de la Mierda because that is what it's good for. But with the bars of San Juan, it's different. It just carries on being the same, with the same kind of people all night." In the same way as Eñaut is uncomfortable in Mosku Plaza, Aurkene and Josu feel uncomfortable in the bars of San Juan Plaza, even though people speak Basque there. My impression, although this is something that has never been explicitly said to me, is that this is the case because the Basque of San Juan Plaza is spoken by people who are ideologically different to them. As for Elsa, her understanding of what is a 'Basque atmosphere' contrasts with that of other people who feel equally Basque. And despite her efforts to integrate with the crowd in Mikel, for example by the use of such markers as the badge in support of Basque convicts, she stands out for her slightly different behaviour, manner of dress and choice of drink.

By analysing the use of space on the part of a number of young people in their choice of bars during a night out in Irun, I have shown how spatial boundaries are used in the construction of personal and collective identity. Their choice of bars indicates who they wish to identify with and who they wish to avoid identifying with, as part of their personal strategies in relation to their sense of belonging to the area. Boundaries of language, politics, dress style and taste in drinks, while at first apparently straightforward, are in fact used and interpreted differently by different individuals for their personal self expression. Beneath the general image of partying together in the same way, subtle markers indicate differences between the different groups of bar-goers. Equally, behind such supposedly universal Basque symbols as the lauburu and the ikurriña, different individuals express a personal sense of Basqueness that is very different from one person to the next. The different ways in which they perceive the social order and the reality in which they live and position themselves in response to it and to each other provide an illustration of how people use a system of shared meanings to help interpret and make sense of the world around them. These meanings are embodied in the material and social world in the symbolic boundaries and markers which surround us. While the fact of sharing common "maps of meaning" gives us a sense of belonging to a common group and a sense of 'who we are', we also interpret these meanings individually (A.P. Cohen, 1994a; 1994b; 1998).

As we have seen from this account, a person's relationship with his or her spatial surroundings is an important factor in creating a sense of security and comfort. Individuals' choice of one bar or another was related to their identification with and sense of control over specific symbols, such as language, Basque cultural markers and Basque nationalist ideas. The 'frame' that results from social interaction and markers within the space creates an atmosphere which the person coming in may either accept or reject, depending on his or her desires and capabilities. We saw how some people chose to go to certain bars because of a feeling of affinity for the social and cultural context which they perceived these bars to represent. Such behaviour corresponds to the way in which place, as noted by Hall (1995), can act as a sort of symbolic guarantee of cultural belonging, as it establishes symbolic boundaries around a culture, marking off those who belong from those who do not.

In other cases, by contrast, we saw how some individuals chose not to go to a certain bar because they did not accept or wish to adapt to the social or cultural boundaries implicit in such a choice, or because they sensed that the symbols present within that space had already been appropriated by people with whom they did not wish to associate. And in yet other cases, we saw how some individuals, rather than adapting to the boundaries or attempting in some way to change them, chose simply to blend in, while interpreting and using in their own way certain symbols important to their personal sense of self, even though their approach differed from that of the other people present within the bar. Here again, I join Hall in his identification of place as part of the system of meaning and, as such, open to different interpretations, since the definition of the place depends on the person's individual experience and memories and the people with whom he or she is. Each person can use place in their own way to express what they mean. Within larger social contexts, people maintain "micro-orders" on which they can depend for the maintenance of their sense of self (Berger, 1986:xvii).

Language, taste and politics have all revealed themselves as equally important boundaries in this process of organising and presenting one's sense of self. Identity is forged from a conglomeration of different features, selected by individuals for their construction of their selves. Within this context, the symbols of nationalism are one of a series of markers available for individuals as they assert the boundaries that provide a framework for their identities and are reflected in their use of space. In all cases, those involved in this process of identity formation require an audience, not only in terms of a contrasting 'Other', a 'You' and 'Them', but also in terms of solidarity between members of a group who identify in similar ways, the 'We'.

What we observe on our brief excursion into Irun nightlife is indicative of this. When Stéphane goes out in Irun, he and his friends hang out in specific bars with other people from Hendaia, in a joint affirmation of their sense of Francophone Iparralde identity. Aurkene and Josu, when they cross the frontier to attend a bertsolari evening in Xaia, find themselves partying in the company of people whose identity is forged through similar cultural, linguistic and political boundaries to their own. Similarly, Elsa, in choosing to go to "the abertzale places" in Irun with her friends, demonstrates her abertzale identity, not so much to local people from Hegoalde in the bars she frequents, as to her friends from Iparralde who accompany her.

In the wider context of life in Irun, Hondarribia and Hendaia, such considerations help to shed light on the limitations facing efforts by the Partzuergo to promote a local 'Bidasoa-Txingudi spirit' or sense of 'Bidasoa-Txingudi citizenship'. While some people from both Iparralde and Hegoalde enjoy going out in all three towns, others stay within the locality where they live, in effect imposing boundaries on their mobility and their ability to participate in the social and cultural interaction of the broader area. In shaping their personal identities in this way, both sets of people are invoking and responding to invisible boundaries beyond those of physical space. Even those who go out to bars in all three towns tend to stick to certain places.

CHAPTER 7

Belonging and Excluding
in the Alarde

The framed photos that dominate the sitting room of the home of Josefa and Nicolás are placed in full view of anybody walking in. On the wall, a near-lifesize photo portrait shows their four-year-old grand daughter Idoia sitting on the floor wearing a smartly tailored blue and white jacket and skirt, a red beret on her head and a white sash round one shoulder hanging down to her waist. On her feet, she wears white boots over white tights. Smiling sweetly, she holds a fan in one hand while the other rests on a miniature brandy keg attached to her waist. Idoia is dressed as a cantinera, the female figure who accompanies the all-male 'soldiers', most of them marching on foot, in the annual Alarde, a pseudo-military parade that is the highlight of the annual fiestas of Irun, where her family lives, and neighbouring Hondarribia.

Below this photo, a smaller one shows a real cantinera – Iulene, the youngest daughter of Josefa and Nicolás, aged 25. Wearing a blue and white tailored skirt and jacket and gracefully sitting astride a horse, she holds the reins in her white-gloved hands. The bright red of her lipstick matches the red of the festive beret atop her neatly bunned hair.

Across the room, three other photos hold pride of place on a book-shelf by the television set. In one, Iulene's sister, Amelia, a cantinera in another year's Alarde, is shown in profile, smiling a delicate smile of bright red lipstick under a red beret, her hair pulled back in a bun and held in place with a big pearl hairpin. In another, her brother David, wearing a smart blue, gold, red and white old-style military outfit, is shown as a lieutenant in the Alarde. His short brown hair is neatly brushed back, and he smiles proudly at the camera. Finally, a third photo shows Nicolás himself, dressed like David in a military outfit, but grander, with the insignia of a captain. Smiling broadly under his bushy white beard, he sticks out his chest in pride.

Looking fondly at the photographs, Nicolás tells me that he has de-cided to relinquish his position as captain this year "in order to give the younger generations a chance". So popular is the Alarde amongst the men of Irun that the list of would-be participants is extremely long and it can take several years before an applicant is allowed the honour of joining the parade. Having reached the elevated position of captain, Nicolás says he is happy now to carry on participating as a simple soldier. "David will probably carry on as lieutenant for a couple of years", he says. "But I believe I have had my time. And I am happy to have had two daughters chosen to be cantineras."

Josefa brings out albums containing yet more photos of members of the family in past Alardes. In one, there's another photo of Idoia dressed as a cantinera. This was the year that Iulene was cantinera and, on this very special occasion, Josefa made Idoia a little cantinera outfit identical to Iulene's. Pointing at the picture, Nicolás exclaims laughing "and I hope one day to see Idoia grow up to be a real cantinera too!"

Here we see a strongly 'Irunés' or 'Irundarra' – Irunian – family for whom the Alarde is of typical importance. "It is something I feel very deeply", Josefa remarked on another occasion. "It is part of our tradition", added Nicolás, "It is part of feeling 'Irunés de toda la vida'".[1]

Neither Nicolás nor Josefa were actually born in Irun. Nor does either of them speak Basque, other than a few key words. Both were born in other parts of Spain, moving to Irun as children in the 1940s with their parents who came here to find work.

Turning to me, Nicolás asks: "In France, they don't have such fiestas, do they? The gabachos don't have these kinds of traditions so much now, hey?" Looking mournful, Josefa observes: "And now, some people have decided in the last few years to mess up the fiesta, deciding they want to change it". Nicolás chips in again: "Now how would you like that? If people told you in France that your village celebration should be changed?" To which Josefa continues: "It is so sad, the Alarde has now become such a tense thing, now that these people try and impose themselves. It used to be such a lovely fiesta, the colours, the costumes, the excitement. But now there are tensions because of these people, and so, even though the Alarde is still wonderful, it makes me really really sad".

At this moment, the doorbell rings and in walk six-year-old Toni and four-year-old Maxim. Nicolás opens his arms wide and exclaims in Basque to the children: "Aupa haurrak! Zer moduz?"[2] *Knowing that their grandfather cannot speak Basque, Toni and Maxim reply in Spanish. Behind them comes Pedro, another son of Josefa and Nicolás. Pedro, however, is not in any of the photos that Josefa, Nicolás and I have just been looking at. In fact, he is one of those asking for change,*

---

[1]   This is an expression which I heard many Irunians using when talking about their attachment to Irun and the Alarde. It literally translates as 'Irunian all one's life' and is meant to evoke an image of Irunian 'authenticity'.

[2]   Basque for "Hello, children! How are you?"

*to make the Alarde open to the participation of women on an equal basis
to men, i.e. not just as cantineras but as soldiers, lieutenants, captains
and so on. On this matter then, Pedro is a filius non gratus. While happy
to see him, Nicolás and Josefa change the subject of conversation.*

The word Alarde literally means a military review. In the context of
Bidasoa-Txingudi, it refers to two parades which constitute the high
point of the annual fiestas of Irun and Hondarribia. In Irun, the Alarde
takes place on 30 June, the feast day of San Marcial, or Saint Martial,
and in Hondarribia on 8 September, the feast day of the Virgin of Guadalupe. The Alarde originates in historical events involving the inhabitants of the two towns. In the case of Irun, it relates to a victory by the
people of the town over the French army in 1522. In the case of Hondarribia, it commemorates another battle against French military and naval
forces which besieged the town for more than a month in 1638. In both
cases, the inhabitants of the towns built shrines to commemorate the
event, dedicated to San Marcial and the Virgin of Guadalupe on whose
feast days the victories occurred. They then vowed to enact a military
parade and make a pilgrimage to these shrines every year on the same
date.

Historically, many towns in Gipuzkoa had militias made up of the
male inhabitants who together formed the militia of the foral community
of Gipuzkoa. So the annual enactment of the Alarde is also a celebration
of the province's former foral privileges. Today, however, its importance lies in its role as a generator of a sense of local belonging.[3] As the
high point of each town's annual fiesta, the day of the Alarde is very
much looked forward to by local inhabitants. For weeks beforehand,
participants in the Alarde, particularly those who will be playing the
txistu, a Basque flute, or the drums, rehearse in small groups parading
through the streets. When the fiesta time comes, many people take a few
days off work, including, in Hondarribia, most of the fishermen, so as to
enjoy the festivities and spend time with friends and family. People with
origins in Hondarribia and Irun but living in other parts of the Basque
Country or elsewhere in Spain often take their holidays at this time in
order to be present.

Structured around particular rules and ideas, the Alarde evokes and
reaffirms a local concept of social order. Interaction around the Alarde
reveals a series of social, family and gender markers and boundaries
common to Irun and Hondarribia and not found in Hendaia. As an
orchestrated ritual taking place in what is in effect an exceptional moment, the Alarde is perceived by participants as a sacred event whose

---

[3] For further historical information on the Alardes of Irun and Hondarribia see amongst
others, Portu (1989), Aramburu (1978), Rodríguez (1975), Urbeltz (1995), Bullen
(1997; 1999; 2000), and Kerexeta (2001).

fixity and stability must be vehemently defended, to the extent of making them untouchable. Actors within the ritual are assigned specific roles in which they must act out symbolic gestures. The privilege of fulfilling these roles provides an occasion for participants to reassess their status within the social group and for social order to be re-affirmed.

In sociological terms, events of this sort typically serve as a way of enabling the community to show itself to itself at the same time as imposing itself on others. As a central site of construction and reinforcement of common identity, such events participate in the constitution of identificatory references, allowing individuals – consciously or unconsciously – to feel themselves to be members of the parading group. The reconstitution of a so-called common past, backed by a mythology retracing the heroic stories and accompanied by music and visual effects also presented as inherited, reinforces a feeling of belonging that is challenged by other forms of sociability during the rest of the year. In this way, such parades occupy the role of a ritual in the Kertzerian sense (Kertzer, 1988), exerting a particular power by providing boundaries for inclusion and exclusion.

Outside the context of the Alarde, Hondarribians often draw a distinction between themselves and their Irunian neighbours, reflecting their different experiences of Basque and Spanish identification and Irun's higher percentage of non-Basque Spanish among its population. Many Irunians, meanwhile, regard Hondarribians as "vikingos"[4] or "barbarians", uncouth in manner and excessively proud of their small town, often to the extent of hostility to non-Hondarribians. The organisation of the Alarde brings together participants to experience and reinforce a sense of solidarity and belonging as Irunians and Hondarribians, a status which during this time becomes a great source of pride and a pretext for celebration.

Preparations for the Alarde take place throughout the year. A *Junta*, or council, consisting exclusively of male inhabitants of each of the two towns, takes responsibility for organisation. Until 1997, the municipalities played an important role in the Juntas of the Alarde, reflecting their financial support for the event. A few members of each town's council formed part of the Juntas and the mayors would choose the general of the Alarde. Since 1997, by contrast, the general has been elected by the members of the Junta who themselves are chosen by the active members of the Alarde. The reasons for this will be explained later. These men are usually people who have dedicated much work to the Alarde and who often have served in the past as commanders, captains or lieuten-

---

[4]   According to local lore, Hondarribia was once the site of a Viking settlement, a factor often cited as a reason for the fiery nature and blonde hair and blue eyes said to be characteristic of long-established Hondarribians.

ants, "people with a good reputation in the area, people of social influence", explains Nicolás.

In Irun, the Alarde is made up of nineteen companies, each with at least 350 men, and in Hondarribia of twenty-five companies. Some represent specific sections of society, such as the fishermen, the local youth, and non-Hondarribian holidaymakers with vacation homes in the area, while others represent neighbourhoods. Most participants take part as members of the infantry which makes up the main body of the Alarde, bearing their own rifles following the tradition according to which, on hearing the approaching enemy, the men of the two towns seized their guns from home and gathered ready to fight. Other companies represent specific functions within the military, such as the cavalry, artillery, drummers, or the music band.

Each company is headed by a captain, supported by two lieutenants. Over the course of the year, these figures are chosen by the Junta. It is not necessary to actually live in Irun or Hondarribia or to have relatives there in order to parade in the Alarde, but it is necessary to be invited by other participants. Some men who live in Iparralde or other parts of the Basque Country are able to take part in the Alarde because they have friends in Irun or Hondarribia who do so. Participants choose which company to parade with according to the practice of their family, relatives and friends or their attachment to a certain neighbourhood. Some men start off by parading with their father, uncle and grandfather in one company but then join friends parading in another or, when they marry, join the company of their father-in-law. I encountered men from a wide range of social and professional backgrounds taking part in the Alarde. What linked all of them was their enjoyment of the Alarde and their pride of feeling Hondarribian or Irunian. "What is important", said Esteban, a Hondarribian fisherman whom I asked about the criteria for joining the Alarde of Hondarribia, "is that you feel the fiesta. That you feel Hondarribitarra.[5] That you are with us". "It is", he stressed, "a very open fiesta. All we want is to celebrate tradition together".

Despite the Alarde's strong traditional base, however, it has become a focus of extreme tensions, causing discomfort for many local people, as we have seen in the case of Josefa and Nicolás. These tensions first arose in 1993 in Hondarribia when a group of women organised under the banner of *Bidasoaldeko Emakumeak*[6] expressed the wish to take part in the Alarde on an equal footing with the men on the grounds that they felt as strong a sense of local belonging as their male counterparts. Their

---

[5] Hondarribitarra is the Basque way of referring to someone from Hondarribia. Curiously, there is no Spanish equivalent as there is for Irun-Irunés (Basque for this is Irundarra).

[6] Meaning 'Women of Bidasoa'.

request was rejected by the authorities and the general public as being in conflict with tradition and threatening to destroy the essence of the Alarde. In June 1996, an attempt by this group, together with the support of some men, to join the Alarde in Irun caused uproar, prompting both verbal and physical violence. This was repeated in Hondarribia the following September, when men and women together with the local women's association *Emeki* took up the demand for the participation of women in the Alarde of Hondarribia. The case was taken to court and in 1997 a judge ruled that since these parades were funded with public money from the municipality they should respect sexual equality, with women being allowed to take part in them freely. However, the vast majority of the two towns' inhabitants, including many women like Josefa, refused to accept this ruling, arguing instead that it was the sovereign right of 'the people' to decide their own affairs. These so-called traditionalists criticised those who supported female participation in the Alarde on two accounts: as being mainly people from outside Irun and Hondarribia who understand nothing of the fiestas, and of being in their majority adherents of the left-wing Basque nationalist movement HB who only want to ruin the celebration.

Despite such opposition, the mayor of Irun upheld the court ruling and stated that women should be allowed to take part. The traditionalists responded by setting up an association called *Betiko Alardearen Alde-koa*[7] in support of the organising boards of the Alardes which, to avoid legal action on the grounds of sexual discrimination, reconstituted themselves as private entities.[8] Since 1997, there have been two Alardes in Irun, the 'official Alarde'[9] supported by the municipality, in which men and women march together, and the much larger 'traditional Alarde' which continues to reject the participation of women. In Hon-darribia, the mayor avoided the issue by denying any municipal author-ity over the Alarde and handing over responsibility for the event to its organising board. Members of Emeki, Bidasoaldeko Emakumeak and other supporters of women's participation ended up regrouping them-selves as an association called *Juana Mugarrietakoa* and creating their own company, *Jaizkibel*, with the backing of the Basque government but with no support from the mayor of Hondarribia. The choice of name for the association is significant, as is the name of the company: Juana Mugarrietakoa was the name of a nun who, according to local lore, hid

---

[7] Meaning 'Those in support of the traditional Alarde of Irun'. The choice of calling the association by a name in Basque, rather than Spanish, is significant, as will be explored later.

[8] These took the names of *Irungo Alarde Fundazioa* and *Hondarribiko Alarde Fun-dazioa*.

[9] *Alarde oficial* in Spanish and *Alarde ofiziala* in Basque.

the statue of the Virgin Mary during the siege of Hondarribia by the French army. In an interview, Ixabel Alkain, captain of the company Jaizkibel, explained that the names were part of their effort to prove that they too were faithful to 'tradition' in their demands for the participation of women on equal terms to men. Since 1997, Jaizkibel has attempted unsuccessfully each year to join the traditional Alarde along with the other companies as they blocked their entrance. The mayor makes clear his support for the traditional Alarde by acknowledging the general in a public ceremony the day before and marching with other members of the town council in the rear of the parade.

The conflict has given rise to two clearly distinct camps: the *tradis*, short for traditionalists in Spanish, or *Betikoak*, from the Basque word 'always', coming from the name of the association and alluding to their passionate attachment to an idea of tradition as permanent and immutable; and "the women", shorthand to refer to supporters of women's participation in the Alarde or, in the case of those in Irun who support the official Alarde, as "those of the official" and, in the case of those in Hondarribia who support the mixed company of men and women by that name, "those of Jaizkibel".

The controversy over the Alarde brings to the fore political tensions and conflicting ideas about community belonging and its criteria. It illustrates the way in which political tensions in Hegoalde find expression in debate over such issues as the 'correct' version of Basque 'history', 'tradition', and ideas of Basque authenticity, all of which are of central concern to Basque nationalists. Alarde traditionalists claim that they resist those calling for change on the grounds that the latter are a minority seeking to impose themselves on the majority. In the tense political climate of the Basque Country, it is an easy step for supporters of the traditional Alarde to draw a parallel between the supporters of women's participation, perceived as imposing themselves on the majority of Irunians and Hondarribians, and ETA and its supporters imposing themselves on the rest of Basque society, prompting the sort of insults that I often heard shouted at them of "terrorists" and "extremists".

In reality, the situation is more complex and the positions of the members of the two camps and of representatives of regional and local political parties are far from overlapping as neatly as such accusations suggest. Nonetheless, the political connotations that have been given to the controversy over the Alarde are revealing of the manner in which symbolic boundaries are used for the construction of different local cultural and political realities and identity. In exploring these constructions of 'us' and 'them', I will also consider what consequences they have for peaceful cohabitation among the citizens of the three towns and for efforts in favour of the construction of a 'Txingudi identity'.

30 June 2000 has arrived, and with it the eighth and most important day of Irun's annual fiesta. Many of Irun's young people, from late teens to early thirties, have been out all night on gaupasa,[10] *dressed in white, red and black and partying in the bars of Irun. Some went to bed around 3.00 a.m. for a quick nap before waking again at 4.00 a.m. in order to hear the "Alborada", the 'réveil' which marks the beginning of the most important day of the town's week-long festivities. As one of my companions explains to me, "following the tradition", a member of the local foral army will sound his horn to warn the inhabitants of Irun that the enemy is near, calling them to get ready to fight and to gather for the Alarde, the review of arms.*

By 6.00 a.m., a big crowd is gathered around the church of the Virgin of Juncal to hear the band of the traditional Alarde play the 'Diana de Villarrobledo', a special tune that calls for the rallying of troops. It is still dark and, despite the tired state of most people, there is a buzz of excitement. People of all ages huddle together on the grass slopes between the trees and on the square in front of the main entrance to the church. The men who will be parading in the Alarde are gathered in groups, chatting and joking. All are dressed in the customary uniform: black jacket, red beret, white trousers, white shirts and white rope-soled alpargatas. Each carries his own rifle upright against his chest.

Those women who have got up early in order to see their husbands, boyfriends, sons or brothers off in the Alarde stand to one side, chatting. Some teenage boys who are not taking part in the Alarde joke in Spanish with a group of teenage girls holding on to each other arm in arm and jostling about laughing. The girls all have long hair and are wearing white dresses or jeans and tight tops, with red scarfs around their necks or on their heads.

Six o'clock strikes and everyone tells each other to hush. Silence, and then a horn rings out. Far away on the other side of the crowd, a member of the Alarde cries out in Spanish and Basque that the inhabitants have to prepare for battle. He ends by shouting "Gora Irun! Gora San Marcial! Gora Irungo Alardea!"[11] *To which we all shout back, "Gora!" At this point, the municipal band by the entrance to the church strikes up the tune of the Alarde. Everyone begins to dance on the spot, holding each other by the shoulders, smiling and laughing. In this fashion we head down to Urdanibia Plaza. There, explain my companions, the men will organise themselves into their respective companies – or troops, so that the review of arms can take place with the general.*

---

[10]   Gaupasa is a Basque expression used by both Spanish and Basque-speakers in the Basque Country to mean 'partying all night'.

[11]   Gora is Basque for 'Long live' or 'Up with'. Irungo Alardea means the 'Alarde of Irun'.

In Urdanibia Plaza, still amid great hubbub and excitement, the infantrymen who make up most of the participants in the Alarde join their respective companies. The captains and lieutenants of the artillery and cavalry companies ride on horseback, accompanied by other men with cannons and mules carrying ammunition. The company of the woodcutters stands out from the others because of its members' large leather aprons and big saws.

Each company has a cantinera, a young woman wearing a military outfit in the company's colours and a sash across one shoulder giving the company's name: Olaberria, Meaka, Bidasoa, Uranzu, San Miguel, Buenos Amigos, Santiago, Lampize, Azken Portu, Anaka, Ama Xantalen, Ventas, Behobia or Belaskoenea. The cantineras all wear make-up, with bright red lipstick matching the red of their berets. Each holds a small keg in one hand, while with the other she wags a fan and waves and smiles at the admiring onlookers. The men of the company keep close to their cantinera and, although not necessarily speaking to her, show their pride by sticking out their chests, glancing regularly in her direction and smiling at the onlookers watching her.

It is now full daylight and time for the Alarde to head up to San Juan Plaza for a review of arms in front of the town hall before setting off on their march. The band plays the Alarde tune, to the accompaniment of the txistu and the drums of a troop of musicians. All nineteen companies march one after the other up San Marcial Kalea. The noise of music, stamping feet and cheering is tremendous. Women and children on the side of the street jostle to get a better view of their men. Each time they catch a glimpse of those they are looking for, they jump up and down and cheer and wave. Josefa, her sister and her daughter-in-law are amongst them, dressed in white and red with white skirts and shirts, a red sash and a red neckerchief and beret. Beside them, little children holding onto their mothers are dressed in white and red as well. A few, like Idoia in the photograph, wear special outfits: some little boys are dressed as generals or captains with smartly cut old-style uniforms and matching hats, while some little girls are dressed as cantineras with a touch of make-up. Holding onto their miniature kegs, they practise waving their fans in the same way as the cantinera, to the indulgent laughter of their families. As the men march past, they wave and call out flirtatiously to the women. Amongst them, Josefa catches sight of Nicolás marching with one of his sons-in-law at his side. She waves excitedly at him as he marches past with a big self-satisfied smile.

On San Juan Plaza, the red of the berets is dazzling. Waiting for the signal of the Alarde general, the participants chat animatedly, trying out each other's guns and occasionally letting off a bang as they fire into the air, leaving a cloud of smoke above them. The women and children have walked up and stand watching from the sides of the plaza. Others look out from the balconies and windows of the apartments of relatives and friends. Nearly all the windows and balconies have flags with the insignia of San Marcial. The women look out at the crowd of men below and each time they spot someone they know they shout and wave.

Finally the general gives the signal to depart. The Alarde forms ranks and begins marching through the streets of Irun in a long line of soldiers with guns, horses, artillery, flute players, drum players, one company after the other, each with their cantinera waving and smiling at the onlookers shouting compliments at her, "Aupa la cantinera! Zer polita!"[12]

In 2000, after heated discussions with the town council, which fixes the itineraries and timetables of the two Alardes, Irun's traditional Alarde began a little later than usual and in a different part of town than had previously been the custom. The official Alarde was given precedence, starting earlier and following an itinerary closer to the previously established one. To the outrage of the Betikoak, the official Alarde was given the right to sound its Diana in San Juan Plaza, in accordance with custom, while the traditional Alarde's Diana had to take place by the church. This was designed to prevent the two Alardes from crossing paths, and so to avoid conflict.

Tensions, nonetheless, were visible around the official Alarde's parade. As its members gathered on San Juan Plaza, surrounded by supporters giving them encouragement by continuous cheering, a group of Betiko youths who had partied all night whistled and shouted, some of them throwing bottles and glasses at them. Trying to ignore them, participants in the official Alarde proceeded with the ritual of the Diana and then set off in procession, accompanied by their supporters. The contrast between the official Alarde and the traditional one was stark as the rest of the population stayed away and the streets through which the procession went remained practically deserted.

Betikoak in Hondarribia and Irun support each other in their common cause against those whom they see as the usurpers of their Alarde. Many are active in Betiko Alardearen Aldekoa initiatives to raise funds throughout the year for the Juntas, in the form of fairs, lottery prizes and private donations, maintaining what they call a spirit of 'defence' against 'the women'. On the other side, a few people who parade in the official Alarde in Irun also participate in the Jaizkibel company in Hondarribia. These particular supporters explained to me that they did so for reasons of principle, rather than for a sentiment of town belonging. The importance they give to their personal attachment to their town is made secondary to their idea of civic priorities. Stickers declaring

---

[12]   "Long live the cantinera! How beautiful!"

support for one or other of the two camps provide visual markers creating inclusive boundaries for fellow sticker wearers and other supporters and exclusive boundaries against others.

In this climate of tension, the mayors of both towns attempt to ensure calm by calling on the assistance of the ertzaintza, Euskadi's regional police force, armed with truncheons and wearing hoods, helmets, bullet proof jackets and in some cases carrying video cameras. In the sky above, an ertzaintza helicopter oversees the event, its loud buzzing adding to the tension. During the annual parade in Hondarribia, supporters of the traditional Alarde block Jaizkibel members from participating, threatening them verbally and physically. In such emotional moments, it is not rare to find people of both camps in tears. During the rest of the year, supporters of Jaizkibel in Hondarribia and the official Alarde in Irun face abuse from traditional Alarde supporters. I have seen them being insulted and assaulted in the street, while some shop-owners have suffered from boycotts and vandalism.

Anthropologist Maggie Bullen (1997; 1999; 2000) has described in detail the social background to this polemic around the Alarde. She provides enlightening insights in her analysis of gender issues in which she observes that a certain minority is challenging a particular understanding of traditional gender social structure that is essentially macho, sustained by a majority. Explanations based on gender issues or the importance of tradition only touch the surface, however, of a much more deep-rooted conflict, based on Alarde participants' interpretations of political difference and foreignness (Bullen, 2000).[13] My interest in the Alarde stems from its importance as part of a process of creation of boundaries for identity in Bidasoa-Txingudi.

Boundaries of Belonging: Being Irunian or Hondarribian

Other fiestas and parades – or 'rituals' – also play a role in both Hondarribia and Irun in the continuation of 'tradition'. In Hondarribia, for example, another important festivity is Kutxa Eramaitea, or the carrying of the box, a one-day celebration for the fishing community, when a box containing all the legal papers of the Hondarribiko Arrantzaleen Kofradia signed by the clergy and municipal council of Hondar-

---

[13] With various local people, I had the opportunity of discussing other theories to explain the vehement opposition to change. For many men, parading in the Alarde is a unique time in the year when they can feel particularly important, acquiring a special status that is completely unrelated to their lives during the rest of the year as a plumber, an unemployed person, a local shopkeeper, etc. Women, too, by becoming devoted defenders of the traditional Alarde have gained special status in the community which they did not have before. They have now become heroines amongst their relatives, friends and acquaintances.

ribia is brought in a big procession by the fishermen from the seat of the Kofradia to the church in the medieval part of town. Every year, a fisherman's daughter is chosen for the honour of carrying this excruciatingly heavy box on her head all the way up to the church, to the sound of music. At Easter, during *Aste Saindua*, or Holy Week, a great procession takes place in which inhabitants of the town re-enact the stations of the cross. While traditional Catholicism is hardly practised at all by many local people, this procession remains a strongly passionate religious event which is given great importance by Hondarribians.

In 1999, an association representing the inhabitants of the marina area was founded under the name of *Portuarraken Asoziaziyua* with the aim of bringing back to life festivities that had been lost in Hondarribia over the years. The word asoziaziyua, as was explained to me by a member of the association's committee, comes from the Hondarribian fishing community's dialect which is made up of a mixture of Basque with French. Such a choice of vocabulary is indicative of the strong emphasis placed again on 'tradition' as well as diffidence towards the establishment of Batua (in Batua, the word for association would be *elkartea*). Their main initiative has been to bring back into existence a day-long fiesta which celebrates the blessing of the Fishermen's Virgin, abandoned for many years. The main activity of the day involves carrying the statue of the Virgin out of the fishermen's church, where it is usually kept, and parade to the old fishing port where a service takes place to bless the fishing boats. A similar service takes place in the port of Hendaia, with the *fête de la mer* in July. However, with the fishing port now redundant, the priest comes principally to give a blessing to the yachts and other leisure boats.

In Irun, the feast day of Saint Thomas, the patron saint of Irun, is known as the day when in former times tenant farmers would come to town from the surrounding countryside to pay their dues to the *jauna* or main landlord. These dues were largely paid in farm products. In modern times, participants in celebrations of Saint Thomas's Day dress in traditional Basque rural garb, the women wearing full dark-coloured skirts and aprons, white blouses and blue checked headscarves and the men knee-length black trousers, thick woolly socks and espadrilles laced up around the calves, large blue shirts buttoned at the neck, and black berets. As this is the time of year when a particular kind of sausage is made, the *txistorra*, this is the main food of the day.

Other fiestas include *Euskal Jira*, or the Basque tour, invented in the early 1900s as a fiesta to celebrate Basque folklore involving both Irun and Hendaia. It consists of a procession of floats with Basque themes in which everyone taking part is dressed up in traditional Basque clothes. Since the mid 1990s, dance groups in Irun have organised a Folk Dance Festival on the Island of the Pheasants in July, when the island is under

Spanish jurisdiction. This event, which is supported by the municipality, involves inviting a folk-dance group from another country to perform on the island, facing the audience sitting on the river bank in Irun. Saint John's Day, in midsummer, is celebrated on both sides of the frontier, though when I was in Bidasoa-Txingudi, I saw it being celebrated with more specific events in Irun than in any of the other towns. In the evening, looking across the Bidasoa to Irun from Hendaia, one could see the bonfires customarily set alight on this day blazing away in the various Irunian neighbourhoods. In all three towns, in addition, neighbourhood – *auzoa/barrio* – fiestas are organised by the local neighbourhood associations.

Undoubtedly, however, the Alarde is the social highlight of the year for most of the two towns' inhabitants, playing a central role for them in the evocation of a sense of community by giving concrete and visible form to abstract community links. In social terms, the Alarde evokes boundaries of 'insider', those who are 'true' Irunians or Hondarribians, versus 'outsider', those who are 'non'-Irunians or 'non'-Hondarribians. It serves this purpose even for people who have moved across the frontier to live in Hendaia but who continue to participate in the Alarde. One such is Juan Etxebarria, a thirty-year-old man who moved with his parents as a child and now works in his father's firm in Hendaia. "Definitely, I am Hendaian, but I carry on feeling at home in Irun and for nothing in the world will I give up my participation in the Alarde", he explained to me. "I feel at home on both sides. Yes, I am Hendaian, but Irun is also in my heart." He dismissed the conflict around the Alarde as the work of "troublemakers who don't understand what the importance of community feeling is all about".

Many people who recently moved to Hendaia hang Hondarribian or Irunian flags from their houses during these towns' fiestas, demonstrating their continuing sense of Hondarribian or Irunian belonging. When I asked about this, they replied that living across the frontier did not prevent them from following hometown traditions. "I don't see why I should alter my customs just because I have moved to live just a few hundred meters away", explained a woman who had a big Irunian flag hanging from her window in a residential area of Hendaia. "I still feel Irunian." Reactions on the part of other Hendaians to these flags ranged between a tolerant shrugging of the shoulders to hostility. Monique Lambert, a former primary school teacher in Hendaia in her early sixties, commented that "it's only normal that they should carry on their traditions even if living here". By contrast, Corinne Delgado, a middle-aged woman who says she hardly ever crosses the frontier into Hegoalde, remarked: "It just shows what little effort they make to integrate here. Not just that, but they impose their ideas and habits on us".

For Nicolás and Josefa, as we have seen, the Alarde is an opportunity to demonstrate that, despite their non-local origins, they are legitimate members of the community. They adhere to the 'tradition' of the Alarde and by defending its immutability demonstrate the constancy of their belonging. When the traditional Alarde is perceived as being threatened by change, they and other people with similar backgrounds whom I met convert the marker of support for the traditional Alarde into a boundary demonstrating and reinforcing their belonging to the 'Irunian' camp, in contrast to the 'outsiders'. 'Tradition', as embodied in the Alarde, is taken to be a fundamental part of Irun or Hondarribian identity. Any attempt to bring about changes to the Alarde is perceived as an assault on 'tradition'. The Alarde serves as a boundary between those who participate in it and support it, and so belong, and those who do not participate, and so do not belong.

Language is used in a similar way, as when Nicolás addresses his grandchildren in Basque even though he does not know the language. Both adherence to the traditional Alarde and the use of Basque words and phrases form part of his strategy to signal identification as a 'local'. The traditionalists' choice of a Basque name for their association is a similarly important marker. The use of Basque, often presented by Basque nationalists as the language of the oppressed indigenous minority, helps to buttress their claim to 'tradition' and local belonging, reinforcing the legitimacy of their cause in confrontation with the supporters of a mixed Alarde also advertising themselves in Basque.

Unfortunately for Nicolás and Josefa, Pedro is not the only member of their family who has chosen to support a mixed men and women Alarde. Another son, Juan, also supports them. In a conversation with me, both Pedro and Juan recalled how their decision to back the alternative Alarde was a serious blow to Josefa and Nicolás. They maintain that no discussion about it has ever been possible. Instead, Pedro reminisces, he and Juan were accused of "betraying the family" and "going against the traditions of Irun and of the family". Pedro and Juan tell me they cannot understand such vehement outrage on the part of their parents. "It's just about the equality of men and women. I really don't understand why it has to be such a big deal. The importance of the Alarde for bringing people together in a fiesta shouldn't be affected just because women are also taking part", says Pedro. "My wife", he continues, "feels Irunian and would like to express this too, like the men in the Alarde. And I don't see why she shouldn't".

In some other families, similar dissension has led to rupture, with parents refusing to talk to their children because of their support for the alternative Alarde. Josefa and Nicolás, by contrast, have chosen to avoid discussing the matter altogether. In conversations with me, they spoke about the issue in terms of the need to keep the Alarde "as it has always been" and unaffected by "modern whims and changes". In taking this stance, they adopt markers and draw up boundaries which help them to demonstrate their belonging to Irun and its community and reinforce their identity as such. They ignore the existence of the alternative Alarde – and omit to include Juan and Pedro's photos with the others in their sitting room. When the Alarde comes, they share the excitement of the event with the other traditional supporters in the family and enjoy themselves with friends and acquaintances in Irun, not seeing their nonconformist sons until the day is over. The year I was with them for the Alarde, Pedro's and Juan's families were excluded from the customary family lunch. "That really hurt me", recalled Pedro's wife Silvia, "I just don't understand".

In effect, Nicolás and Josefa react to Pedro and Juan's support for a mixed Alarde not only as a boundary between them and their sons but also as a threat to their identity construction. To counteract this threat, they join the majority in defence of the traditional Alarde, showing that they are more Irunian than their dissident sons. During our conversation, when I repeatedly tried to get Nicolás to explain the situation concerning the Alarde, he stressed his desire to speak only of the 'real' Alarde.

Spatial boundaries reinforce the gulf between the two camps. During the fiesta, Nicolás and Josefa avoid areas where supporters of the official Alarde are likely to be. In Irun, this means most of the old part of town, around Urdanibia Plaza and parts of the San Marcial Karrika. Similarly, other friends of mine who supported the traditional Alarde and who frequented the bars in Urdanibia Plaza throughout the rest of the year did not want to go there during the fiestas, dismissing it as "the hangout of those of the official (Alarde)". In Hondarribia, the association supporting the traditional Alarde set up a bar to raise funds at one end of San Pedro Kalea. None of my friends who supported Jaizkibel wanted to go there or to other bars in the same street. Instead, they remained within the area bounded by the old city walls, with Muara as one of their main meeting points. The only place that was fairly neutral, with a mixture of young supporters of both camps, was the old fishing port area where temporary stalls selling drinks and food, fairground attractions and a concert stage were set up. Among them was a stand erected by the associations supporting Basque 'political' prisoners with huge photo portraits of these prisoners hanging from the old fish market building, providing a rallying point beneath which sympathists could gather. The crowd in this area also included people who, while supporting female participation in the Alarde, were not necessarily committed left-wing nationalists but who felt safer in this area than in the marina area, mainly frequented by Betikoak.

It is about 7.00 p.m. on a sunny September afternoon. Hondarribia's fiestas are already in full swing, with only a few days to go to the day of the Alarde. For weeks beforehand, people have been preparing, the men busy with rehearsals for the Alarde while their wives and mothers have been occupied preparing the special clothes that the men will wear on the big day. Many shopkeepers have decorated their shop windows with the local festive colours – green for Hondarribia and red, white and black for the Alarde.

Gradually, the marina area of Hondarribia is filling up after the late lunchtime lull. Groups of teenage boys and girls gather near a 'chucherrias' shop selling a wide array of sweets, crisps, pipas – dried sunflower seeds – and pastries. Most of the boys wear t-shirts and baggy jeans or corduroy trousers with Spanish or American surfing labels. Many of the girls wear bell-bottom trousers, also with brand labels, and tight tops, their long hair loose or in ponytails. Together, they sit on benches or on mopeds chatting in a mixture of Basque and Spanish. Some wear stickers on their chests with an abstract black and green picture of Hondarribia and the phrase "Betiko Alardea".

Suddenly, the sound of drums and txistus rings out from behind a block of houses. From around the corner, five young men wearing black berets march into San Pedro Kalea, one playing the drums and the others following behind with txistus. Several of the young women sitting on the benches run to join them and, holding hands, skip behind them to the tune. Older people standing around drinking glasses of beer, some accompanied by young children playing together, stop to look, smiling. Some of the mothers, holding on to their children's hands, begin to dance, encouraging their children to do the same. A pot-bellied man wearing casual jeans and a check shirt picks up his small daughter and places her on his shoulders, breaking into an impromptu dance. Marching at a fast pace, the five young men reach the end of San Pedro Kalea and disappear round the roundabout of San Kristobal. As the music dies down, the young women, laughing and jostling each other, skip back to their friends by the chucherria shop.

Within an hour or two, the marina area is buzzing with people. Elderly men and women in couples or single sex groups, families with small children and babies in prams, and groups of teenagers walk around socialising, slapping each other on the back and greeting each other with kisses on the cheeks, talking loudly as they stand outside or inside the numerous bars, many of them holding a 'zurrito', a small glass of beer, or red wine in their hands. Children run around playing, the little girls smartly dressed in frilly dresses with ribbons in their hair and little gold studs in their earlobes, and the little boys in neat shirts and knee-length shorts, some with their hair gelled down. While the adults order pintxos, the teenagers gather together or walk around in small groups, nibbling pipas, jelly sweets and crisps. A few more groups of men practising for the Alarde have been parading around. In between re-

hearsals, they stop to take a drink with their friends or rejoin their wives and children standing on the pavement.

Amid this general atmosphere of jollity and family togetherness, a rumour runs through the crowd that "ellas"[14] – the women, in reference to Jaizkibel – are also going to rehearse. Sure enough, the melody of txistus and drums can soon be heard approaching. "It's them", says a teenage boy wearing a red Mendi Loreak sweater and long beige baggy shorts, sitting on his moped with friends. "They're coming this way", confirms one of his friends, another teenage boy similarly dressed and with his hair cut mid-length with a long fringe, pointing down the street. As a group of men and women, all with black berets on their heads, and dressed casually, most of them in jeans or dark trousers and t-shirts, march into Beñat Etxepare Kalea playing the txistu and the drums, the two boys and lots of other teenagers rush towards them. Before they can reach them, a cohort of ertzainak in dark blue and red suits and big red helmets, their faces hidden behind hoods, emerges from a series of vans parked by the roundabout of San Kristobal to create a barrier between the marchers and the onlookers. Standing behind the ertzainak, the teenagers peer through.

A black-coloured banner hanging between two trees on either side of the roundabout proclaims in big white letters "Gora Betiko Alardea".[15] (The banner has probably been hoisted especially for the passing of this parade because less than an hour later, once the rehearsal is over, it is no longer there.) "Out! Out!"[16] the teenagers shout at the marchers, while other opponents of the Jaizkibel whistle and hiss and boo. One teenage girl, still sitting on her moped, beeps its horn incessantly in order to drown out the melody played by the marchers and gyrates to the sound of it as if it were music, a big insolent smile on her face. Down the street, the paraders march past the hostile crowd. Some of the women in the crowd deliberately stand with their backs to the procession and carry on chatting to their friends or stare up at the sky with a stern expression on their face, ostentatiously ignoring the paraders. Both women and men shout, "Out! Out! Feminists! Lesbians!" in Basque and Spanish. One man with a big bushy mustache wearing a casual dark blazer manages to get particularly close to the marchers and brandishes his fist in their faces, shouting "Get out of here! We don't want you here! Leave us in peace!" A woman following him chimes in, shouting "Terrorists!" A few small children standing on top of a wall behind, next to their parents, join in the general shouting, crying "Out! Out!"

---

[14] In Spanish, this is the feminine third person plural.
[15] "Up with the Alarde of Always".
[16] "Fuera! Fuera!!"

The marchers continue to play, marching in unison down the street, their faces clearly focused on their task and seemingly ignoring the insults. Some have stickers on their t-shirts and jumpers with a picture depicting red berets and the words Emakumeak Alardean[17] in big black letters. Excitedly, some of the teenagers rush off down another street, where they know the parade will continue, in order to carry on booing at them. On the street corner, a teenage girl with a Betiko Alardea sticker plastered on her shirt is standing on her own, her fingers plugged in her ears, making it obvious that she is trying to block out the sound of the paraders' music. Tears run down her face as she watches the marchers parade past her. Shaking her head and muttering to herself as she wipes her tears from her cheeks, she walks slowly behind the marchers who are disappearing down the street amidst a torrent of abuse. Reaching the roundabout where the marina area ends and the streets of the medieval part of Hondarribia begin, they stop playing and disband. A few walk off towards the bar Muara or up to the old centre.

This typical scene of the conflict that has ridden the annual festivities of both Hondarribia and Irun for the past few years took place in Hondarribia in 2001. On other occasions, I heard the mixed Alarde supporters called "traitors" (alluding to their alleged letting down of local values and destruction of the town fiesta), "faggots" and "whores". I also saw people attempting to assault them by pushing and hitting them and grabbing their guns and their berets as they paraded past. The drawing of a boundary by the Betikoak between themselves and supporters of a mixed Alarde, continuously emphasised outside the period of the festivities, was illustrated one year earlier in a meeting organised by the Junta of Hondarribia's Alarde in September 2000, following the arrest by the police of over a dozen young women who had used physical force to block Jaizkibel members from parading on the day of that year's Alarde. In an atmosphere of cheerful solidarity, about a hundred people had gathered in the basement room of a five star hotel in Hondarribia called Bidasoa to discuss how to respond to the heavy fines to which the women had been sentenced. The meeting included men and women of all ages, but particularly of two age groups, between 16 and 26 – the age of most of the women arrested – and between 50 and 70 – the age of most of the mothers and grandmothers.

As those present chatted excitedly in small groups, the Spanish word "*ellas*" repeatedly came up. Some people had copies of a recent edition of the newspaper Diario Vasco featuring on its front page a photo of some of the young women detained by the ertzaintza during the Alarde. Prominent in the photo was the face of a pretty young woman dressed in red and white like the others, looking at the policeman arresting her with

---

[17]   Meaning 'Women in the Alarde'.

an insolently flirtatious smile. Sitting behind a long table on a podium, the seven members of the Junta, men mostly in their forties and fifties, wore serious expressions emanating an aura of authority. Calling the meeting to order, a member of the Junta greeted those present in Basque before reverting to Spanish. Explaining that the Junta wished to organise fund-raising events to help pay the fines imposed on the women, he declared: "We are all in this together". The supporters of Jaizkibel, he added, "are doubtless preparing another *coup* against us (referring to the legal battle being fought out between the two camps at the high court). So we must make sure we are ready". At his invitation to the women who were arrested to identify themselves by putting their hands up, one revealed that she came from Pamplona. "From Pamplona?!" the Junta representative exclaimed: "Well! I didn't know we had friends that far away!" Amid the general laughter, everyone clearly shared a sense of fighting together for a great cause.

Solidarity between supporters of the traditional Alarde does not however efface boundaries between Irunians and Hondarribians. On the contrary, the issue of the Alarde is sometimes used as a way of emphasizing the differences between each other. Josefa, for example, commented that "in Hondarribia, with regard to the fight against the women, they are much more violent than here". A young Irunian man similarly told me: "They are real barbarians there, in Hondarribia, really quite cavemen-like in their attachment to traditional values and their sense of clan. Whereas we are quite a mixed, cosmopolitan people… we are more tolerant and open-minded".

Conversely, Kepa, a 25-year-old Hondarribian, painted this portrait of Irunians: "Irunians really lack a sense of tradition and a proper identity. I mean… in Hondarribia we would never let such a thing happen as in Irun (alluding to the creation of an official Alarde). We Hondarribians have an extremely strong sense of identity. And much more respect for the traditions of the town". Kepa's parents are originally from Irun, but he now emphasises his belonging to Hondarribia by distinctly drawing up a boundary with Irunians.

While inclusive boundaries create a sense of positive belonging, the construction of the 'other' or the 'outsider' is based on a series of identifiers that define difference in negative terms. As we have seen, the outsiders in the conflict over the Alarde are not just those who do not live in Irun or Hondarribia but those who support the mixed women and men's Alarde. The distinction between outsider and insider cuts across culture and gender in a process of identity construction which is subject to a specific set of socio-cultural values. Men from other towns can acquire insider status by being invited to take part in the parade. Women can only participate as insiders if they are from one or other of the two towns and if they accept a clearly defined gender role.

Women who defend the traditional Alarde reject accusations of kow-towing to male supremacy. As Paula Aizu, a woman in her mid-twenties living in Irun, passionately explained to me, "Of course I believe in women's rights. I am a modern woman myself. And I defend myself as one. But the Alarde is something else. I don't see why there is any need for women to take part in it. It's ridiculous. It was not like that in his-tory. So why should we change tradition now?" However, an initiative launched in 1998 by a group of women who support the traditional Alarde confirms the separation of roles. In order to show that women were not excluded from the traditional Alarde, these women organised a complementary parade to the traditional Alarde in which women could take part dressed in traditional clothes. The parade involved carrying of torches through the streets of Irun on the eve of the Alarde, in a refer-ence to the role said to have been played by local women in the battle against the French army: by lighting torches in the middle of the night and walking up the mountain behind the town, the women succeeded in confusing the enemy as to the whereabouts and size of the Irunian army.

The Alarde and Politics

In fact, the Alarde has been subject to change in the past without causing crisis, for example through the creation of new companies and changes in timetables, costumes and choreography. In Irun, the figure of the cantinera was only introduced at the end of the nineteenth century. In this case, however, the polemic has gone beyond gender issues to become a political controversy in which local politicians have also got involved. At the local council level, representatives of the left-wing Basque nationalists have shown support for the mixed male-and-female Alarde. But the stance of other parties has been less clear-cut. On the regional level, both the PP and the conservative Basque nationalist parties have taken positions firmly in favour of women's rights, but their local representatives have tailored their attitudes to what they perceive to be the dominant view of their electorate. In Irun, Maribel Castelló, an EA representative with responsibility for cultural affairs on the town council, was initially one of the most adamant defenders of women's rights. However, as the conflict developed, she was asked by her col-leagues to step down. Local PSE representatives have similarly wavered between a desire to uphold the law and the need to retain the favour of their electorate, especially in Irun. In the municipal elections of 1999, mayor Alberto Buen won re-election after a last-minute declaration of support for a traditional Alarde.

Some Betikoak supporters to whom I spoke branded the women who seek to join the Alarde as radical feminists, and them and their male supporters as leftists and dangerous nationalist extremists who want to use the parade for political subversion. Both Nicolás and his daughter

Iulene, for example, told me that they reckoned at least two thirds of the mixed Alarde supporters must be HB voters. Betikoak followers accuse supporters of the mixed Alarde of recruiting from outside Irun and Hondarribia and even, according to rumours, of paying supporters to take part. Both feminism and nationalism are perceived by the Betikoak as being outside the agenda of the Alarde, which they claim is not an appropriate forum for political campaigning. By dismissing mixed sup-porters as trouble-making radicals, the Betikoak are able to discredit their demands for sexual equality.

Since the outbreak of the conflict, a series of letters published in lo-cal and regional papers have added to the venom. Letters from the "tradis" associating supporters of a mixed Alarde with various left-wing political groupings have prompted defensive but also sometimes vindic-tive replies from mixed Alarde supporters. Public statements by repre-sentatives of the mixed Alarde supporters, for example on the occasion of the presentation of the cantineras taking part in the official Alarde in Irun, in which they express support for Basque prisoners and their return to Euskal Herria, have served to provide the "tradis" with what they regard as additional proof of their political associations.

While many supporters of the mixed Alarde are associated with the extreme left-wing nationalist movement, however, the connection is not straightforward. Many in the mixed Alarde camp do not share these political views and there have been numerous lengthy debates between the women campaigning for participation in the Alarde over the best strategy for achieving their aims. Furthermore, there have been divisions within the left-wing nationalist camp arising from the clash between the desire to defend equal rights and social justice for all and the wish to protect local traditions as markers of Basque cultural identity. Even among those who support the idea of a mixed Alarde, some, including left-wing nationalists, have carried on parading in the traditional Alarde, refusing to confuse their political commitment with their enjoyment of taking part in a traditional event.

The Alarde and Gender Issues

Many local men defend the traditional Alarde by arguing that their womenfolk are its most ardent defenders. This is borne out by state-ments made to me by women like Josefa and Paula and the strong presence of women in the meeting in Hondarribia called to discuss a response to the fines levied on the women who had blocked Jaizkibel's participation. Many women supporters of the traditional Alarde to whom I spoke argued that they do not feel excluded in the fiestas and that, on the contrary, they take part in their own way through the prepa-rations for it and as spectators. As we have seen, the behaviour of the women spectators, dressed up coquettishly in red and white and makeup for the day, running with the children after the band of musicians as they play and march down the street and pushing tourists out of the way to get into the front row to wave at their men, reveals a seduction play that would surely disappear were the women to parade as well.

In the traditional Alarde, the only woman honoured with participation is the cantinera, elected by the men of her neighbourhood. According to Alarde participants, her principal role is to keep up the morale of the troops with her good nature and beauty. In the past, the cantinera was chosen by the people of the neighbourhood, but with the increase in population it was decided that candidates should make a formal application, enclosing a photo of themselves, and then rely on the lobbying of male relatives and friends in the company in order to have their names put in a lottery. Each company has its own cantinera and to be chosen to play this role is perceived as a public recognition of her and her family in the locality, her social status and her good looks.

As the status of the cantinera has risen, so has the intensity of competition for the position, to the extent that I have been told that some young women even delay getting married in order to increase their chances of being chosen. Such is the glamour surrounding the role, according to some informants, that the day when a young woman serves as cantinera can rank as 'the happiest day of her life', surpassing even her wedding day. The rules of the Alarde of Irun actually stipulate that the most beautiful young women of the town should be chosen. Cantineras are required to be unmarried, not more than 28 years old, and Hondarribian or Irunian in the sense of having either been born in the towns or having lived there at least fifteen years (Aramburu, 1978).

During my fieldwork, I sometimes heard jokes about such and such a cantinera who was not exactly a classic beauty, sometimes involving suggestions of possible corruption in the voting process. I also heard suggestions that candidates are more likely to be selected for the role of cantinera if they are from a well-off socio-economic background, and that some families seek to increase the chances of one of their family members being chosen by paying favours to the Junta. While I have no evidence to support such assertions, it is undeniable that economic status plays a role since, according to the custom that has developed over the past several decades, the cantinera's family is expected to pay for her costume and treat all the members of the company to drinks at the end of the Alarde. In my experience, however, rather than their economic profile, what stood out amongst the families of those young women selected as cantineras was their adherence to certain ideas of tradition.

On the day of the Alarde, the cantineras are one of the main focuses of the festivities, praised for their beauty and their 'nobility' as 'ambassadors' of their neighbourhood and town. Hardly surprisingly, it is the dream of many young women to be given this role. Photo portraits of the cantineras of the year adorn shops in Irun and Hondarribia. They are invited to speak on local radio and television programmes. Local papers feature their names and photos with the programme of the fiestas. Some bakers prepare special cakes on which they stick photos on rice paper of the cantineras. Some old women proudly told me that in their youth they were chosen to be cantineras several times. Today, due to the intense competition for the role, a girl can only be a cantinera once, enhancing the specialness of the role. One reason why women are the most vociferous defenders of the traditional Alarde is that a mixed Alarde would diminish the importance of the cantinera. Being a cantinera fits with the romantic image entertained in Irun and Hondarribia of the beautiful respectable woman who will then get married and who will continue to be honoured in the town. On several occasions, I saw women who had been cantineras in the Alarde in the past being pointed out in the street by passers-by whispering to each other in admiration "she was a cantinera".

The importance given to the role reflects an aspect of Hegoalde society relating to the gender roles of men and women evident both in social values and in the way in which certain public spaces are used. In cake shops in Hegoalde, one finds women sitting and chatting together, while bars generally remain the domain of the men. Young people form cuadrillas – groups – to which they often remain loyal throughout their life. These cuadrillas are most often formed at school or in their neighbourhood, where children will make their first friendships, and largely consist of friends of the same sex. In their teens, when boys and girls form romantic relationships across cuadrilla boundaries, the importance of their respective cuadrillas does not diminish. Going out in the evenings, each often stays with his or her own cuadrilla. If they bump into each other in the same bars, they will take a few drinks together but will eventually move on to the next bar and carry on with their cuadrilla. In such a context, peer pressure for social conformity can be strong, as I was able to perceive from personal observation and from conversations with various young people. Expressing a different opinion poses the risk of ostracism from the rest of the cuadrilla and further repercussions on family and other relations in the town. In fact, two young women told me it was best simply to keep one's opinions, if one had any, to one's self. In such circumstances, the need to reaffirm one's belonging and acceptance by others is translated in relation to the Alarde into a refusal to reflect further on the issue and instead to adhere like the rest of the majority to the vehement defence of the traditional Alarde.

The same process is evident in the construction of masculinity which emerges in the debate over the Alarde and reflects the models predominant in society (Bullen, 1997; 1999; 2000). Supporters of the traditional

Alarde project the dominant model of masculinity built around the notion of the man as principal protagonist of the public arena, transmitter of certain masculine values, attached in this particular case to military practice and male diversion. Anthropologist Gilmore noted how a certain dominant kind of masculinity is enacted in public performances in many Mediterranean countries in such a way as to ascertain its perpetuation in the local society (1994). In the Alarde, the men are the protagonists of the fiesta and the minority women, as cantineras, appear as if on virtual pedestals. The arrival of the supporters of a mixed Alarde is an intrusion into a neat social order that threatens to ruin the traditional Irun and Hondarribia's respectable self-image. As one woman, her hair permed a shade of purple and wearing a large silk white blouse and a small red neckerchief, angrily exclaimed to me, "these women supporters, they are people who do not like the Alarde, who do not care about it. It doesn't mean anything to them. They have turned the Alarde into a masquerade, a complete joke". In Irun, a young man dressed as a soldier with a beret on his head and holding an old air gun, his face bright red from the heat and the passion, muttered to me under his breath just after the official Alarde had marched past: "They look like clowns. Ridiculous and pathetic".

On the side of the mixed Alarde, campaigners for sexual equality have retained the role of the cantinera in their parade, in apparent contradiction with a model of femininity that would normally be seen as sexist by most feminists. This contradiction however, is acknowledged by supporters. As one woman parading in Irun's official Alarde explained to me, "yes, it is true, I recognise it is quite contradictory. I think this cantinera image is ridiculous... But we can't bring in too many changes, otherwise we really will be lost in our effort to persuade the traditionalists to accept the simple change of having women as soldiers". She adds, "I must say, I am pretty anti-military too. So all this parading around does make me quite sick. I parade out of principle for the right for women to express their Irunian identity like the men".

Perceptions of the Alarde on the Other Side of the Frontier

For some Hendaians with relatives and friends in Irun and Hondarribia, the Alarde also serves part of their identity construction and expression. Until recently, for example, Iñaki Beitia, a sixty-year-old man born in Hendaia to parents from Irun and Hondarribia who settled in Hendaia in their youth, took part in the Alarde of Hondarribia. "I would take a day off work – not so easy to use the excuse of the Alarde in Hendaia though – and I marched with my cousins and friends, friends I have kept since I was young, from just partying on the other side. It's part of my feeling Hondarribitarra I suppose. And it is this special day in the year, when all the family gets together."

Despite such links, however, he and others expressed awareness of a boundary drawn between Hendaians and Irunian or Hondarribian co-paraders in the Alarde. "The jokes and remarks you get about being French, gabatxo, … it does go on a bit", says Mr. Beitia. "I don't take it personally. You laugh along, but it is a bit tedious. There definitely are rivalries, a strange ambivalence between us. I suppose it's all about the pride of being Hondarribitarra. They are a funny lot. With their pride in tradition, their particular Basqueness and their fishermen. What is amusing too is that sometimes they pat me on the back after such a joke and say, 'but we know you are different, hey, you are one of us'!"

People in Irun and Hondarribia with whom I spoke denied any anti-French aspect to the Alarde, despite its origins as a celebration of victory against the French. But a sense of difference between the inhabitants of Irun and Hondarribia, on the one hand, and Hendaians, on the other, was regularly evoked, signalling a drawing of boundaries. As Nicolás explained to me: "O.K., the origin of the fiesta is a celebration of a victory against the French. But now, it is more just a fiesta. The Alarde is no longer specifically against the French but against what was then an enemy. This is just the fiesta of the people of Irun and Hondarribia. And if the gabachos come, they just enjoy themselves as well. There is nothing for the Hendaians to feel excluded about. They have their own fiestas… though quite lame ones!!"

A few Hendaian musicians are occasionally invited by the municipality of Irun or Hondarribia to join in their municipal bands when these are in need of extra musicians. Monique Lambert, a lady in her sixties who was once headmistress of a school in Hendaia, recalls how she was once invited by some Irunian friends to come and watch the Alarde in Irun from the balcony of the town hall. "It was a great honour", she recalls, "and I dressed up carefully in red and white for the occasion. Of course, I felt conscious of not being from there. But I have immense respect for their fiesta, the importance they give to their Alarde. It is their fiesta. And they understood that and I think they very much appreciated me for this".

Among the younger generations, however, while many young Hendaians in their twenties to whom I spoke went out at night in Irun and Hondarribia during the fiestas, few had actually been to see the Alarde. "They start so early in the morning, and then all it is is watching men troop past", says Emmanuel Lecumberry. "It's only exciting if you are from there. This is a fiesta for them."

In their reactions to the conflict about women's participation in the Alarde, many Hendaians to whom I spoke revealed a similar sensation of a boundary between them and their neighbours in Irun and Hondarribia. Hendaian women, while making an effort to understand the point of view of the traditional supporters, all concurred with Sandrine Irazu, a 25-year-old woman working in a transport agency close to the frontier, that "nothing of this kind could ever take place here, I don't think. We are not such a traditional society in this way". Tonio Bergouin, a young man in his twenties who regularly competes in rowing competitions with people from Irun, Hondarribia and other parts of Hegoalde, remarked that "all this fuss simply about the participation of women is really quite ridiculous. And so... well, you know how they are always criticising us, saying we are boring, stingy, cold... well, here we can now strike back, criticising them for being so old-fashioned and narrow-minded".

Fiestas in Hendaia

By comparison with the passions that surround the festivities of Irun and Hondarribia, fiestas in Hendaia seem a pale affair. Hendaia has its own annual fiesta in mid-January, known in Basque as the *Bixintxos* after Hendaia's patron saint, Saint Vincent. Until the 1970s, this was a lively one-week event including an open-air ball with live music, Basque folk dancing, games and convivial communal meals under marquees set up for the occasion. Many elderly Hendaians recalled to me how people from Irun and Hondarribia would come to join the festivities. Over the intervening years, however, excitement around the Bixintxos has largely fizzled out and during my stay in the area they were in no way such a thrilling subject of conversation amongst Hendaians with whom I spoke as were the fiestas of Irun and Hondarribia for the inhabitants of those towns. Many young people whom I knew in Hendaia did not even bother to take part.

One reason for local indifference to the Bixintxos may be the time of year in which they take place, often marked by poor weather. In January 2001, the fiesta committee of Hendaia which, although not an organ of the municipality, depends on the municipality for 90% of its budget and is made up primarily of municipal councillors, organised a series of activities for children for the Bixintxos, including a competition in which children dressed up as pirates, in memory of the locally famous naval mercenary Etienne Pellot who fought successfully with Napoleon Bonaparte against the English navy at the turn of the nineteenth century and who, later, managed to negotiate a peaceful entente with the Duke of Wellington when his forces invaded Hendaia in 1813 and threatened to destroy Hendaia yet again. The poster advertising the Bixintxos was adorned with a Walt Disney-style cartoon figure of a pirate, to evoke Pellot. But while the fiestas were declared a success in the local papers, they remained largely frequented only by children and their parents.

Many people to whom I spoke, on both sides of the frontier, concluded from this that there is little sense of tradition in Hendaia. "Hendaians have little sense of Hendaian identity, as compared to us", a woman from Irun remarked. For others, it was confirmation of "the dullness of the French". Hendaia does, however, have a exceptionally high number of local associations, several of which organise their own events, during which they set up stands serving different kinds of food and play music. Rather than dwelling on tradition, as is the case in Irun and Hondarribia, the citizens of Hendaia seem to be more ready to innovate and look beyond the frontiers of the Basque Country for inspiration.

This may be a reflection of Hendaia's calmer political environment. While tradition draws its justification from the past, its utility in social terms is firmly anchored in the present. Tradition serves to identify people who belong together, but it also serves as a rallying point in a social context characterised by political insecurity and cultural tensions. Seen in this light, it is easier to understand both the obsessive insistence on tradition of many citizens of Irun and Hondarribia and the apparent indifference to tradition of many Hendaians. In less than a century, Spain has undergone two dictatorships, a civil war and several attempted *coups d'état*. Today, Spanish democracy is still less than thirty years old, and in Hegoalde, it continues to be challenged by conflicting political, social and cultural attitudes, exacerbated by the violence of ETA. This has the consequence of sustaining a culturally and politically polarised society. As frontier towns, Irun and Hondarribia have had to come to terms with a large influx of immigrants and with the social and economic changes brought about by the ending of frontier controls and the removal of the once seemingly secure boundaries that these entailed. In such a context, the value of a tradition such as the Alarde, which until the outbreak of the current controversy incorporated a majority of inhabitants in a harmonious way, becomes evident.

Hendaia, by contrast, though it has an even more mixed population given the presence of so many Spanish citizens, has benefited in recent years from a less confrontational political context. Rather than setting up exclusive barriers to keep people out, Hendaia makes a point of inclusiveness, with numerous associations whose role is to welcome people in. The municipal elections of March 2001, rather than being a contest between opposing political parties as would have been the case in Hegoalde, provided an occasion for Hendaia residents to assert their identification with the town. The winning list of Mr. Ecenarro, Hendaia's mayor, included people with radically contrasting political views, from conservative to Communist and abertzale. All five competing lists of candidates – Mr. Ecenarro's *Hendaye Plurielle*, *Agir pour Hendaye*, a group following a French conservative trend, *Cap Alternance*, a group gathering local entrepreneurs, *Vivre Hendaye*, an alliance of French Socialists, Communists and Green party sympathists, and Biharko

Hendaia, the local Basque left-wing nationalist group – expressed in one way or other their priority as being to work "for Hendaia".

In addition to the Bixintxos, the municipal fiesta committee organises another fiesta in mid-August, a so-called *fête basque*, whose highlight is a parade through the streets of Hendaia with floats representing themes or subjects linked with the town. The insignia of Hendaia, a whale and the initials HE,[18] adorn much of the décor, together with Basque flags. For the occasion, people wear traditional Basque garb and dance to Basque folk music.[19] Several Hendaians I spoke to about this event stressed that they did not dress up in traditional Basque dress, thus making it clear that this was not a carnival but "part of their identity" as one woman put it to me. As a fiesta taking place in the middle of the summer tourist season, the fête basque is very much a source of entertainment for tourists. While Hendaians take part in it as their fiesta, a few expressed to me their irritation with the tourists dressing up as Basques, for whom, as one friend commented, "it means nothing, it's just a laugh". Others, however, did not seem to mind too much the presence of the tourists: "tourists have always been part of the life of Hendaia. We're a mixed kind of town anyway, with so many people coming from other places".[20]

Many festivities in Hendaia are organised by clubs or associations. In August 2000, a band called Zarpai Banda[21] organised a fiesta to celebrate its thirtieth anniversary, involving street parades, concerts and food stalls, in which numerous Hendaians, young and old, took part. As one friend told me afterwards, "it was a real thing for Hendaians. Everyone was there". Most participants, at the request of Zarpai Banda, wore white clothes and red berets, sashes and neckerchiefs, the typical festive dress of Hegoalde now increasingly common in Iparralde. Spanish and Latin American themes were evident in the music, decorations and the kind of food that was served. The poster advertising the event was adorned with the words "Viva la fiesta" with cartoon figures of a fla-

---

18   The whale symbolises whale hunting which was the main source of economic revenue of Hendaia until the late nineteenth century. H. and E. are the last letters of Hendaia written in French (Hendaye). The insignia of the crown was bestowed by Louis XIV on making Hendaia independent from Urruña in 1654.

19   An explorer, astronomer and Bascophile, Antoine d'Abbadie is credited with initiating the idea of a Basque fiesta in the late nineteenth century as a way of celebrating Basque traditions (Michelena, 1997).

20   During the summer months, the population is estimated to triple.

21   Zarpai does not have a specific meaning but, according to its former president Michel Lambert, is meant to evoke "craziness, non-conformism, adventure and temerity. Basically letting loose". A banda is a type of music band, similar to a *txaranga*, a Spanish Basque-style steel band which is now also extremely popular in festivities in Iparralde, as well as other areas around, such as Les Landes.

menco woman dancing alongside a drummer with a Mexican hat, big moustache and Cuban cigar, a Basque man dressed in white with a red beret and neckerchief and holding a *gaita* – a Basque wind instrument, and a black bull banging on a big bass drum.

Other annual fiestas include the *fête du chipiron*, a day-long fiesta named after a local type of fish, which involves a big convivial meal with seafood organised by various local associations, and the *Corso Lumineux*, a convoy of floats made by local associations and groups of friends which parades through the streets at night. In addition, many smaller festivities are organised by associations and the fiesta committee of Hendaia. Over recent years, there have been Andalusian fiestas, recreations of the fiestas of Pamplona, with specially set up stalls serving red wine and tapas, and an omelette fiesta, involving making a giant omelette. Zarpai Banda has also been extremely active in the organisation of such celebrations. Through its link with a band from Sulzbach in Germany, it organised a Beer Festival. On several occasions too, it included floats for the fête basque which followed the theme of the Alarde of Irun and Hondarribia. Three young local women were dressed as cantineras and seated on the float waving their fan to the passing crowds. In early 2002, it was decided by the municipality in collaboration with local associations that another annual festivity would be organised in June, called the *fête du printemps*, the spring fiesta, and which would revolve around the participation of one or other of the towns with which Hendaia has been twinned since 1999, Viana do Castelo in Portugal or Peebles in Scotland. This was considered as having been successful, although turnout was not very high, and it has been decided to make it a fixed annual event.

CHAPTER 8

Cross-Frontier Cooperation

In the council chamber of Irun's town hall, a dozen men and women stand chatting. They are here for a meeting of the General Council of the Partzuergo, and the way they interact with each other reveals a lot about local politics in Bidasoa-Txingudi. On one side, Ion Elizalde, a 28-year-old student with very short hair, wearing a woolly jumper recognisably made by the Spanish Basque fashion firm Mendi Loreak, jeans and earrings, is joking in Spanish with Borja Semper, in his mid-20s, more formally dressed in a dark blue suit with his hair slicked back with gel, and Guillermo Echenique, a round-faced, bespectacled man in his 50s in a dark business suit and open-necked shirt. Next to them, Raphaël Lassallette, a 74-year-old man in a casual grey suit, chats in French with Elena Etxegoien, whose well-groomed dark brown hair matches the sophisticated cut of her clothes. Nearby, Jean-Baptiste Etcheverry, dressed in flannel trousers and a sports jacket, is engaged in a more serious conversation in Spanish with Alberto Buen, a short man with thick-rimmed glasses, brown hair and wearing a casual suit.

The atmosphere is relaxed and amicable, even though these are politicians representing parties of opposing views. Mr. Elizalde represents the moderate Basque nationalist party EA on the town council of Hondarribia, and Mr. Semper represents the Spanish conservative party, PP, in Irun. Mr. Echenique is the director of Bidasoa Bizirik. Mr. Lassallette is the Socialist mayor of Hendaia, while Ms. Etxegoien is EAJ councillor for Irun. Mr. Etcheverry is an independent Basque nationalist on the Hendaia council and Mr. Buen is the Socialist mayor of Irun.

Somewhat apart from this group, seated on the benches to one side of the council chamber, a man and two women are watching in silence. Marije Zapirain, a smartly but simply dressed woman with tidily brushed short blonde hair, sits alongside Joxan Elosegi, a serious-looking man with a bushy greying moustache, wearing a casual suit. Behind them, Amaia Navarro, an elegantly dressed woman with well-groomed curly shoulder-length hair, sits on her own. All three are opposition councillors. Ms. Zapirain and Mr. Elosegi represent the left-

wing Basque nationalist party EH[1] *in Hondarribia and Irun respect-*
ively. Ms. Navarro is an independent member of the municipal council
of Irun.

They are waiting for the mayor of Hondarribia, EAJ member Borja
Jáuregui, to hold what will be the last board meeting of the Partzuergo
under the presidency of Mr. Lassallette.[2] *In the front row of the seats*
reserved for the public, two journalists representing Sud-Ouest *and* La
Semaine du Pays Basque, *the two most widely read French-language*
newspapers in Iparralde, have come to cover the event. Beside them,
two Irun-based journalists, one representing El Diario Vasco, *the main*
Spanish language newspaper in Hegoalde, and the other the Spanish
radio station Ser, are chatting to each other. A journalist for La Bahía,
a Spanish-language magazine distributed free in Irun and Hondarribia,
walks in and sits down beside a reporter from Txingudi Telebista.

Sitting behind the journalists, a pensioner from Hendaia is appar-
ently the only person present for reasons of personal interest rather than
professional duty. Beside him, Pilar Fuertes, an employee of the town
hall of Hendaia working for the Partzuergo, is joined by Felipe Sara-
gueta, casually dressed with creased trousers and an open shirt, who is
the director of the Partzuergo, and Eva Fernández, one of the directors
of Bidasoa Bizirik, *smartly attired in a skirt and jacket. The three chat*
animatedly together.

At last, a tall man with thinning hair and glasses, wearing a casual
dark blue suit, walks in. It's Mr. Jáuregui. He shakes hands with a few
of the people standing, and everyone takes their seats. The three mayors
sit behind a table at the end of the council chamber, facing the public.
Mr. Lassallette, sits in the middle with Mr. Jáuregui to his left and
Mr. Buen to his right. The other councillors of the majority parties sit on
benches to one side, opposite the councillors of the opposition.
Mr. Echenique and PSE councillor from Irun, José-Antonio Santano, sit
at one end of the front bench and Mr. Elizalde and Ms. Etxegoien sit
together at the other end. Mr. Semper jokingly whispers that he "won't
sit with the nationalists", instead taking his seat behind them on his
own.

The session begins. Mr. Lassallette greets the audience in Basque,
Spanish and French: "Egun on deneri, buenos días a todos, bonjour à
tous". From then on, however, he speaks only in French. Praising the
success of the three towns' cooperation up until now, he stresses its

---

[1]   Since this meeting took place in March 2001, before EH was re-born as Batasuna, the
       councillors were still members of EH.

[2]   A few weeks later, were due to take place the municipal elections in Hendaia and, as
       Mr. Lassallette did not plan to stand again as mayor, the new mayor would continue
       as president of the Partzuergo in place of Mr. Lassallette for the rest of the mandate.

importance not only for other cross-border projects but also for the local population. Once he has finished, the secretary of the Partzuergo, Juana Maria Herrador, who is also general secretary of the municipality of Irun, and Serge Peyrelongue, general secretary of the municipality of Hendaia, take it in turns to read the various motions proposed by the Partzuergo. Mr. Peyrelongue speaks in French and Ms. Herrador speaks in Basque and Spanish. The motions are all passed unanimously.

After making a few suggestions for future Partzuergo projects and listening to the comments in Spanish of Messrs. Buen and Jáuregui, Mr. Lassallette invites questions from the audience. Two technical questions are posed and answered. Then Mr. Elosegi, one of the two EH councillors, puts up his hand to speak. He addresses the session in Basque, and the three mayors and Messrs. Semper, Echenique and Santano reach for their headphones to listen to the interpretation. As an opposition councillor, Mr. Elosegi has no participation in the running of the Partzuergo, and he uses this occasion to give voice to his frustration. Not only are the representatives of some political groups, such as EH, excluded from the Partzuergo's management, he observes but, "despite the Partzuergo's successful cooperation, members of the Partzuergo continue to talk of the frontier as if it were still in effect". They "should not speak about one side of the border and the other side of the border, or Irun, Hondarribia and Hendaia all separately", he argues. Instead, he urges, "it is the duty of the Partzuergo to promote the area as a unified whole".

To reply to Mr. Elosegi, Mr. Lassallette switches on the microphone in front of him and proceeds to talk in French. He explains that the issue of non-representativity was already brought up in another meeting recently, when it was decided unanimously by members of the Partzuergo's board to keep participation to the present three seats per municipality, giving the representatives of minority groups only a consultative role. This, he recalls, was agreed upon on the basis that having all political tendencies represented would cause disunity within the Partzuergo and hamper its effectiveness. Personally, he adds, he is not opposed to the idea of full participation. But he points out that it is a difficult issue to resolve if everyone is not in agreement. Having said that, he notes that indeed the inhabitants of Irun, Hondarribia and Hendaia are all one people. However "there is also the reality, that of the frontier, which still exists whether we like it or not, with its different cultures, habits and languages, in spite of there also being a common Basque character on either side".

In conclusion, adds Mr. Lassallette, "if only I could speak Basque, I would have answered you in Basque... This is another reality that remains and which continues to separate us... We must all work to protect the Basque language, though I do not think it is necessary for us to go as far as to create one country. Rapprochement is at the moment the most important step, so that we can know each other better and learn to like each other better... One last thing: your comments have not shocked me. Actually, I was expecting them".

Following these remarks, the final valedictory speeches are made, with Messrs. Jáuregui and Buen expressing their appreciation of Mr. Lassallette's efforts in "directing the destinies of the three towns together". Having listened to them wish him all the best in his retirement, Mr. Lassallette takes their hands in his and thanks them warmly. The session is brought to a close.

(Friday 2 March 2001, town hall of Irun).

In this description of a meeting of the Partzuergo's General Council, we can clearly see the deployment by the various participants of a range of symbolic boundaries to assert and affirm their personal notions of self. Some were used consciously by the individuals present in their interaction with others in that particular context. Others can be said to have been used unconsciously. Since this meeting of the Partzuergo's General Council took place in March 2001, some of the actors on the Bidasoa-Txingudi political stage have changed, but the behavioral mechanisms witnessed here remain as relevant to our theme as ever. Four main boundaries can be immediately identified, in individuals' use of language, their personal appearance, their physical behaviour and their use of space.

Let us begin with the linguistic boundary. At the start, we witness various actors altering their usual language of communication in an inclusive manner. Mr. Elizalde, for example, although he considers himself euskaldun – he speaks Basque and has told me he feels Basque first and foremost – speaks in Spanish in order to communicate with Mr. Semper. Introducing the session, Mr. Lassallette uses all three languages to greet the assembled company, before resorting to French, the only language with which he feels completely comfortable.

When Mr. Elosegi takes the floor, he chooses to speak in Basque, even though he is fluent in Spanish and can understand and speak French more or less well. He uses Basque as a matter of principle, as he claims to feel first and foremost euskaldun living in Euskal Herria rather than Spanish and a citizen of the Spanish state. In using Basque, Mr. Elosegi can also mark himself off deliberately from the other councillors, of whom many, as he knows, have only a rudimentary knowledge of Basque or no knowledge at all. By responding to Mr. Elosegi in French, Mr. Lassallette reasserts his right to his own notion of self in the common space in which they are both interacting.

In terms of the construction of boundaries, and thereby identities, what does not happen in this brief exchange is as important as what does happen. In choosing to answer in French, Mr. Lassallette eschews two other possible boundaries. As it happens, he at one point took Basque lessons with AEK. In this particular context he could have drawn on what Basque he does know in order to answer Mr. Elosegi. He also speaks a little Spanish, and could have chosen to address Mr. Elosegi in that language.

The fact that Mr. Lassallette chooses not to use Basque can be ascribed to two non-exclusive motives. Firstly, such an option would almost certainly be too laborious, considering the intricacies of what he has to say. Had he done so, his effort would have been greatly appreciated by the Basque speakers present. But by continuing as before in French, Mr. Lassallette preserves his own boundary of identity, thereby asserting his right to speak French and yet simultaneously to feel Basque in his own personal way.

As for his possible use of Spanish, this would most likely have been taken as a great insult by Mr. Elosegi, who could have interpreted it as a condescending and imperialistic reaffirmation of his status as a Spanish citizen over and above all his claims to being Basque. In the event, we may assume that Mr. Lassallette did not consider either of these options, and if someone had suggested one or other to him he would almost certainly have rejected them as counter-productive in such a situation, in relation to his own personal identity and in the political diplomacy sought.

Personal appearance is the most immediately visible marker of identity. With language, the linguistic boundary is only evident when a person speaks, while with dress, the identity markers are physically visible. The choice of dress can be either conscious or unconscious. Whatever the case, preferences relating to dress are revealing about the person's sense of self. They provide a message about the person relevant to his position in society and in his direct relations with other people. They are also often in line with the person's identification: they can say much about the person's political affiliations, taste and social associations.

On this occasion, we see how different individuals use their choice of dress to express political boundaries. In the general socio-political context of the Basque Country, the smooth, clean-cut and close-shaven style of Mr. Semper is easily recognisable as fitting the image of the PP. In direct contrast, left-wing Basque nationalists often distinguish themselves by a particular kind of dressing-down. They rarely put on business suits, though casual ones are sometimes worn. Instead, young and old often sport t-shirts distinctly marked with Basque slogans or long-sleeved and striped purple or turquoise and black, and out-door clothing, such as walking boots and anoraks. Many women wear their hair in a short crop, or long with a bandana covering their forehead and rarely wear skirts. Many young men choose to wear their hair short in the front and long in the back, and earrings, while the older men may choose to adopt a beard or bushy moustache. In the council meeting, the only distinctive marker which goes along with any of these stereotypical descriptions is Mr. Elosegi with his thick moustache. While a seemingly small detail, in the socio-cultural context of the Basque Country, this is very significant.

However, again, such boundaries are not always clear or fixed, high-lighting in this case the unreliability of stereotypes. Mr. Elizalde, for example, with his short hair, ear-rings and jeans, would appear from first impressions to fit the image of the left-wing Basque nationalist, on the basis of the stereotype depicted above. Through his personal choice of dress, Mr. Elizalde adopts the vestimentary boundaries for his own personal expression of identity. He gives his choice of dress his personal meanings. As for the other council members, at first sight their mode of dress appears rather indeterminate. The Socialist councillors generally adopt a casually formal style of dress, while the representative of EAJ and the independent councillor from Irun are in more conservative smart dress. Seemingly not very conspicuous at first, these different styles are nonetheless markers of a general trend within these distinct socio-political circles.

Boundaries of dress are here subtly exposed. Often, when such boundaries are played out discreetly, others will be asserted more force-fully. It is therefore in the actual moment of social interaction that these and others become evident, as we have seen with the use of language and as we shall now see with the use of space.

Spatial boundaries can be noted not only in the use of space by the council members in the chamber but also in the way they talk about other spatial features, such as the frontier. Let us begin with the actual space of the chamber. At the beginning of their mandate, municipal councillors are allotted their seats in their respective municipal council chambers. While the councillors of Irun attending this board meeting of the Partzuergo in their own town hall tend to occupy the same seats in which they ordinarily sit, the seating choices displayed by the council-lors from Hendaia and Hondarribia are more significant. While many, despite their different political affiliations, have friendly relations with each other, in the context of the Partzuergo meeting they choose to place themselves next to their political colleagues. So we see Mr. Elizalde taking a seat next to Ms. Etxegoien, after chatting with Mr. Semper and Mr. Echenique, and Ms. Zapirain sitting beside Mr. Elosegi. A return to the political boundaries that affirm each of the councillors' identities is thus evident.

The fact that Mr. Elosegi and Ms. Zapirain are not members of the board of the Partzuergo's General Council is an additional factor, which sets them consciously apart in space. At a Partzuergo meeting one week previously in Hendaia, in a conference hall where there were no allotted seating plans, Mr. Elosegi and Ms. Zapirain also set themselves well apart from the rest of the council members by sitting together a few rows of seats away. At this meeting, by already being seated while waiting for the council meeting to begin, Mr. Elosegi and Ms. Zapirain effectively set themselves apart from the other councillors who are standing about chatting in the center aisle. But they are also seated some distance away from the other councillors who are not members of the board of the Partzuergo, such as Ms. Navarro.

Mr. Elosegi's objection to the repeated use of the word frontier by members of the Partzuergo says something about his perception of himself within a Basque space. A similar criticism was made by Mr. Elizalde, in other General Council meetings last year. However, within the complex context of Basque nationalist politics, despite their supposedly common visions of a united Euskal Herria, both contest each other's actual commitment to the eradication of the frontier both as a physical and symbolic boundary. EH partisans criticise EAJ and EA for their vague way of talking about fighting for the independence of Euskal Herria, while EAJ and EA partisans express doubts about the realistic and democratic aspects of EH's independence-seeking process.

In contrast to both Mr. Elosegi and Mr. Elizalde, Mr. Lassallette insists on his own 'reality' of the existence of the frontier, as a physical and symbolic border, marker of two separate social contexts affected by the presence and control of two different states. At the same time, he presents a different interpretation of the *raison d'être* and objectives of the Partzuergo to that of Mr. Elosegi, corresponding to his contrasting notion of self and different perception of a Basque space.

We also see facial expressions and physical comportment serving to demonstrate boundaries in this context of the Partzuergo General Council meeting. When Mr. Jáuregui walks in, he does so in a quick and rather abrupt fashion, greeting some people but not others, notably Ms. Zapirain and Mr. Elosegi who are positioned directly in front of him and so immediately within his eye range. Another example of how individuals choose to mark boundaries by their behaviour during the meeting is the choice by some members of the council who do not understand Basque to not pick up the translation headphones when Mr. Elosegi speaks. By not doing so, a message is transmitted about the indifference or rejection of what Mr. Elosegi is saying. Ms. Zapirain and Mr. Elosegi, meanwhile, also engage in boundary-drawing which separates them from their colleagues. With their stern expressions, the two EH councillors make their own detachment from the social mingling taking place in front of them particularly manifest.

Another detail that is of equally great significance in the sociopolitical context of the Basque Country, evident in this account of the Partzuergo meeting, is the spelling of names. For reasons of homogeneity, as I explained in the introduction, I have chosen to use place names in their Basque version, and specifically in accordance with Batua, or unified Basque, rather than their Spanish or French equivalents. In this vignette, however, I have spelt some names the Spanish or the French way as I have often seen them written in various official texts, press releases and newspaper articles. Echenique follows Spanish spelling, in contrast to Etxenike in Basque, while Etcheverry is written the French way rather than Etxeberri in Basque. I have also sometimes seen the name spelt Etxeverry, an alternative way of writing with Basque connotations. Similarly, Jáuregui is written the Spanish way instead of Jauregi in Basque, though I have seen it, on very few occasions, written in Basque. Elizalde, Etxegoien, Saragueta, Zapirain and Elosegi, on the other hand, are written the Basque way, as I have always seen them. The choice of spelling Elosegi instead of Elósegui, or Etxegoien instead of Etchegoyen in Spanish and Etchegoin in French is significant. This shows a propensity on the part of the nameholders or the writers to play with the markers implicit in the choice of language spelling, revealing identification with French, Spanish or Basque values to the detriment of the others. Basque spelling, in particular, can be used for particular political purposes, setting inclusive boundaries, for example, to please a culturally or politically Basque audience or exclusive boundaries to mark a difference with other people whose names are written the Spanish or French way.

Finally, the identity markers and boundaries that we have seen used by the participants in the Partzuergo General Council meeting are only a few aspects of the notion of reality held by each of the contenders. The manner in which they each actually 'live out' the frontier and react to the way the Partzuergo operates sheds further light on the ways in which they construct and give meaning to their own identities in relation to the boundary area in which they live. In other words, the uniform of the politician left in the closet and the political lingo put aside, the way these participants behave and talk – in short, live in their social environment – reveals other aspects of their notions of self. The implications of this are relevant for an understanding of the human interaction on which social and political structures are based and the thorough analysis of the functioning of a political project such as the Partzuergo.

Political Organisation in Bidasoa-Txingudi

In Iparralde, local politics tend to be dictated more by local influences than by political party considerations, and Hendaia, as we saw earlier, is no exception. In Hegoalde, by contrast, local politics and the passions that they arouse are much more polarised along political party lines. Due to the pro-Republican sentiments of a large proportion of its population, Irun suffered severely at the hands of Franco's forces during the Spanish Civil War. Under Franco, Irun and Hondarribia, like other towns in Spain, were run by officials close to the regime. Hondarribia was a vacation destination for members of Franco's family and for supporters of his government.

Soon after the meeting of the Partzuergo's General Council described above, Mr. Lassallette, a former teacher who had been mayor of Hendaia since 1981, relinquished his post and handed over his mantle to his deputy, Kotte Ecenarro, like him a member of the *PS*,[3] the French Socialist party. As of the time of writing, Mr. Ecenarro leads a so-called 'plural' coalition made up of twenty-five councillors of disparate political allegiances. This coalition includes five members of the PS,[4] six of the French Communist Party (PCF)[5], one adherent to the French moderate conservative coalition group UDF, another to the radical left-wing *Mouvement des Citoyens*,[6] four councillors who claim to be Basque nationalists but do not regard independence as their primary goal and condemn ETA violence, and three with no declared links with any party. Mr. Ecenarro proclaims himself an abertzale, giving importance to Basque culture and the Basque language and the campaign for the creation of a département du Pays basque, although without siding with any Basque nationalist party. He is fairly fluent in both Spanish and Basque, but insists on his feeling Hendaian and a French citizen. In order to work together harmoniously, both he and other members of his coalition with differing political sympathies claim to adapt their positions to what they think are the particular needs of Hendaia.

In Hondarribia, as of the time of writing, the municipal council has been headed by moderate Basque nationalists since 1979, reflecting the strong traditional Basque character of Hondarribia's population. Borja Jáuregui, the mayor, took office in 1995 and in May 2003 was reelected for a third mandate. A member of EAJ, he succeeded Alonso Oronoz, a member of EA, leading a coalition of EAJ and EA councillors. Mr. Jáuregui is from a well-known local family which owns a hotel, bar and restaurant in the centre of town. However, he does not speak Basque

---

[3] This stands for *Parti socialiste*.

[4] At the time of writing, only Mr. Ecenarro was an official member of the PS. Three councillors were due to renew their membership, while the other two expressed no need or hurry to officialise their support to the PS. While it was necessary for them to be members for the election campaign, so as to ensure the support of the PS, now that they are in the municipal council, this is no longer necessary.

[5] This stands for *Parti communiste français.*

[6] This literally translates as the 'Movement of Citizens'. This is Jean-Pierre Chevènement's French nationalist and Jacobin party.

and professes no interest in learning it.[7] As of early 2003, Hondarribia also had one councillor representing the PSE-EE and another representing the PP. Until the banning of Batasuna in September 2002, the town council also included four representatives of Batasuna. With municipal elections due in Spain in May 2003, the composition of Hondarribia's council was set to change, although EAJ seemed likely to retain control.

In Irun, the conservative Basque nationalist party EAJ won seven councillors in the previous municipal elections, thanks to strong support in some of the old neighbourhoods of the town. But this was not enough to give it control of a municipality characterised by a large population of people with origins outside the Basque Country, many of whom voted for representatives of national political parties. The mayor of Irun since 1983 was a PSE-EE member, Alberto Buen. Mr. Buen had been active in the Socialist movement before and during Spain's transition to democracy, and had served as a Socialist councillor in Irun between 1979 and 1983 under an EAJ mayor. He knows a little French and once took Basque lessons, but is most comfortable speaking Spanish. After he resigned in 2002, his deputy, José-Antonio Santano, also a PSE-EE member, took his place. In the opposition, the council also included one independent and, until September 2002, four representatives of Batasuna. Forthcoming municipal elections held out a significant prospect for change, with the likelihood that EAJ might win a majority for the first time in twenty years.

The different political make-up of the three towns, reflecting the constrasting socio-political identifications and ambitions of their populations, has made the task of rallying people together under a common programme through the Partzuergo a considerable challenge. Within the three towns' populations, individuals have different understandings of what it is to belong to the area and to feel Basque and perceive different social and cultural symbols as important to their identificatory process. The three municipalities have responded in the Partzuergo not so much by erasing exclusive socio-political boundaries as by seeking to create new inclusive boundaries common to the whole area.

---

[7]   In an interview in May 2002, Mr. Jáuregui explained to me that, as a child and whilst growing up, for various reasons, he did not have the opportunity to learning the language. He continued: "I do not need to learn Basque in order to feel any more Basque. I am now in my fifties and it is not now either that I am going to go off and learn the language. Anyway, I don't see why I should always have to justify myself for not speaking Basque".

The Creation of the Bidasoa-Txingudi Mugaz Gaindiko Partzuergo

In May 1980, the European Convention Framework on Cross-Border Cooperation between collectivities or local authorities provided a point of departure for the development of European laws to promote and facilitate cross-border cooperation. It was not until 1989, however, that cross-frontier co-operation took on a new form in the Western Pyrenees, with a protocol between the regions of Aquitaine and Euskadi. In 1991, the establishment of the European Single Market and the INTERREG programme led to the launching of a cross-border regional cooperation initiative under the name of Euro Region Aquitaine Euskadi, primarily focused on economic cooperation, particularly in the development of transport and business exchanges along the Atlantic coastal area. At a local level, the mayors of the towns of Bayonne, Anglet and Biarritz in Iparralde teamed up in mid 1993 with the mayor of San Sebastian to launch a cooperation initiative under the name of *Euro Cité Basque* in French, *Euro Ciudad Vasca*, in Spanish, and *Euskal Euro Hiria* in Basque. This initiative largely revolves around exploring options for the development of urban construction, transport and communications infrastructure in the area, which stretches from Bayonne along the Atlantic coast to San Sebastian and has a total population of more than 600,000.

In this context of cross-frontier cooperation and reconfiguration of space, the Partzuergo stands out as being deliberately motivated by the realisation on the part of local politicians in Hendaia, Irun and Hondarribia of the need to cooperate as neighbours in an increasingly open European context. Even before the introduction of the European Single Market and the extension of the Schengen agreement to include Spain led to the dismantling of the border controls that had provided both Irun and Hendaia with much of their economic activity, it was clear that these developments would lead to numerous job losses with repercussions for the rest of the local economy. Contacts between the three towns in the late 1980s led in 1990 to the submission of a proposal to the French and Spanish governments for inter-municipal cross-border cooperation and, subsequently, to an application for INTERREG funds. That same year, in an "Institutional Declaration of the Lower Bidasoa", the three towns formally agreed to cooperate with each other on potential cross-border projects. Following further reflection and analysis by the three municipalities, joint committees were set up in the domains of culture, social and economic affairs. In 1992, Irun and Hondarribia created the development agency Adebisa to promote innovation in the local economy on their side of the frontier.[8] A year later, together with the municipality of Hendaia, Adebisa contracted two French and Spanish consultancy firms to carry out a study on possible medium to long-term economic and urban development in the area, known as the Strategic Development Plan of the Bidasoa.

In 1995, in a further step at state level towards enhanced cross-border cooperation, the French and Spanish states signed the Treaty of Bayonne recognising the value of cooperation between communities on either side of their joint frontier. This provided the municipalities of Irun, Hondarribia and Hendaia with the legal backing to join together and form what they called the *Euro District Bidasoa-Txingudi* in French, *Euro Districto Bidasoa-Txingudi* in Spanish and *Bidasoa-Txingudi Euro Barrutia* in Basque. Under its aegis, they launched a series of cultural projects, financed by funds from their own budgets, from the INTERREG programme and regional bodies.

Support for cross-frontier cooperation was initially far from unanimous, however. In Hendaia, members of the PCF and of the conservative RPR and UDF parties expressed scepticism regarding the proposed cooperation pact on the grounds that it "risked threatening the sovereignty of France".[9] In Irun and Hondarribia, members of the PP similarly showed little enthusiasm for the project in its initial stages. The lack of an appropriate legal vehicle for the Euro Barruti limited its functioning. Only in the late 1990s did the three municipalities find an appropriate solution in the form of a "consorcio", a Spanish juridical concept which allows for collaboration between local public institutions.[10] Agreement was reached on the constitution for a Consorcio

---

[8] The change of name took place following the appointment of Guillermo Echenique as new director. According to Mr. Echenique, the name Bidasoa Bizirik was favoured "to reflect the dynamism of the area" and the use of the word Bidasoa made it sound more local and "so closer to the people" (Interview January 2002).

[9] Interview with PCF member Jean Navarron.

[10] The choice was between this and two French legal entities, the *Société d'Economie Mixte* and the *Groupement d'Intérêt Public*. An SEM allows for the creation of a *société anonyme*, a partnership of various municipalities for the use of public services for common interest, while a GIP allows local public institutions across EU state borders to create a partnership with their own financial autonomy from their respective states. Both were deemed too restrictive because they favoured the French entity, thereby creating an unequal partnership. Nor was the GEIE considered a possible option as it does not provide flexibility for the launching of specific projects (the Euro Hiri will be able to launch specific projects by creating consorcios specially for them) (Interview with Felipe Saragueta, May 2002).

By contrast, the framework of the 'consorcio' under Spanish law allowed the three municipalities to enjoy equal standing in their partnership, despite being located in different state territories, and carry out projects together. The consorcio is "the union or association of local entities with other public administrations or non-profit private entities for the management of an initiative of common interest with its common or-

Bidasoa-Txingudi – or Partzuergo – in December 1998. The Partzuergo finally became operational in October 1999, following ratification by both the Spanish and French states of the Treaty of Bayonne and their formal approval of the Partzuergo initiative.

By endeavouring to promote a common local identity based on a heritage combining non-political elements that are Basque, Spanish and French, the Partzuergo seeks to go beyond the frontier as a political and social boundary. As an associative entity with full juridical capacity for carrying out its objectives, the Partzuergo divides its development priorities into four main areas: Tourism, involving a series of initiatives for promoting the three towns together internationally; Culture, involving activities of "historical and cultural interest" and "linguistic development" designed to gather the populations of all three towns together; Social Affairs, including the provision of information about social services in the three towns and coordination in specific areas; and Economic Development, involving projects to promote the mobility and collaboration of the local population and local businesses, including the setting up of a business exhibition ground aimed at attracting foreign investment.

As we shall see later in more detail, the Partzuergo has drawn on tradition and fiesta as part of its strategy to foster a sense of Txingudi belonging. One of its projects, conceived and promoted by the municipality of Hendaia, is the creation of a cultural itinerary, a path around the bay and through the three towns adorned along the way with panels giving information about the history of the area. These panels, according to the preliminary draft of the project, will explain how people on both sides of the frontier have many things in common, including the Basque language and Basque culture and how, despite the frontier, they have always succeeded somehow in maintaining these links. Another project is the annual hosting of a *Txingudi Eguna* or Txingudi Day in which local associations are invited to present themselves to the public, and a series of cultural and sports activities are organised for the enjoyment of the population of the three towns. By promoting a selective account of the area's history and providing a common space within which people can celebrate together, the Partzuergo is implementing a strategy to bring together the local population under new markers. These new inclusive boundaries may eventually replace the old boundaries still evident in institutions like the Alarde and still a factor in the daily lives of the inhabitants of the area.

---

ganisation and personal juridical identity" (Saragueta, 2000:31). It also has the advantage of being flexible in that it allows the possibility for members to choose the statutes themselves.

In organisational terms, the Partzuergo is headed by the Presidency, under whose leadership the General Council oversees the activities of the Committee of Directors and votes on its proposals. The mayors of the three towns take it in turns to act as president for a year while the other two are vice-presidents. The first president, from October 1999, was Alberto Buen, the mayor of Irun. In October 2000, it was the turn of the then mayor of Hendaia, Raphaël Lassallette. In March 2001, following municipal elections, his successor as mayor, Kotte Ecenarro, took his place. In October 2001, Borja Jáuregui, the mayor of Hondarribia, took over the rotating presidency. In October 2002, Mr. Buen's successor as mayor of Irun, José-Antonio Santano assumed the Presidency of the Partzuergo.

The General Council is made up of the three mayors, each with two deputies. At the time of writing, as the municipal council of Irun was led by a coalition including the PSE-EE, the Spanish conservative party PP and EAJ, the two deputies for Irun in the General Council were a PP councillor, Borja Semper, and an EAJ councillor, Elena Etxegoien. As for Hondarribia, where EAJ ruled in a coalition with EA, its two deputies were an EAJ councillor, Aitor Kerejeta, and an EA councillor, Ion Elizalde. Finally, in Hendaia, in an attempt to reflect its plural composition, the two deputies were ex-UDF member Jean-François Durandeau and moderate Basque nationalist councillor Jean-Baptiste Etcheverry.

The Committee of Directors includes three municipal representatives from the General Council along with two employees of the Partzuergo. One of these two employees included the director, Felipe Saragueta, until October 2002 when he resigned. At the time of writing, the Partzuergo had still not replaced him. Two town hall secretaries also take part, providing administrative and legal support on behalf of the municipalities. Finally, there were also two members of staff from Bidasoa Bizirik, the director, Guillermo Echenique, a former Socialist head of the diputación of Gipuzkoa, and the person responsible for cross-frontier issues, Eva Fernández.

Under the Partzuergo's constitution, Bidasoa Bizirik is responsible for the Partzuergo's administration and accounts. In 2000, when the bulk of my research was undertaken, Mr. Saragueta, together with the other two members of its staff, Pilar Fuertes and Javier González, were employed by Bidasoa Bizirik. Initially, the Partzuergo had its headquarters in the offices of Bidasoa Bizirik in Irun, where Mr. Saragueta and Mr. González were based, while Ms. Fuertes worked in Hendaia at the *Service des Relations transfrontalières*, or Service for Cross-Frontier Relations, set up by the town council to liaise with the municipalities of Irun and Hondarribia and Bidasoa Bizirik. Since the end of 2002, the

Partzuergo has shared its offices with Bidasoa Bizirik in a newly re-stored building that was formerly the French consulate in Irun, known as Villa Ducourau.

As a project set up by the mayors of the three towns with the backing of their supporters in each town's municipal council, the Partzuergo's statutes restrict membership of the Partzuergo's organising bodies to members of the majority parties in the three town councils and their nominees. The director of the Partzuergo and minority members of the three town councils can attend meetings of the General Council but only with consultative roles. This effectively excluded members of the left-wing Basque nationalist party Batasuna in Irun and Hondarribia from the decision-making process of the Partzuergo, a fact which was a source of continued complaint on their part.

The main areas of activity of the Partzuergo are dealt with by committees, with the participation of members of the majority parties in each town council and municipal and Partzuergo employees responsible for the relevant topics. Under the committees, working groups handle specific projects in such areas as sport and communication, with the participation of relevant local figures such as representatives of associations, journalists and entrepreneurs.

The Partzuergo's budget is funded by the three municipalities and by contributions from local and regional funds on both sides of the frontier and the EU. Hondarribia and Hendaia each contribute a quarter of the three municipalities' share of the budget, while Irun, as the biggest town, contributes half. Despite Irun's significantly bigger financial contribution, it has the same voting rights and veto powers in the General Council as Hendaia and Hondarribia, following a proposal along these lines by the mayor of Irun designed to ensure harmony between the three towns.

CHAPTER 9

The Partzuergo:
Using Boundaries to Unite

Just as the "cultural branding of its flock" (Gellner, 1983:40) has been an essential element in the creation of the modern nation-state, the creation of a sense of 'Txingudi identity' is considered by the promoters of the Partzuergo as a fundamental step to its success. Although its promoters repeatedly stressed to me in interviews that the Partzuergo is an 'apolitical' initiative, it clearly is a political project drawing on a "projection" at an intercommunity level of concepts of community identity found within each of the three towns in the same way as partisans of closer European integration attempt to rally together national populations under an EU banner (Stråth, 2000:13). The Partzuergo's rhetoric is a political discourse which entails a certain vision and interpretation of reality. Its emphasis on cultural projects and its repeated evocation of the importance of the Basque language and culture are part of its drive to create a common sense of 'Txingudi belonging'. By developing a common sense of self-understanding and belonging to a so-called Txingudi culture and society, the Partzuergo is laying the foundations for further initiatives of an economic and political nature.

In all communities, shared myths, legends, symbols and ritual help to provide a sense of belonging. In some cases, the Partzuergo draws on symbols and rhetorical devices used by Basque nationalists, as in a reference to *Hiruak Bat*,[1] meaning 'Three make One', echoing the Basque nationalist phrase *Zazpiak Bat*, or 'Seven make One', a reference to the seven provinces that make up Euskal Herria. Such actions mirror Basque nationalist tactics aimed at mobilizing people by using and manipulating certain symbols for political purposes. In other cases, the Partzuergo makes use of historical or quasi-historical references and inherited or invented ritual to press home its message. By creating a sense of Bidasoa-Txingudi identity, the Partzuergo seeks to establish legitimacy for its actions, even though most local inhabitants play no role in its everyday running and conceiving of projects.

---

[1] *Bidasoa-Txingudi*, October, 1999, No. 12, p. 4.

In the way that it has attempted to construct a social trend in its favour through the use of social values such as language and emphasis on common history, the Partzuergo is an example of how "administrative organisations create meaning" (Anderson, 1983:55). A touch of romanticism helps to boost its credibility and with it the popular appeal of the Partzuergo. By picking out certain facts from the past at the expense of others, the Partzuergo is constructing its own historical reality, creating in effect its own mythology. This strategy, which Alonso (1988) calls "departicularisation", is a familiar tactic in the process of nation-state formation (Foster, 1991:242). A touch of romanticism helps to boost its credibility and with it the popular appeal of the Partzuergo. Just as the bureaucratisation of French society over the course of the late nineteenth century helped to transform "peasants into Frenchmen" (Weber, 1977), the Partzuergo hopes to transform the diverse inhabitants of Irun, Hondarribia and Hendaia into 'Txingudians'.

In this context, it is interesting to contrast the Partzuergo's initiative with that of the European Commission's.[2] Like the European Commission, the Partzuergo is inherently a political initiative with economic objectives. While the promoters of European cooperation began by introducing the legal bases for implementing economic initiatives and only started to worry about obtaining legitimacy in the eyes of public opinion in a second stage, however, the promoters of cross-border cooperation in Bidasoa-Txingudi have done the opposite. Unable for legal and financial reasons to launch its economic initiatives from the start, they began by stressing the importance of popular participation and identification. In a public interview in October 2001, Mr. Etcheverry reiterated that the Partzuergo "is not just a Partzuergo of elected people. This would not serve its purpose, not without the support of society". Only in a second stage has the Partzuergo now moved on to give more practical emphasis to economic projects.

The importance of getting the local population to "feel like inhabitants of Txingudi"[3] is repeatedly stressed in the three towns' public communications. They talk about the changing local environment in the wider context of the EU, the importance of historical, cultural and political links between the three towns, and the idea that as neighbours they share much in common despite a turbulent and often conflictual past. In a public statement in October 2000, Aitor Kerejeta, the EAJ councillor in Hondarribia in charge of cultural affairs, insisted that "this Partzuergo, this union between the three towns, this town of towns, must

---

[2]   See Shore (2000) for an anthropological analysis of the European Commission's attempt to 'build Europe'.

[3]   Iñaki Iturrioz, sports technician at the municipality of Hondarribia, quoted in the opening article of *Bidasoa-Txingudi*, June, 2001, No. 20, p. 3.

serve to develop those elements we have in common. If the frontier has served as a barrier, if it has signified a wall between our two sides, finally if it has been a scar in history, we now have to heal this wound and make up for lost time".[4]

It is interesting to note Mr. Kerejeta's portrayal of the frontier as a barrier when, as we have seen earlier, the frontier was for a long period the economic mainstay for much of the local population. This is clearly part of a Basque nationalist discourse, which Mr. Kerejeta backed up again in an interview to me: "Of course I want to see the three towns together. I am a nationalist, and for me this is the most natural thing that could ever happen. The frontier and all the Spanish and French politics behind it prevented this from happening, but at last this can change". At the same time, Mr. Kerejeta's logic goes along with that of other pro-moters of the Partzuergo who readapt their way of speaking about the frontier to fit the new situation of emerging cross-border co-operation and the ending of police and customs controls.

Nonetheless, although Mr. Kerejeta claims that "we can begin to see Bidasoa-Txingudi as our home", he adds that "of course, that doesn't mean that we have to give up our attachment to our town. I will, for example always continue to feel Hondarribitarra. It's just like you and your neighbourhood. You always prefer your own neighbourhood". A "veritable cross-border identity", as two other organisers of the Partzuergo called it, will take time to develop, and, as they said, the Partzuergo is merely taking the first steps in the dismantling of physical and symbolic boundaries as part of a larger process. Recognizing the challenges, a former spokesperson of the Partzuergo, Vicky Alquezar, admitted in a press conference that "our objective is that the local popu-lation take up little by little the idea that we belong to one city made up of three. But it is clear that someone from Irun will never become Hendaian".[5]

One of the first acts of the promoters of cross-frontier cooperation was to create a new name for the area. Prior to the three towns' coopera-tion initiative, the name of the river Bidasoa had been used to define the Spanish *comarca*, or district, which groups Irun and Hondarribia as the *Comarca del Bajo Bidasoa*.[6] But there had been no common name covering the broader area also including Hendaia. The name Txingudi, written in accordance with modern Basque orthography, was originally

---

4   *Bidasoa-Txingudi*, September, 2000, No. 16, p. 3.

5   *Diario Vasco*, 1 October, 2000.

6   The full name of the comarca is *Bajo Bidasoa*, meaning 'Lower Bidasoa' in Spanish, so making a difference with the rest of the Bidasoa area further upstream in Nafarroa. Often however, I have heard local inhabitants of Irun and Hondarribia talk about their area as simply the *comarca del Bidasoa*

applied to a small marshy bay on the edges of Hendaia. In recent years, it had also come to be applied to a marshy area between Irun and Hondarribia which was made into a nature reserve under the protection of the Basque government in 1998,[7] and, by extension, to the area around the Bidasoa estuary. By combining this name with the name of the river, the initiators of the cross-border project invented a catchy new name, Bidasoa-Txingudi.

As Bourdieu has pointed out, the act of naming a place involves a re-conceptualisation of the space in question and its acquisition of a new status in the eyes of those people interacting with and within it (1991:220-21). In anthropological terms, such an action can be understood as a way of imposing authority through symbolic control. The bestowing of a new name for the area of Bidasoa-Txingudi supported efforts to create a sense of common identity among people on either side of the frontier and thus bolster acceptance of cross-frontier cooperation. The fact that the promoters of the cooperation project chose to spell the new name in Basque rather than French or Spanish was both a way of emphasizing the common Basque culture on either side of the frontier and a deliberate ploy to impose a stamp of Basque political correctness on the project.

According to Juan San Martín, a locally renowned linguist and historian residing in Hondarribia, the choice of a Basque-sounding name was a classic tactic on the part of local politicians. Even though, in his view, a more appropriate name for the area would have been the Latin place-name Oiasso or Oarso, used by Roman settlers to refer to the general area covered by the three towns today, he acknowledges that this name lacks the appeal of Txingudi. "Why they discarded a Latin word as an alternative is quite obvious: why go for that, devoid of any useful political and cultural significance, when one can go for a Basque one?" As for the orthography, he adds, "of course they chose Txingudi written that way, it sounds so conveniently more Basque".

The new place-name, formalised in the name of the cross-border Bidasoa-Txingudi Euro Barruti, has been maintained in the name of the Bidasoa-Txingudi Mugaz Gaindiko Partzuergo. Introducing its use on an everyday basis has taken longer, however. In Hegoalde, amongst the references I heard were *comarca del Bidasoa-Txingudi, comarca de Txingudi* and *comarca del Bidasoa*. Some local newspapers also occasionally talk of the *Consorcio Bidasoa* or *Bidassoa*.[8] This confusion was

---

[7] This nature reserve is officially called Playaundi. However, it is known by both the local population and people in other parts of Hegoalde as the *parque natural de Txingudi*. A book (Etchaniz *et al.*, 1999) entitled *Txingudi* was published in 1999 by the Basque government about this nature reserve.

[8] See for instance *La Semaine du Pays Basque*, 9-15 October 2003, p. 21.

also noticeable amongst local politicians. The word 'Txingudi' is none-theless frequently used now by Partzuergo and municipal officials when addressing the population of the three towns. In the Partzuergo's official literature, references to an actual *city* of Txingudi gently drum the notion into people's heads. This is sometimes done in a subtle manner, for example by simply mentioning the number of craftsmen in "the city of Txingudi"[9] or the opinion of local youth on living in "the city of Txin-gudi".[10] On other occasions, as for example in a communiqué which talks about the Partzuergo's and "our" desire to constitute a "CITY OF TXINGUDI" (its capitals),[11] the process is more blatant. In its official magazine, *Bidasoa-Txingudi*, the Partzuergo regularly runs a competi-tion called "Ideas City of Txingudi", inviting local inhabitants to imag-ine how they would like 'their' city of Txingudi to be in the future.[12]

An example of deliberate invention of ritual is provided by the cere-mony organised to formalise the Partzuergo's constitution on 23 De-cember 1998, for which the mayors of Irun, Hondarribia and Hendaia met on a boat in the middle of the Bidasoa estuary, each having set out by boat from their side of the river. In a 2000 edition of the *Bidasoa-Txingudi* magazine which sets out the composition of the Partzuergo's first budget begun in late 1999, the Partzuergo is likened to "a newly married couple". Another example is that of the ceremony for the inau-guration of a "Eurofair" in June 2001, organised by the Partzuergo with the support of regional funds as part of an information campaign about the euro. Two representatives of the Partzuergo stood on one side of a ribbon drawn across the international bridge linking Irun to Hendaia, while a dancer performed a Basque dance called the *aurresku*. Over the following ten days, seminars and workshops were organised in the three towns to explain the euro, while a bus linking the three towns was decorated as a "Eurobus" for three months. In this way, the Partzuergo sought to build 'Europeanness' into their ideal of a Txingudi identity and citizenship.

A project first mooted in the mid-1990s but still not implemented at the time of writing provides for a cultural itinerary round the bay and through the three towns, by means of which both local people and visitors would be able to get a sense of community in the area. As Mr. Etcheverry, the councillor in charge of cross-frontier affairs for the municipality of Hendaia and one of the principal promoters of the project, explained in an interview, the idea "is to encourage local inhabi-tants to explore their own surroundings more. By going through the

---

9   *Bidasoa-Txingudi*, December, 1997, No. 7, p. 2.
10 *Bidasoa-Txingudi*, May, 1998, No. 8, p. 4.
11 *Bidasoa-Txingudi*, July, 1997, No. 6, p. 3.
12 For example *Bidasoa-Txingudi*, July, 1997, No. 6, p. 18.

three towns and across the Bidasoa, it will become evident that the area is geographically bound together. Like that, the people walking along the path will feel more in touch with their neighbourhood and thus with each other". As a path symbolically crossing the frontier and traversing the three towns, the proposed cultural itinerary can be perceived in anthropological terms as having a quasi-ritualistic function. By offering those who embark on it a 'journey' between time, status and place, it provides what Victor Turner (1967) defines as a key "meaning-creating experience".

Under plans drawn up by *Maîtres du Rêve*, a French consultancy firm based in Aix-en-Provence contracted to carry out the initial phase of the project, the trail would be equipped with information boards "explaining the history of the area" in order to give users a holistic vision of the area. After a year of interviewing local associations and public figures, the consultancy came up with a presentation in June 2000, focusing on the "natural space", the "historical space", the "cultural space" and the "escapades" of the bay. Faithful to the wishes of the Partzuergo, as a representative of Maîtres du Rêve explained to me, "the idea behind the project as we have conceived it is to encourage *la rencontre*,[13] enable the inhabitants to get to know each other better, and so reinforce a common identity. To learn to live together, basically". In this vein, the text of Maîtres du Rêve's presentation seeks to evoke a sense of community and belonging, with titles such "Txingudi, my bay" and phrases such as "Txingudi, tell me who I am." Information on the panels along the way would remind readers that despite the frontier the inhabitants of the three towns share common social and cultural links.[14] Historical references to battles between the French and Spanish armies over the centuries would explain how political events at the nation-state level sometimes created a situation of official enmity between the three towns. At the same time, however, they would stress how members of the local population continued to cooperate across the frontier through family and social links and through smuggling, an activity highlighted as "an early form of cross-border cooperation"[15] in opposition to the nation-state.

The figure of the smuggler, well-known in Basque literature and folklore and in the Basque nationalist imagination, thus provides quasi-mythical input into the efforts of the Partzuergo to forge a 'Txingudi identity'. In the border area of Behobia, a neighbourhood of Irun, there are plans to restore a derelict nineteenth century customs building as a

---

[13]   Meaning 'Meeting' in French.
[14]   Interview with technicians of Maîtres du Rêve, February 2001.
[15]   *Bidasoa-Txingudi*, April, 1995, No. 0, p. 4. and also *www.bidasoa-txingudi.com/ presentation.html*.

museum about smuggling. The information panels of the planned cultural itinerary, meanwhile, would evoke anecdotes about the smugglers' daring and adventurous life – "a real culture of its own"[16] – and how, dressed in special dark clothes and armed with a multi-purpose knife, they scurried along secret paths through the mountains in the dark of night to carry out their *gaulana* – or night work in Basque – smuggling goods and helping refugees. Little, by contrast, is said about the darker sides of clandestine border-crossing, such as the activities of those who during the Second World War took money from Jews fleeing Nazi persecution only to abandon them to their fate half way across the mountains, or those who today supply arms, information and money to ETA militants.

When I asked an employee of Maîtres du Rêve involved in the project whether these panels would also touch upon the more recent and contemporary political, socio-economic and cultural issues, my question was received with uncertainty and finally with the answer that the project was "not a political manifesto or propaganda tool". This illustrates not only a concern with political correctness in the confection of the history of the area but a voluntary refusal to acknowledge other realities present and to confront the tensions in the area that still exist. Instead, the answer indirectly suggests that alternative historical accounts are precisely that.

In the context of the cultural itinerary project, Maîtres du Rêve suggested to the Partzuergo the idea of documenting the lives and reminiscences of local inhabitants. In response, the Partzuergo bought a movie camera and in January 2002 invited the anthropology department of the University of Euskal Herria in San Sebastian to put a group of undergraduate students in charge of producing a documentary film on the local inhabitants. This project, in process at the time of writing, intended to gather 'live' information about local customs, ways of living and kin relations, thereby contributing to the preservation of some kind of "heritage" that "would otherwise be lost".[17]

To paraphrase Geertz (1973:5), the Partzuergo is trying to create an idiom or a web of shared meanings, in the form of a collection of symbols which the population of the three towns can understand and identify with. Building on the cultural itinerary project, the Partzuergo plans to assemble and publish a collection of didactic material about *Bidasoa-Txingudi* for use by children in local schools. In parallel, the Partzuergo initiated discussions with the French Ministry of Education to resolve

---

[16] *Maîtres du Rêve*, "Chemin de la baie de Txingudi – programmation thématique et contenu des panneaux d'interprétation", June, 2000, p. 2.

[17] Interviews with Felipe Saragueta, director of the Partzuergo, and Jean-Baptiste Etcheverry, councillor of Hendaia.

certain legal issues that currently make it difficult for schools to take spontaneous trips across the frontier, so as to enable school children from either side of the frontier to be in closer contact with each other.

Implementing Cross-Frontier Cooperation

Pending formalisation of the legal status of the cross-frontier cooperation project, the Partzuergo's precursor, the Euro Barruti, launched a number of cultural and social projects, including the *Bidasoa-Txingudi* magazine and the annual localfiesta Txingudi Eguna. Such projects, needing no formal structures for their execution and thereforeeasy and quick to put into effect, were perceived as important for the success of the project. As Serge Peyrelongue, the secretary-general of the municipality of Hendaia explained to me, "when the three municipalities first got together to think about projects to do together, culture and social events were the main things we all thought of". In other interviews, representatives of the three town councils insisted on the importance of "culture" and "social activities" for encouraging participation on the part of the local population and promoting a new sense of local belonging.

As part of its inclusive approach to the concept of "a Txingudi spirit", a term which repeatedly crops up in Partzuergo publications or media coverage of the Partzuergo, the Partzuergo promotes Basque, French and Spanish equally. All of its public information leaflets, posters and cultural programmes, as well as the minutes of its council meetings, are produced in all three languages. On public occasions, the mayors of the three towns, though none of them are fluently trilingual, always begin their speeches by greeting the audience in the three languages. Other Partzuergo spokespersons are chosen for specific occasions for their fluency in one or another language. So, for example, the director of the Partzuergo, as a native Basque speaker of Spanish nationality, may give part of a presentation in Basque and then be followed by a councillor from Hendaia speaking in French and a municipal employee of Irun or Hondarribia speaking in Spanish.

The Partzuergo lays particular stress on Basque, repeatedly referring to it in public statements as the common feature of both sides of the frontier. The mayor of Irun, for example, wrote in the magazine *Bidasoa-Txingudi* in 1995 that "over the centuries, we have ignored the call of a common nature and of a common language: euskera".[18] In another editorial in the magazine, written in all three languages, the councillor of Hondarribia in charge of culture stressed that "there is something that this frontier has not been able to eradicate from either

---

[18]   *Bidasoa-Txingudi*, April, 1995, No. 0, p. 6.

side of the Bidasoa, and that is its common CULTURE, the BASQUE one, and a common LANGUAGE, BASQUE" (his capitals).[19]

In early 2002, the Partzuergo announced plans to launch a project aimed at developing knowledge of Basque amongst the staff of the three municipalities and local businesses. While the municipalities of Irun and Hondarribia make knowledge of Basque a condition for employment, significant numbers of municipal employees do not know Basque, having taken up their posts before the establishment of the Basque government and its bilingual policy.

Reflecting the Partzuergo's drive to promote Basque as a common cultural element, many of its projects have only Basque names. This is the case, for example, for Txingudi Eguna, first launched by the Euro Barruti in 1995 and always referred to in Basque, rather than in French or Spanish. The main feature of the event, whose location rotates each year between the three towns, is a fair bringing together local associations, each with a stand where it can give out information about its activities. According to official statements, Txingudi Eguna aims to "bring together the inhabitants of the three municipalities in a festive atmosphere (by) providing an annual rendez-vous which allows us to get to know each other better through a common celebration".[20]

A couple of months prior to the festivity, a competition for the design of an official poster encourages the active participation of local people. On the actual weekend, other activities and competitions are organised for children and teenagers, as are shows involving adults in local choirs, drama groups and folk dancing. At midday on Sunday, a series of long tables are placed under a marquee where a cooked lunch is served to all comers by a local association. In 2000, a concert with a famous Basque singer from Hegoalde, Kepa Junkera, was organised on the Saturday night in the stadium of Irun. Art associations of the three towns set up a joint exhibition of paintings in the town hall of Hendaia. Mr. Etcheverry explained the Partzuergo's support for such a project by alluding to the "typical" character of the local population: "Here, we like to party. We are a convivial kind of people – on both sides of the frontier. Much of the social life here revolves around partying, sport, eating... So what could be more natural than to organise a big fiesta?"

In 2000, the Partzuergo organisers decided they would like to have a stand serving simple, local-style food at the Txingudi Eguna. A group of women from Hondarribia who made *taloak*, a kind of unleavened maize-flour bread served with cheese, cooked ham or sweet fillings,

---

[19] *Bidasoa-Txingudi*, September, 2000, No. 16, p. 3.
[20] *Txingudi Eguna. Rapport de Présentation*, 1999, Municipality of Hendaia, p. 9.

offered to give their services. It happened however, that these women were supporters of the participation of women in the Alarde. In an effort to create inclusive boundaries, the Partzuergo agreed to allow this group of women to set up their stall. However, that year, the Txingudi Eguna took place in Hondarribia, and many of the town's inhabitants who were supporters of the traditional Alarde reacted to the presence of these women with insults and threats to demolish their stall. Despite their effort to produce harmony, the Partzuergo organisers failed to realise the implications of ignoring certain tensions between local inhabitants. While politics of the Alarde are taken very seriously by local politicians, the organisers of the Partzuergo, in their desire to be "apolitical", as Javier González, an employee of the Partzuergo, described it to me, and to rally together the local population in cultural and festive events, fail to take into account the continuing existence of this conflict.

Another area where cross-frontier cooperation has achieved concrete results is sport. The Partzuergo organises a series of sports competitions during Txingudi Eguna where local sports clubs take part in competitions and give demonstrations. The first tentative steps to encourage local sports clubs to get together and organise local competitions began in 1998. Since then, the Partzuergo has subsidised cross-frontier initiatives between different clubs, including a bicycle race along the Bidasoa, a basketball tournament and a canoe race down the Bidasoa. Txingudi Korrika, an event launched by running clubs in Hondarribia and Irun, has been extended to include runners from Hendaia, thanks to additional financial backing from the Partzuergo. In 2000, the Partzuergo set about publishing a directory of sports clubs in the area, with a view to improving mutual awareness and communication, and the three municipalities agreed to make their sports facilities available to each other for sports events organised by the various clubs.

The Partzuergo's sports working party has succeeded in solving administrative and legal obstacles which made it difficult for teams of one country to play in competitions of the other. It also encouraged the creation of teams composed of players from different clubs in Irun, Hondarribia and Hendaia to represent Bidasoa-Txingudi as one place, all wearing the same uniform with the logo of the Partzuergo.

Building on such initiatives, the Partzuergo has launched a number of cross-frontier economic projects. One of the recommendations of the area's first Strategic Development Plan had led to the decision in 1999 to construct a commercial exhibition area in a disused sector of the former customs area on the Irun side of the frontier with the additional financial help of the municipality of Irun, the provincial government of Gipuzkoa, the Pyrénées Atlantiques département and the joint regional fund of Aquitaine-Euskadi. The project, completed in 2003, aims to welcome business conferences and exhibitions, thereby attracting more entrepreneurialism in the area and increasing local investment.

A second development plan launched in 2000 targeted the development of social services, business development and the environment. As part of a drive to encourage a sense of Txingudi belonging, it added to this list "development of the zone with its very own identity",[21] recommending the continuation of such activities as the *Bidasoa-Txingudi* magazine and Txingudi Eguna and the enactment of plans for a cultural itinerary around the bay.

Another project involves promoting the three towns together as a single tourist destination, Bidasoa-Txingudi. In July 2000, brochures were launched advertising Irun, Hondarribia and Hendaia jointly and the tourist offices of the three towns now present themselves together in tourist fairs across Spain and France. In 2001, they released a CD-Rom featuring Bidasoa-Txingudi as "the city of cities" in Basque, French and Spanish. Distributed for free in the tourist offices of the area, it shows attractive images of the three towns and, with a soft lull of new age music in the background, has a male voice repeatedly pronouncing the words "Bidasoa-Txingudi... Bidasoa-Txingudi".

In the commercial sphere, Hendaia's economic development bureau worked with Bidasoa Bizirik on ways of helping small and medium-sized businesses. Since May 2000, the three municipalities have been exploring the possibilities of establishing a common sewage and garbage collection system. At present, Irun and Hondarribia share a joint waste management service, called *Txingudi Zerbitzuak* in Basque and *Servicios Txingudi* in Spanish, while Hendaia shares sewage and garbage collection services with neighbouring towns in Iparralde. With EU environmental regulations requiring more ecological solutions to waste disposal, a joint solution for the three towns might be able to benefit from EU funds.

In April 2002, another project discussed at a meeting of the Partzuergo's General Council concerned the need to find a solution to the traffic problems in the three towns. Currently, the road network between and around the three towns is too small to deal with the increased amount of traffic, particularly of lorries going through. As there are plans at a regional level for a high-speed train service across the frontier which would affect the area common to Irun, Hendaia and Hondarribia, the Partzuergo has been working on a proposal to build a deviation from the motorway. Such a project would require the approval of the provincial government of Gipuzkoa and the Basque government as well as the Spanish state since the motorways are beyond municipal

---

[21] *Minutes of the General Council of the Partzuergo*, 8 February, 2000.

competence. In an effort to give more weight to their project, the municipalities of Irun and Hondarribia have presented this as a Partzuergo project.

Communicating Cross-Frontier Cooperation

When the Euro Barruti was launched in 1995, its promoters decided that they needed a newsletter to inform local inhabitants about the project and its objectives. The *Bidasoa-Txingudi* magazine was launched "to develop a means of communication between the inhabitants of the three towns that make up Bidasoa-Txingudi".[22] Lacking the means and expertise to produce the magazine itself, the Euro Barruti contracted the task out to a local media enterprise, Txingudi Telebista, one of three firms that responded to a call for tender. The media company, now renamed Localia Txingudi following its acquisition by a larger private television channel in April 2001, continues to produce the magazine. The contents and presentation, however, are decided on in collaboration with the organisers of the cross-frontier cooperation project. Aimed at reaching the population of Txingudi in its entirety, the magazine is produced in 33,000 copies and sent by post to all the households of the area.

As the voice of the Euro Barruti and now the Partzuergo, the magazine provides a case study in communication of a cross-frontier cooperation initiative. It features articles explaining the Bidasoa-Txingudi project, as well as reports about local public figures who lead a cross-border or international lifestyle. The choice of subject matter is supported by a certain choice of words, presentation of ideas, particular narrative tone and other rhetorical devices, such as the constant use of the pronoun "we" to underline the theme of cooperation and convey a sense of community, where everyone is made to feel together in a united effort. In their writings, the mayors of the three towns often adopt a somewhat nostalgic tone, reiterating calls to overcome differences and make up for lost time.

Catchwords such as 'the future', 'building', 'constructing', 'solidarity', 'together' and 'in common' emerge repeatedly, evoking positiveness, optimism and success. In the same vein, the concepts of Europe and citizenship are often cited as values for moving forward. Similarly, words and phrases such as "our bay",[23] "*Txinguditarrak*",[24] which in Basque means 'those from Txingudi', and the more directive "what we

---

[22] *Bidasoa-Txingudi*, April, 1995, No. 0, p. 3.
[23] For example December, 1995, No. 2, p. 3 and September, 2000, No. 16, p. 17.
[24] For example June, 2001, No. 2, p. 3.

call the city of Txingudi"[25] all serve to convey the idea of a Txingudi people. Again and again, through the evocation of "we", "our patrimony" and "our obligation", references to common kinship are made. As anthropologist Borneman noted in his study of how the West and East German states sought to exert influence on the populations of the two Berlins prior to the coming down of the Berlin Wall, "kinship is the *topos* on which 'nationness' as a subjectivity is mapped. Because kinship is a constitutive element of nationness, it indexes categories of belonging essential to a state's claim to legitimacy in representing a nation. The ability to name or categorise becomes significant when the name serves to classify either a category of ownership or membership" (1992:19). By invoking a sense of 'Txingudi belonging' and of community across municipal, national and linguistic boundaries, *Bidasoa-Txingudi* magazine contributes to the reification of what its articles "describe or designate" (Bourdieu, 1991:220).

In order to make the magazine attractive to its targeted readers, its promoters decided from the start that it had to be relevant to the lives of local people. The aim, recalls Pilar Fuertes, an employee of the Partzuergo, was to provide a magazine "that could reflect the reality of cross-border life of the local inhabitants and thus the *raison d'être* of the Euro District". The trial-run issue of *Bidasoa-Txingudi* magazine explained its aim in an editorial as being "to develop a mode of communication for the inhabitants of the three towns located around Bidasoa-Txingudi".[26] The ninth edition gave a run-down of the different types of cross-frontier cooperation that had taken place in the EU over the twentieth century, setting the context for cooperation in Bidasoa-Txingudi. The editorial stated that the magazine was "born out of the conviction that cross-frontier cooperation is not decided only in the spheres of state or regional administration (but) must place itself at the first level of society, the closest possible to the citizen".[27] From the beginning, too, the magazine occasionally dedicated a page or two to extracts of letters from readers which, according to its editors, have become increasingly numerous over the years. By featuring these letters, the magazine conveys an image of popularity and democracy, demonstrating the openness of the Partzuergo to public opinion and readers' suggestions.

In contrast with local commercial media which mostly restrict news coverage to what happens on their respective side of the frontier, *Bidasoa-Txingudi* magazine was conceived as disregarding the existence of the frontier. By concentrating on events in all three towns, it defines a

---

[25]   For example October, 1998, No. 9, p. 13.
[26]   April, 1996, p. 3.
[27]   *Bidasoa-Txingudi*, April, 1995, No. 0, p. 3.

certain concept of space, as defined in its title. The same concept is reiterated in articles recounting local success stories, such as one about the Hendaia-born member of France's national football team, Bixente Lizarazu. In an interview with him, the magazine asked about his childhood in "Bidasoa-Txingudi". Such citations of local famous public figures also help to emphasise some kind of legitimate image of the cross-frontier cooperation initiative. By evoking the local attachment of these public figures, the magazine stresses the idea of a homeland and makes cross-frontier cooperation an important part of this experience. Such devices are all examples of virtual flag-waving in the manner analysed by Billig (1995) in his study of "banal nationalism" – every-day, mundane, subtle gestures that powerfully evoke and emphasise a sentiment of belonging to a place and a group.

A fundamental feature of *Bidasoa-Txingudi* magazine is the fact that it is written in all three local languages, French, Spanish and Basque, with a view to avoiding exclusion and appealing equally to everybody. In addition to demonstrating the magazine's cross-frontier character, this is a way of rejecting linguistic boundaries in local society. In the trial-run edition, the mayor of Hendaia evoked in French the challenges overcome by the three municipalities and stressed the need "to know each other better, to better understand our needs and ways of function-ing, in order to better decide together". Below his statement, the mayor of Irun pointed out in Spanish that "I firmly believe the obligation of our generation is to overcome these concepts (artificial difference and distance) and embrace firmly both banks of the Bidasoa within the indispensable context of the EU".[28] Finally, in Basque, the mayor of Hondarribia reiterated the need to carry on with "our efforts" as key players in Europe.

Articles in the magazine typically appear in full in one of the three languages, with summaries in the other two languages. The choice of language for the main version of each article is tactical. For example, the main text of an article about an aspect of Hondarribia will be written in French, with summaries in Spanish and Basque, thereby addressing readers from Hendaia who are less likely to know about Hondarribia than people from Irun or Hondarribia itself. Likewise, an article about something in Hendaia is likely to be in Spanish or Basque rather than French. Such a tactic ensures that the reader, looking for articles in his or her language, will read about aspects of Bidasoa-Txingudi with which he or she is less likely to be familiar. It also allows readers to broaden their linguistic horizons by reading articles in other languages as well.

In friendly and optimistic tones, articles about cross-border coopera-tion are interspersed with others about local life and traditions, typically

---

[28]   *Bidasoa-Txingudi*, April, 1995, No. 0, p. 3.

covering such themes as the cross-frontier composition of the municipal symphony orchestra of Hendaia, plans to filter waste water in Irun and Hondarribia in order to meet EU environmental standards and how EU regional funds can help to finance cross-frontier initiatives.

In December 1998, to mark the signing of the constitution of the Partzuergo, the magazine published an article giving the history of local cross-border cooperation and explaining the structure of the Partzuergo.[29] The theme was given visual reinforcement by the inclusion of photographs showing a meeting of the Partzuergo's General Council, children enjoying themselves at Txingudi Eguna, and visitors picking up information leaflets in one of the recently set up tourist offices. An article entitled "Before the Frontier, Now Europe. The INTERREG program works to eliminate borders in order to construct Europe" explained the role of EU regional aid and its relevance for Bidasoa-Txingudi. A feature humorously entitled "The guinea-pigs of Maastricht" introduced the association of cross-frontier workers founded by people of Spanish nationality who established residence in Hendaia but continue for the most part to work in Hegoalde. Such articles seek to demonstrate the Partzuergo's relevance in the context of an already existing cross-border lifestyle.

But though the magazine reaches an increasingly large audience, not everything has been smooth sailing. In November 1999 and January 2000, I attended editorial meetings at which the format and content of forthcoming issues of *Bidasoa-Txingudi* magazine were the topic of discussion. Partzuergo officials and magazine journalists had recently recorded the criticisms of some local inhabitants with regard to the magazine, focusing particularly on what was perceived as its excessively institutional character. In brainstorming sessions at these editorial meetings, participants reviewed the aims and methods of the magazine and discussed ways of improving its format and content in order to make it more attractive to the local population. While one person stressed that the magazine could fill a significant gap in the local press by focusing on the area and keeping people up to date with cultural events and other news in the three towns, another person acknowledged the role of the magazine as a propaganda tool of the Partzuergo and emphasised the need to find a way of "disguising the fact that it is so".

However, as local initiatives increasingly began to produce their own cross-frontier papers, it was eventually decided to make the magazine simply the Partzuergo newsletter. Its April 2001 issue, for example, featured the Partzuergo in the main news item, while another section provided a report on recent meetings of the three councils and news of their future projects. The close connection between Europe and feeling

---

[29]   *Bidasoa-Txingudi*, December, 1998, No. 10.

'Txingudian' continues to be regularly evoked. The June 2001 edition of the magazine sported a blue cover with a picture of a gold coin marked "EuroTxingudi" on it. Above it, the title of this edition declared that the euro had "already arrived",[30] advertising its "Eurofair" project six months before the euro was introduced.

What is not featured in the magazine is as significant as what is featured. Contributions from outsiders are by invitation or in the form of letters selected for publication. Controversy is carefully avoided, and no articles mention any of the conflictual issues that affect people in the area. Several editions of the magazine featured articles about the various festivities existing in the three towns. However none of these mentioned the Alarde. Articles about cross-frontier cooperation make no mention of the differing views of the various political actors in the area with regard to the frontier and cross-frontier cooperation. Articles explaining how the Partzuergo works fail to comment on the fact that minority groups within the three town councils are excluded from active participation in the Partzuergo or on the difficulties encountered in trying to get some associations or local institutions to work together across the frontier. In short, information is provided on a selective basis, carefully presented in order to maintain a positive image of the Partzuergo and to keep any potential sources of conflict at bay.

The Partzuergo has also made use of other modern means of communication. In 2000, it commissioned a Spanish image consultancy to produce a logo. The result was a design showing three circles coloured red, yellow and green set against a blue background evoking the sea and the river and linked by a white ribbon ending in a spiral in the centre: "Strong colours and curvy lines to represent the dynamism of the union of the three towns" was how *Bidasoa-Txingudi* magazine presented the logo.[31] In a press release in July 2000, the Partzuergo acknowledged its commercial purpose as being "to identify the Partzuergo in all its marketing plans, communications and publicity". Since then, the Partzuergo has used it in all its public communications.

In January 2001, the Partzuergo launched its website, www.bidasoa-txingudi.com or www.bidasoa-txingudi.net. Decorated with the logo and glossy photos of the local landscape, people engaged in various social and professional business, evoking a sense of humanity and dynamism, the website features the latest activities of the Partzuergo and its projects, and outlines its organisational framework, in Basque, French, Spanish and English. The text mentions the strategic position of Bidasoa-Txingudi in the centre of the Bayonne-San Sebastian axis as an area of "strong European vocation, in the specific framework of cross-

---

[30]   *Bidasoa-Txingudi*, June, 2001, No. 20, p. 1.
[31]   *Bidasoa-Txingudi*, May, 2000, No. 14, p. 5.

frontier cooperation".[32] There follows a brief history of the area as a frontier site, starting with the Romans who settled in the area, and of the emergence in the twelfth century of Hondarribia as a strategic fishing port. The text mentions the constant movement of people through the area, evoking its dynamic "métissage". It then stresses how the Partzuergo is "at last an opportunity for resolving the divisive crises of the past". Below, three "historical elements" are listed as "enabling the conception of a bond in the area to exist": smuggling, the exchange of students in the last few years, and Basque culture and language.

Significantly, the Partzuergo has chosen Internet addresses ending in .com and .net, rather than country-specific addresses such as .fr for France or .es for Spain. This ensures neutrality in relation to either of the two states in which the area is located, avoiding any risk of accusations of statist or national bias. Its inclusion of English as one of the languages of its website underscores its desire to appear modern, open-minded, European and international. A page entitled "links of interest" provides links to the websites of the various regional governments, the European Commission and other cross-frontier initiatives, thereby giving a distinctly European tone to the Partzuergo initiative.

Targeted communication also takes place at local level. In 1998, Hendaia set up a so-called *Laboratoire de Langues*, with the principal aim, according to Mr. Etcheverry, the councillor responsible for this project, of helping Hendaia residents of Spanish nationality to learn French. Two years later, the municipality of Hendaia, with the help of the Partzuergo, opened up a "Cross-Frontier Information Point" in a building already housing the Service for Cross-Frontier Relations. Directed at recently established Hendaian residents of Spanish nationality, it aims to provide basic information about administrative, legal, social and cultural activities in Hendaia and, for more detailed information, to direct visitors to the necessary municipal services. An employee who speaks fluent French, Spanish and Basque welcomes visitors by appointment. The information point also publishes a monthly newsletter, named in Basque *Ondoan*, meaning "next door" or "nearby", featuring municipal news relevant to Hendaia residents of Spanish nationality, which is distributed to people's homes. According to Mr. Etcheverry, who is also in charge of this project, the aim is to "facilitate the integration of the new population of Hendaia originating from Hegoalde". In collaboration with Bidasoa Bizirik, the information point also eventually plans to provide information to businesses wishing to find out more about setting up in French territory. The cross-frontier character of this information point is further enhanced by its collaboration with Irun's municipal information service, known as the SAC, in an exchange of

---

[32] http://www.bidasoa-txingudi.com/presentation.html.

information, particularly on administrative matters. This initiative forms part of a general endeavour on the part of the Partzuergo to encourage the sharing of information by the three towns in the interest of the local citizens.

CHAPTER 10

The Partzuergo:
Successes, Drawbacks and Challenges

"No to the extension of the airport of Fontarabie. Demonstration with our neighbours from the other side of the Bidassoa. 13 April, at 5.00 p.m. Meeting at the bus stop of Mendelu, Hondarribia" This announcement, written in French, is typed in bold black letters on a sheet of white paper and posted in the windows of numerous shops in Hendaia. It calls on inhabitants of Hendaia to take part in a demonstration against the Spanish government's plan to enlarge the airport located in Hondarribia on the banks of the estuary of the Bidasoa opposite Hendaia, officially known as the airport of San Sebastian. In Irun and Hondarribia, a similar call to demonstrate is posted in most shops. Written in Spanish, it says, "Demonstration. On 13 April 2002 at 5.00 p.m., there will be a demonstration against the enlargement of the airstrip of Hondarribia. Itinerary: Mendelu crèche to the Airport, with a stop there, and back to Mendelu. All Txingudi is concerned. We look forward to your participation".

And so at 5.00 p.m. on a cold and wet Saturday afternoon in the spring of 2002, around 3000 people are gathered in Mendelu, a neighbourhood of Hondarribia bordering on Irun due to be demolished if the airport enlargement goes ahead. The reason for their presence is made evident by the placards and banners that some of them carry. In Basque and Spanish, they read "Airstrip no! Houses yes!" while a banner held up by some people from Hendaia states in French "No to the extension of the airstrip".

In the middle of the crowd, Borja Jáuregui, the mayor of Hondarribia, Alberto Buen, the mayor of Irun and Kotte Ecenarro, the mayor of Hendaia, are surrounded by some of their colleagues from the three town councils. Chatting together amicably, they look around at the neighbourhood of Mendelu, mostly made up of small blocks of flats. The crowd falls silent as the three mayors move forward to lead the demonstration out of Mendelu and on to the main road to the airport approximately one kilometre away.

At the junction with the main road, a municipal policeman with a red beret stops the traffic in order to allow the procession to advance.

Groups of people holding banners walk in front of and behind the three mayors and their entourage. Amongst them, a group of young children from Mendelu carry placards in Basque and Spanish with texts like "Without my neighbourhood, where shall I play? What will happen to my house?" In unison, led by their teacher, they shout in Spanish "Airstrip no! Houses yes!" Most people in the crowd seem to be talking in Spanish, but in the middle of the procession a group of people from Hendaia are chatting together in French, while a few others are speaking in Basque.

Arriving at the airport terminal, the marchers gather around its entrance to watch a performance by the children of Mendelu. Running from one end of the road, past the entrance to the airport building, the children shout their slogan louder than ever to the accompaniment of a man tapping on an African drum, led by their teacher who wears a grotesque model of an aeroplane on his head. The crowd claps loudly in support of the children's message. Journalists from local newspapers and the local television station, Localia Txingudi, interview some of the participants. Eventually, the demonstrators regroup into a procession to walk back along the main road to a roundabout just beyond Mendelu at the entrance to Irun, and finally back to Mendelu itself.

Plans for the enlargement of the airport of San Sebastian made headlines in local newspapers on either side of the frontier as from the beginning of 2001. At present the airport can be used only by small to medium-sized planes which cover the journey between Hondarribia and Madrid ten times a day. The only airport in Euskadi able to take larger aircraft is at Bilbao, an hour and a half's drive from Hondarribia, although Biarritz, less than an hour's drive away, also has an international airport, and another slightly smaller airport is located at Pamplona, an hour and a half away in Nafarroa. Under a proposal put forward by the Spanish government, the airport's runway would be extended to enable it to take larger longhaul aircraft. The plan is designed to improve the air transport infrastructure of northern Spain, but it would cause considerable inconvenience in Hondarribia, Irun and Hendaia. The houses of Mendelu would be demolished and all of the surrounding largely urbanised area would suffer from this extra noise and pollution. In addition to damaging the environment and the quality of life of the local population, opponents claim that the project would jeopardise the area's potential as a tourist destination, turning it merely into a transit point for people heading to more picturesque places in Iparralde and Hegoalde. As a result, the three municipalities have been unanimous in their rejection of the project. Negotiations with the Spanish government have not been easy, however. In September 2001, the mayor of Hendaia, Kotte Ecenarro, went to Madrid to make personal contact with government officials in an attempt to open negotiations. In spite of this, the threat remained that the project might go ahead.

It was in this context of urgency that associations and local business representatives in Irun, Hondarribia and Hendaia began to mobilise in the autumn of 2001. In late November 2001, a federation of neighbourhood associations and local businesses from Irun, Hondarribia and Hendaia formed a coordination to fight against the threat of the airport.

The demonstration on 13 April 2002 was the first major demonstration against the proposed runway extension. Significantly, as a number of participants observed, it was also the first time that inhabitants of the three towns had gathered together for a common cause. As José Ramón Arizu, an inhabitant of Mendelu who is the chief organiser of the coordination, told me in an interview in front of the airport terminal, "it wasn't easy getting everyone together at first. It took at least four months of serious coordinating. But we are very happy with the result. We were expecting around 2000 people to take part in the demonstration today, and I think we are much more than that, about 3000. And we have had a very good response too from the Partzuergo". The president of an environmental association in Hendaia, Claudette Peyrega, also expressed her satisfaction with the mobilisation. "We are all concerned, and we have managed to rally together on this issue. This part of the frontier is also, after all, our home. We are altogether."

Indeed, in spite of the differences that are often voiced and acted out by much of the population, as pointed out throughout this book, this occasion was marked by unanimity. This was clear not only from statements by the demonstration's organisers and the participation of numerous inhabitants, including the three mayors and councillors of the various parties, but also from the wording of the poster announcements. The poster in Hendaia referred to "our neighbours on the other side of the Bidassoa", avoiding reference to the frontier. While it referred to the airport of Fontarabie, using the traditional French name for Hondarribia, it used the Basque version of the town's name, Hondarribia, in accordance with the terminology used by most Hegoalde inhabitants, when it stated the starting point for the demonstration. The posters in Irun and Hondarribia mentioned the importance of this demonstration for the people of "Txingudi", a reference to the inhabitants of all three towns.

Although the representatives of various associations involved in the demonstration talked to me about each other as "the French" and "the Spanish", their being together in this demonstration marked a significant step towards the sort of union of the people of Txingudi to which the Partzuergo aspires. An elderly man from Mendelu whose house is threatened with demolition referred approvingly to the presence in the demonstration of "brothers" from Hendaia. A woman from Hendaia observed while marching that "we are at home" on the Hegoalde side of the frontier as well, to which her husband added that "we are only divided by the Bidasoa". Robert Arrambide, left-wing abertzale from Hendaia noted that, while there had in the past been political demonstrations bringing together people from both sides of the frontier, this was the first time that 'civil society' from both sides of the frontier had come together in this way. There were no speeches or demonstrations by local political parties on this occasion, and the three mayors limited their participation to simply walking at the head of the rally. In this way, the event brought together the inhabitants of the three towns without pomp or political declarations in response to a common concern about the future.

Ironically, it might seem that, despite all the efforts of the Partzuergo to mobilise the populations of the three towns around a series of positive projects, they actually needed a negative incident to bring them together and overcome the boundaries dividing them. Merely by being present without making a show of it, the three mayors succeeded in assisting in the legitimisation of the Partzuergo. Indeed, the word Partzuergo or Consorcio was on the lips of many of the participants that I interviewed in the demonstration. As one member of the coordination put it, "it is the first time that I see people of the three towns together. And we benefit from the support of the Partzuergo".

As this event demonstrates, the Partzuergo's drive to encourage a new holistic perception of the area has begun to bear fruit. It has been aided not only by negative threats such as the proposed airport extension but also by new opportunities in the field of business, leisure and lifestyles following the lifting of border controls. Commercial initiatives have fuelled the process by changing the way local people view their surroundings and encouraging them to perceive the three towns as a whole.

Inevitably, however, social values and traditions specific to each of the two sides of the frontier and to each of the three towns continue to hold great importance. Individuals who have altered their lifestyle, for example by taking up residence or pursuing new leisure activities on the other side of the border or by starting new business initiatives, remain attached to their social group and its local space. And though the socio-cultural projects of the Partzuergo have managed to overcome some of the cultural and political challenges particular to Bidasoa-Txingudi and appealed to a growing number of local inhabitants, major obstacles to effective cross-border cooperation remain. As we have seen, behind the Partzuergo's image of unity and harmony and outside the context of such unusual moments of consensus as the demonstration against the proposed airport extension, the political and cultural boundaries used by local inhabitants in the formation of differing individual notions of identity continue to exercise a divisive influence.

On the positive side of the balance sheet, public awareness of the Partzuergo has grown considerably over the past few years. When I began my field research in late 1999, my inquiries about the Partzuergo frequently elicited comments along the lines of "the Partzuergo? No idea what that is" or "It's some kind of Basque project, isn't it?" Participation by local associations in Txingudi Eguna, mentioned by many people as an example of the Partzuergo's initiatives, has increased significantly. Many participants in Txingudi Eguna expressed positive views of the Partzuergo as a logical initiative, "considering that we are neighbours and we have so much in common in spite of the frontier that divides us", as one non Basque-speaking woman living in Hendaia told me.

In parallel, awareness of Bidasoa-Txingudi as a spatial concept has grown. The local media now talk freely about "the area of Bidasoa-Txingudi", "our district[1] of Txingudi", and "Txingudi citizens". While it is still rare to hear ordinary people talk in this way, it is not uncommon to hear references to the "bay of Txingudi", a place-name that has stretched from the little bay in Hendaia to refer to the three towns together. An annual marathon around the bay, organised by the athletics associations of Hondarribia and Irun under the name Txingudi Korrika, has extended its scope with financial help from the Partzuergo to include runners from Hendaia. New cross-border initiatives between associations include joint concerts by the choirs of the three towns and plays by drama groups, often supported by subsidies from the Partzuergo. In 2000, despite mocking of the term 'Txingudi' on the part of his friends, one of whom remarked that it is something that "no one uses here. It's all part of the 'make-up' of the Partzuergo", Urbil Artola, a popular musician from Hondarribia, wrote a song entitled "Txingudi". In 2001, some young musicians from the Conservatory in Irun decided to name their group Oiasso, the Latin name for the area, "in homage to the cross-border area to which we belong".[2]

Since the mid 1990s, local enterprises have shown awareness of the business potential of this new cross-border space. Firms based in Hendaia and Hondarribia provide boat services between the two towns, while French and Spanish bus companies link all three municipalities. Many local businesses and social or sporting initiatives have adopted Txingudi as part of their name. So the rowing club in Irun formerly known as Santiagotarrak is now called Txingudi Santiagotarrak and the yacht club which manages the leisure port in Hendaia changed its name from Club Maritime Hendaye to Club Maritime Hendaye Txingudi. As its director explained to me in an interview, the name change was "an

---

[1]   "Comarca", in Spanish, "bassin", in French, and "aldea", in Basque.
[2]   Quoted from interview in Irun-based magazine *La Bahía*, January, 2001, p. 5.

endeavour to move with the times". Two influential local initiatives are a commercial centre outside Irun, "Centro Commercial Txingudi", and the television channel Txingudi Telebista/Localia Txingudi. In 2000, a baker in Irun gave the name Txingudi to a new cake that he was selling. The same year, when the Partzuergo announced its intention of creating its website as www.txingudi.com, it turned out that the name had already been taken by a publishing house in Irun.

Associations and other groups have not been indifferent to the financial opportunities offered by the Partzuergo. An employee of the Partzuergo noted that it receives numerous applications from local associations for subsidies for projects with minimal cross-border elements, suggesting that such requests are motivated only by the financial benefits that could be obtained. Other bodies have been skilful in drawing on the discourse of the Partzuergo for their own purposes. When *Gure Irratia*, a Basque radio station based in Bayonne, sought to extend its reach to the border; which it had not previously been able to do because of reception problems, it appealed to the Partzuergo for financial backing. It proposed to create a small local branch called *Antxeta Irratia*,[3] hailing the "Txingudi project" as going "forward step by step, opening its doors to the Europe of tomorrow". Drawing attention to the obstacles in the way of integration, it ended its proposal in terms similar to the Partzuergo's own rhetoric by portraying itself as a "function of integration of the different communities of Txingudi" and as "an assistant in the institutional and social project of the future".[4]

Nonetheless, as Gure Irratia noted in its application, cultural, social and linguistic boundaries used by the local population in the construction and expression of their selves continue to limit the Partzuergo's ability to bring people together as citizens of a common area in a harmonious way. The frontier, as the central physical boundary in the area, continues to influence the identity formation of many local inhabitants. This can be seen in the way some people have reacted to some of the Partzuergo's projects. For example, the Partzuergo's plan to combine the tourist offices of the three towns encountered reluctance in Hendaia, where employees of the local tourist office expressed reservations about working with "those of the other side". During the 1999 Txingudi Eguna, which took place in Irun, Txingudi Telebista journalists were dismayed by the lack of cross-border awareness on the part of some of the people they interviewed at stands representing their associations. When they asked these people what occasions they were looking forward to participating in over the next few months, all listed festivities

---

[3]   Meaning Seagull station both in illusion to the seaside character of Bidasoa-Txingudi and the fact that a seagull, flying around, takes no heed of frontiers.

[4]   *Radio "Antexta Irratia" Avant-Projet*, Hendaia, 1 July 2001, p. 2.

taking place in Hegoalde. None raised the possibility of going across the frontier, even to Hendaia.

Attempts by the Partzuergo during 2000 and 2001 to encourage schools in the three towns to collaborate in specific initiatives met a less than enthusiastic reception. Some teachers in Hendaia told me they did not see any interest in having more contact with schools in Irun and Hondarribia, since so many children from Hegoalde attended school in Hendaia. In Irun and Hondarribia, reactions were similarly apathetic. The French teacher of the ikastola of Hondarribia told me in an interview in February 2001 that she had once expressed interest in making contact with French schools but met little enthusiasm, either from schools in Iparralde or from the parents of her own pupils. Teaching of French in Hegoalde is decreasing radically in favour of English, a trend explained to me by a Hondarribian parent as reflecting the fact that many young parents in Hondarribia come from other parts of Hegoalde further from the frontier and so have little appreciation of the intimate contact with Iparralde neighbours that Hondarribians once had. In early 2002, the ikastola of Hondarribia set up a small radio studio and invited the participation of the ikastola of Hendaia to take part in some of its programmes, an invitation enthusiastically accepted by the school's director. Relations between other schools, particularly with the state schools, as well as the Ikas Bi system in Hendaia, remain minimal or non-existent, however, indicating the importance of different identifications.

Efforts to coordinate the citizens' information service in Irun and the Information Point in Hendaia have had only limited results. In response to several attempts on my part during 2001 to obtain basic information about Hendaia in the office of Irun, I was told that I would be better off asking in Hendaia directly. In other areas of social services, local bodies explore cooperation initiatives further afield, rather than looking for partners in Bidasoa-Txingudi. In Hendaia, the director of the social centre Denentzat, financed by the French government and the town council, explained a lack of contact with similar centres in Irun and Hondarribia as being due to his centre's local and French 'Republican' nature and the fact that its primary concern was with the socially and economically deprived areas of Hendaia. He then mentioned that he was seeking to establish contact with social workers from Peebles, the Scottish town with which Hendaia is twinned, in order to have an exchange of ideas and initiatives. In Hondarribia, a youth programme recently launched by the municipality made contact with a similar initiative in Pau, the main town of the département des Pyrénées Atlantiques, instead of considering possible collaboration with Hendaia.

In response to encouragement from the Partzuergo, several associations have met to explore the possibility of launching projects together.

These, however, have not always had harmonious results. In 2000, members of the sailing club of Hendaia were disappointed with the attitude of their counterparts from the sailing club of Hondarribia when it was their turn to organise the Txingudi fishing competition. According to the Hendaians, the Hondarribians changed the rules of participation from those instituted by the sailing club of Hendaia when it had organised the event the previous year by demanding that participants pay a higher entry fee and hold a Spanish fishing license. As a result of these new rules, would-be participants from Hendaia were put off taking part in the competition. When I went to find out about this event at the yachting club in Hondarribia, however, I heard a completely different story, with a committee member explaining to me that the French had simply not wanted to participate this year. Another instance of miscommunication and discord in the context of a Partzuergo project occurred in a meeting between teachers of Irun, Hondarribia and Hendaia in late 1999 to discuss the possibility of organising a joint choir. A suggestion by some French-speaking teachers from Hendaia to include French songs met opposition from Basque-speaking teachers from Irun and Hondarribia. What was meant to be a collaborative project bringing the different schools together ended in tension and disillusion.

This last case illustrates how tensions surrounding language issues continue to be an obstacle to harmony, despite the Partzuergo's promotion of trilingualism and of Basque as a common language for the area. Within the Partzuergo itself, only the director, Mr. Saragueta, is completely fluent in Spanish, French and Basque. Of the three mayors, Mr. Ecenarro is the only one who is able to converse in Basque and fluently speaks the state language of his neighbours across the frontier. As a result, communication within the Partzuergo takes place predominantly in Spanish.

Mr. Saragueta once remarked to me that he needed to be careful not to appear to be favouring the Basque language too much in Partzuergo projects. He noted little enthusiasm on the part of members of the Partzuergo, particularly those from Irun, notably the Socialists and members of the PP. An example he gave me during the summer of 2001 concerned the possibility of Partzuergo support for the Antxeta Irratia radio project, which appeared to some members of the municipal councils as possibly too closely linked to left-wing Basque militantism.

That is not to say that nothing is being done to address such issues. The Antxeta Irratia project has been taken up. At the insistence of Mr. Etcheverry and with support from the Hondarribian councillor Ion Elizalde, and the agreement of Irun's councillor in charge of culture and the Basque language, Fernando San Martín, the Partzuergo set up in mid 2002 a working group on the Basque language. Interestingly, Mr. Etcheverry was one of the main advocates in the Hendaia municipal council for the proposals made by the survey on the situation of the Basque language in the town, although lack of support from other councillors prevented these from being followed up. So here the Partzuergo provides a forum within which people like Mr. Etcheverry are able to develop projects that they cannot so easily do in the more restricted environment of their hometown.

Nonetheless, many of the boundaries dividing the population of Bidasoa-Txingudi are evidenced in the Partzuergo and its interaction with local citizens. As an organ set up and run by the three towns' councils, which in turn are run by members of the French and Spanish Socialist parties, the Spanish conservative party PP and the conservative Basque nationalist party, the Partzuergo has a clear profile as part of the local political establishment. Olivia Tambou, in her study of the Partzuergo's legal status (1999), states that the Partzuergo is an egalitarian and democratic body thanks to the fact that the three towns have equal voting and veto rights, even though Irun is economically and financially more powerful. However, she neglects the fact that the Partzuergo's political base as it stands today is limited by being run only by the ruling parties of each municipality, without the participation of the opposition parties. As already noted, this excluded Batasuna, the left-wing Basque nationalist party, whose representatives denounced this lack of inclusiveness. While admitting that the Partzuergo could be a step towards their objective of uniting the French and Spanish sides of Euskal Herria, they expressed scepticism in interviews with me about its potential for actually achieving such an objective under its current constitution and leadership.

One contradiction brought up by some councillors of Hondarribia is the dominant role played within the Partzuergo by Irun and the PSE-EE. Until mid 2002, Irun was represented in the Partzuergo's Committee of Directors by José-Antonio Santano, the Socialist deputy of the town's Socialist mayor, rather than by one of its three representatives in the Partzuergo's General Council, the mayor, PP member Borja Semper and Basque nationalist party member Elena Etxegoien. This arrangement, while perhaps expedient in terms of the politics of the Irun town council, was in conflict with the statutes of the Partzuergo, which specify that representatives of the three towns in the Committee of Directors should be drawn from among their representatives in the General Council. Mr. Santano is also the president of Bidasoa Bizirik, which supervises the day-to-day operations of the Partzuergo, while its director is a former president of the provincial government of Gipuzkoa, PSE member Guillermo Echenique. Irun's financial contribution to the running of Bidasoa Bizirik is significantly greater than Hondarribia's, and this is reflected in the influence on its operations of the municipal council of Irun. The strong Spanish Socialist component in the Partzuergo and in

Bidasoa Bizirik once led Mr. Saragueta, the Partzuergo's director, to remark to me that he "work(s) with Spanish people" and that "we want the help of the agency but not its control".

Bidasoa Bizirik was initially meant to assist in the re-orientation of the area's economy following the removal of customs controls at the frontier, by assisting local small enterprises and launching initiatives for job creation. In this context, Bidasoa Bizirik has a section specialising in applications for external funds, particularly from the EU. The growing importance of this activity has sparked criticism from some local people who see this body as a machine that is increasingly focused on getting subsidies. The role of Bidasoa Bizirik in relation to the Partzuergo was a source of much discussion during 2000 and 2001. But despite a decision at the time that its involvement should be only temporary, there has so far been little indication of change. The Partzuergo technicians continue to be employed directly by Bidasoa Bizirik and, until Mr. Saragueta resigned from his post in October 2002, he reported to the director of Bidasoa Bizirik as his boss. Reflecting such ambiguities, Mr. Saragueta's role as director of the Partzuergo continued to be perceived differently by the three municipalities. In Hendaia, he was understood to be the director and in Hondarribia the manager, but in Irun he was considered to be merely the chief coordinator. Nonetheless, when I mentioned such matters early in 2002 to members of the ruling majorities in the various councils, all said that they saw no contradictions and that it was only normal that Bidasoa Bizirik, as an existing service, should be used. Mr. Etcheverry did acknowledge to me in an interview in March 2002 however that "yes, maybe we did a mistake there. But as we were all so eager to get things going, we were ready to take on whatever was necessary for the idea of cooperation to go ahead".

The Partzuergo has also been criticised for failing to encourage genuine participation on the part of local people in its activities. Despite a general invitation issued by the three municipalities in 1993, 2000 and again in 2002 for people to take part in discussions about the strategic development plans for the area, recent events have gone ahead without much public consultation. Rather than invite the local population to take part in the creation of common projects, the Partzuergo turned to outside consultants for the creation of its logo, as well as for the preliminary studies of the area and planning the cultural itinerary round the three towns. Critics complain that the participation and views of local inhabitants are called for only after such projects have already been launched. Consequently, when in October 2000 the Partzuergo organised a conference to present its projects to the general public, the audience included only three people who were not linked in some way or other to the three municipalities or the Partzuergo. As for the regular council meetings of the Partzuergo, although they are open to the public, they rarely attract attendance. As we saw in the earlier account of a meeting of the Partzuergo's General Council, the only outsider present on that occasion was a retired man from Hendaia.

Members of a group of local young people who have launched their own project under the name of *Mugazabaldu*, meaning in Basque "step on – or efface – the frontier", to work on border-related issues in the Irun neighbourhood of Behobia with the involvement of local inhabitants, have complained about the Partzuergo's lack of engagement with them. Repeatedly, they invited Partzuergo representatives to attend their events and take interest in their projects. In 2001, when they organised a three-day conference in which local inhabitants were invited to talk about their experiences of life on the frontier, the only Partzuergo employee to attend was Pilar Fuertes, who came for one evening. In the summer of 2001, when the Partzuergo invited bids for the production of educational material accompanying the cultural itinerary project to be distributed to local schools so that children could be introduced in an educational way to Bidasoa-Txingudi, Mugazabaldu made a bid along with two other organisations, Maîtres du Rêve and *Arkolan*, an Irun-based association involved in the development of an archaeological site and the construction of a museum of Roman times in Irun with the support of the municipality. When Maîtres du Rêve won the contract, it seemed to Mugazabaldu representatives that the bidding process was rigged from the beginning. Early in 2002, they were disappointed again when they found out that the other project related to the cultural itinerary, the production of a documentary film about people's lives in Bidasoa-Txingudi, was not to be put out to tender, as they had been told by Mr. Saragueta, but had already been awarded to the San Sebastian university students.

As it turns out, some members of Mugazabaldu are employed in educational projects by the municipality of Hondarribia and I subsequently learned that relations between the two sides were not always smooth. This served as one of the reasons why Hondarribia representatives in the Partzuergo may not have been enthusiastic about employing Mugazabaldu for Partzuergo projects. Some participants of the Partzuergo also noted to me that they saw advantages in contracting firms from outside Bidasoa-Txingudi, in their so-called desire to preserve neutrality in the development of some projects. I venture to say that, contracting a firm from outside also gives a more 'sophisticated' image. So, below the surface of the Partzuergo's image of harmonious consensus and desire for civic participation, we see that personal and political concerns influence decisions. Since mid 2001, Mugazadaldu has succeeded in gaining support from the municipality of Irun in relation to plans to develop the frontier area in Behobia. It is ironic, however, that an association which appears to have aspirations similar to those of the Partzuergo should not be welcomed by the Partzuergo and should have to continue seeking support from one of the three participating councils as an individual initiative.

Other areas of frustration reflect the sensitivities of particular interest groups. Shopkeepers in the border area have complained that projects like the planned commercial exhibition area, in which the Partzuergo is a participant, will deprive them of customers by preventing lorry and car drivers from parking to go shopping in the area. Local environmentalists have complained about the Partzuergo's failure to mention ecological concerns in its constitution. In January 2002, when the three municipalities made public plans to install an incinerator in Irun, local environmentalists protested against its un-ecological character. Concerns have also been raised over plans by the Irun council to rehabilitate the marshy area and small islands on its side of the Bidasoa in order to incorporate them into an adventure park for canoeing and kayaking as part of the larger project to make Bidasoa-Txingudi attractive for tourists with a series of leisure activities.

The Confraternity of Fishermen in Hondarribia has complained that the Partzuergo ignores it,[5] despite what its president, Esteban Olaizola, described in an interview as the Confraternity's "important role in the economy and traditions of Hondarribia". "All the Partzuergo is interested in is flashy tourism", he added. The director of a transport agency based in Irun, Joxan Garaialde, complained about the lack of interest of the municipalities in the transport industry, reproaching the Partzuergo of being focused only in the domain of tourism. "It is principally thanks to us, to the transport agencies, that Irun and Hondarribia did not go down hill economically after the frontier was opened. And the municipality of Irun have taken their time in providing us the space we need to develop our industry. Just because of this concern always with tourism. So, the Partzuergo... I think it's a complete joke."

The apparent failure of the Partzuergo to take account of such local concerns contradicts its claim to be forging a new consensual social space. During my fieldwork, I also encountered expressions of resistance on the part of some people towards the Partzuergo, on account of their perception of its directive character. *Bidasoa-Txingudi* magazine has been criticised by some as being clearly a propaganda tool. Other people explained the poor attendance at the concert by Kepa Junkera, despite his great popularity in the Basque Country, as being due to uneasiness with the context of Txingudi Eguna in which the concert was organised. In response to my question on whether they used the term 'Txingudi', many people scoffed at the idea, describing it simply as a

---

[5]   *Bidaberri*, January, 1999, No. 7, p. 10.

political ploy and saying that they would continue to talk of the comarca del Bidasoa for Irun and Hondarribia and refer to Hendaia separately. The dominance of Spanish cultural influences in the Partzuergo initiative is made evident in details such as the way information about the Partzuergo is presented. On its websites, texts appear to have been written first in Spanish and then translated into French, Basque and English, often with mistakes. Most of the texts are first written by Bidasoa Bizirik and then translated by them or by Hendaia municipal employees. On the Partzuergo's website, a section listing participants in the committee of directors includes, beside the name of Hendaia's municipal secretary, the Spanish word "secretario". Figures for the Partzuergo's annual budget from 1999 until early in 2002 were cited in pesetas, even though the euro had been in existence as a cross-frontier currency since 1999. The practical reason for this was that the accounts of the Partzuergo are managed by the Bidasoa Bizirik. However, it should go without saying that any endeavour to promote values that are non-nationalist and aim to be 'European' should take advantage of the existence of a European currency.

Although the municipalities of Irun and Hondarribia had roadsigns since the late 1990s announcing "Bidasoa-Txingudi: Irun, Hondarribia", they do not mention "Hendaia". Meanwhile, in Hendaia, there are no similar signs. Instead, visitors to Hendaia are welcomed by roadsigns announcing the town's twinning arrangements with Peebles in Scotland and Viana do Castelo in Portugal.[6] Roadsigns continue to refer to the frontier and state territory, even though they are now in Basque as well as in French or Spanish. As we saw earlier, a road sign in the centre of Hendaia points to the frontier with the words "frontière" and "muga", while in Irun roadsigns point to "Francia" and "Frantzia". The municipalities of Irun and Hendaia have had their own websites since 1999 and 2000 respectively but make little effort to keep their sections on the Partzuergo up to date. On Hendaia's website, for example, the list of activities dates back to 2000. When I mentioned this to Kotte Ecenarro, the mayor of Hendaia, in an interview in April 2002, he replied that "this kind of communication is not our priority. We have other more important things to worry about". At the same time, however, he still insisted that Hendaia's interest in the Partzuergo remains strong.

Even the councillors in the majority have not demonstrated themselves to be as exemplary Bidasoa-Txingudians in their lifestyle as they are in their speeches. When I pointed out how I had noticed few council-

---

[6]   Since 1998, the municipality officialised its twinship with these two towns following contacts made with them by Robert Arrambide and Monique Lambert, two key local figures of Hendaia. This initiative is called by its French and Basque name *jumelage/ parezkatze*.

lors present at Partzuergo events such as Txingudi Eguna, Serge Lonca, a councillor of Hendaia in the majority at the time, acknowledged to me that "what we do in our public life and what we do in our private lives are often two very different things". Another example is provided by Ion Elizalde, the Hondarribia councillor, who protested on several occasions in the Partzuergo's General Council at the continued use of the word "cross-frontier", which he said contradicts the Partzuergo's objective of overcoming boundaries. However, in an interview, Mr. Elizalde joked about the Partzuergo being "*un maquillaje*" – make-up – "we still talk about the gabachos across the frontier, we still complain that they get drunk in our bars. All this about 'Txingudi'… Come on, none of us use this term. I certainly don't!" In mid 2001, Mr. Elizalde moved to live in Hendaia, where he had bought a flat.[7] But he admits that he doesn't know Hendaia well. "Only the supermarket and the way to the beach! What else does Hendaia have that I need to know about?" he says, laughing. "I only discovered where the town hall was the other day, when I had to go there for a Partzuergo meeting!" On another occasion, Mr. Elizalde complained when Txingudi Telebista broadcast some news in French over a period of several months (this was actually done by me), in addition to its customary use of Spanish and occasionally Basque. "It's so annoying", he said. "I can't understand anything!"

In interviews with me, the mayors of the three towns expressed common positive and enthusiastic views of the Partzuergo, sustaining this impression in a wide variety of media shows. In an interview in May 2002, for example, Mr. Jáuregui, the mayor of Hondarribia, noted the "symbolic importance of the Partzuergo". But such an image crumbles when we observe interaction in less public instances. Despite their insistence on mutual understanding and enthusiasm, the interests and priorities of the three municipalities are often quite different. A clue can already be picked up when one takes a look at the different priorities given by each of the municipalities to the choice of twelve projects listed in the second strategic development plan. While Hendaian delegates see cultural projects as one of their main priorities, their counterparts from the other two towns complain about the insistence of "the French" on these initiatives. Hondarribian delegates give more priority to the development of road communications and tourism and Irun delegates favour business ventures along with development of road communications and an intermodal centre to deal with freight traffic.

---

[7] Numerous other councillors from Hegoalde also live in Hendaia. Two of these are Fernando San Martín and Miguel Angel Paez, both PSE-EE representatives at the municipality of Irun. Being in constant need of personal bodyguards to protect them from possible attacks by ETA, living in Iparralde is rendered furthermore attractive as a much less risky place.

Through an examination of life in Irun, Hondarribia and Hendaia, within the Partzuergo and the development of its projects, we see that the official discourse of the Partzuergo is not as harmonious as the promoters of the Partzuergo would represent it in their public speeches and media statements. Despite the mayors' and the councillors' assurance of optimism and general positiveness, each has different interests and visions of the Partzuergo and what can be done with it. We also see that local inhabitants have their own interpretations of what the Partzuergo is about. In all cases, different senses of identity are evident. These accounts reveal a contrast between how individuals see identity as a fixed and homogenous thing and how, in their daily life, they provide evidence of how identity is actually constructed through the flexible use of markers and boundaries very different from such an immutable and holistic notion of identity. In the process, power plays a fundamental role in the discrepancy between discourse and practice. Held back from fulfilling its objectives by the fact that it is an organisation essentially made up of politicians, the Partzuergo's ultimate success hinges on the extent to which its promoters take account of power relationships in the area and the manner in which individuals constantly adapt aspects of their identity and behaviour to different contexts, company and circumstances.

The Challenges of Identification

In this study of identity issues in Bidasoa-Txingudi, I have sought to demonstrate how 'Basque identity', like any other ethnic or group identity, is not something fixed, but rather a composite conglomeration of flexible and changing boundaries. Going beyond emotional and political issues, I have tried to develop a disinterested analysis of how identity is constructed and expressed in a series of interwoven social contexts. Avoiding preconceived definitions regarding questions of underlying identity, I have examined the way in which individuals, social groups and political parties use symbolic markers and boundaries for self-identification and the identification of others. I have shown how individuals construct their own identities in a variable manner, according to the social context within which they are operating at any given moment. In this way, I have presented identity as the product of a fluid and changing application of markers and boundaries by individuals in a constant process of identification and self-identification.

As we have seen from empirical observation, expressions of identity involve an action or reaction in relation to the identity demands and expectations of others. As cultural beings, individuals use the knowledge acquired from their particular cultural experiences in the construction and expression of the self, acting out this knowledge at specific moments in time in ways that may be conditioned by collective considerations but which may also be the result of specific personal choices. This is illustrated in Bidasoa-Txingudi by the choices that individuals make in particular circumstances. At a local fiesta, for example, a person who chooses to participate has to decide how to respond to certain boundaries, such as whether to dress in the customary fiesta clothes or wear different clothes of his or her own choice. At the fiesta, this person has to respond to more boundaries, by deciding for example whether or not to engage in drinking the beverages on offer, whether or not to start singing and dancing, whether to sing some songs and not others, dance some dances and not others, and so on.

Sökefeld, in his study of the management of the self in situations where potentially conflictive social relations are maintained, concludes that "there can be no identities without selves", having defined "self" as "that reflexive sense that enables the person to distinguish self-consciously between him – or herself and everything else" (1999:424). Amid the clash of conflicting ideological forces in the Basque Country, issues of identity are a source of frequent polemic, imposing constant negotiation and compromise on individuals' expression of the self. As in any cultural system, not all symbolic boundaries are accepted and interpreted by different people in the Basque Country in the same way. In the fiesta context, a person who adopts the markers used by the group becomes part of this group and contributes to the drawing up of the boundaries that distinguishes it from others. At the same time, however, the person may not use all of the available markers in the same way as others in the group. In such cases, this person may draw up boundaries between himself or herself and the others, while not necessarily diminishing in his or her own eyes his or her membership of the group.

In a broader context, similar considerations have implications for the way in which the phenomenon of Basque nationalism is understood and expressed. Reflecting the emergence on both sides of the state frontier of a range of 'nationalist' movements with different tendencies and objectives, the term 'nationalism' in the Basque context has become ambiguous and unclear. In Hegoalde, both the conservative Basque nationalist party EAJ and the left-wing abertzale movement in the orbit of the now outlawed Batasuna party lay claim to the term, despite their very different ideologies. In Iparralde, a small minority condones violence in pursuit of Basque independence and maintains links with sympathisers in Hegoalde, while a larger group of more moderate nationalists seek to distance themselves from the conflictive political and social situation in Hegoalde by stressing the specific nature of their demands. Nonnationalists, meanwhile, frequently show pride in cultural and ethnic symbols of Basque identity while rejecting the political goals of the nationalists.

Given the way in which boundaries can be interpreted differently depending on where a person stands in relation to them, one of the starting points of my research was the realisation of the close relationship between constructions of group identity and the exercise of power in a context of different visions and understandings of 'reality'. In the Basque Country, as we have seen, competing versions of history and tradition are used by individuals as components of identification strategies for the purposes of inclusion or exclusion. While the French and Spanish states have constructed their own versions of 'national' history, Basque nationalists have followed a similar strategy with regard to their identification of 'the Basque people'. In highlighting the interconnection between the use of symbols and the exercise of power, I have emphasised the impossibility of establishing any one 'true' version of history or tradition. I have also shown how, just as individuals use identification strategies as part of a process self-affirmation, the promoters of the Partzuergo resort to the fabrication of identity as part of a strategy for obtaining and holding onto power. The symbolic struggle over the definition of who qualifies as a 'real' Basque person has inevitable consequences for the Partzuergo, as those involved approach it with different understandings of what it is meant to do. Viewed from afar, the Partzuergo, in its use of Basque symbols and its attempts to promote the Basque language, seems to some people like an abertzale initiative, even though this is not the case. Such misperceptions were illustrated to me by the way in which some local people referred to it as "this Basque thing" when I first asked them about it in 1999. Other people, who identified themselves to me as primarily French or Spanish, were initially suspicious of the Partzuergo as heralding a move in the direction of Basque national reunification. At the same time, as we have seen, the Partzuergo is subject to criticism from the left-wing abertzaleak, who question its motives. In its attempt to promote a new common perspective of the local space and a new sense of belonging amongst the local population, the Partzuergo has to grapple with the challenges of a symbolic struggle which creates boundaries of division and tension amongst its inhabitants.

In conversations with the organisers of the Partzuergo, I often heard statements such as "we need to know each other better" and "we still have some way to go". Such statements seem to suggest that the creation of an overarching 'Bidasoa-Txingudi' sense of belonging is simply a matter of stimulating awareness of a shared cultural heritage. Such an idea, however, is based on questionable assumptions. One is the idea that because individuals have fluid, changing and situational identifications, these 'identities' will logically fit together in a harmonious hierarchical arrangement like "concentric circles which would encourage compatible loyalties from the local to the European level" (García and Wallace, 1993:172): this ignores the political aspect of identity construction. Another is the idea that a Bidasoa-Txingudi identity can be forged simply by exploiting locally existing symbols such as language, history, myth, memory, folklore and tradition: this ignores the fact that it is precisely those cultural elements from which existing identities are constructed that presently are the factors that most divide local inhabitants.

The Partzuergo's organisers have tried to get round this by saying that a sense of Bidasoa-Txingudi belonging, made up of 'difference' and 'plurality', is a greater whole than the sum of its parts and therefore 'naturally' transcendent. Such an assertion mirrors at a local level the EU's slogan of 'unity in diversity'. However, not everyone may grasp this bigger picture of Bidasoa-Txingudi belonging or do so in a uniform way. Moreover, the question of who defines this sense of belonging is itself a politically loaded one. There is also a contradiction between attempts to mobilise public support for further integration, through populist rhetoric about 'being all together' and 'needing to know each other', and attempts to 'de-politicise' matters by focusing on the legal/rational and 'technical' aspects of an integration process that in fact raises far-reaching issues of history, evolution and destiny.

As we have seen, the Partzuergo's public statements frequently cite 'Europe' as a central concept in the context of cross-frontier cooperation. The Partzuergo features the European flag and other markers linked with the European Union in its publications and public events. Frequently, in interviews, officials told me how important 'Europe' is in relation to the Partzuergo's contribution to contemporary social, political and economic developments, and how the Partzuergo initiative is an essential part of the 'consolidation of Europe'. Often, too, they stressed the importance of 'Europe', for example in talking about 'the need to remain competitive within the widening economic currents of Europe' and the possibility of benefiting from EU funds. By contrast, few of the people outside the Partzuergo with whom I spoke explicitly mentioned a sense of identification with 'Europe', and some even told me they were not keen on the idea of feeling 'European'. Attitudes to 'Europe' as embodied in the EU frequently appeared to reflect merely a recognition of it as a current social, political and economic reality, without any deeper personal involvement in a 'European project'. Interestingly, this analysis was also expressed to me by many individuals leading a cross-frontier lifestyle.

How best to enable citizens to participate in the democratic polity is a longstanding subject of debate. In an EU context, the European Commission has launched various campaigns over the years to foster a sense of European identity. One of the best known, the Lexcalibur project, aims to create a kind of 'European public sphere' (Risse, 2002) by providing a space on the Internet for individuals to voice their opinions about current legislation and policy-making in the EU. Such initiatives, however, as MacClancy (2000:16) has pointed out, are likely to be restricted in their impact, catering principally to members of the middle class who have the time and resources needed to take part. This risks happening, too, with the Partzuergo. As an elite-led enterprise, rather than an elected body, it is ill-equipped to seek popular legitimacy through manufactured symbols.[1] As long as the debate around the idea

---

[1]   This issue has also been brought up by scholars in the social and political sciences with relevance to efforts by politicians, bureaucrats and intellectuals to construct new formal notions of identity such as 'European' (e.g. Shore, 2000; Stråth, 2000) and 'transnational' and 'border' (e.g. Persson and Eriksson, 2000; Die Erde, 2002). While they all acknowledge the important role played by the elite in the popular adoption of specific symbols, they stress the need to empower citizens with the right to participate in the democratic polity.

of Bidasoa-Txingudi space and identification remains essentially political and partial, with the circle of people supporting and constructing it restricted to those for whom such a reality is politically and economically appealing, the Partzuergo is likely to have only superficial success.

In an effort to open up participation in local affairs, the municipal council of Irun has taken a number of steps over the past few years. In 1999, it set up a citizens' information service, the SAC. A year later, it launched a municipal website, www.irun.org, with a series of special public tents on Ensantxe Plaza for free internet access. In January 2002, it launched a so-called Citizens' Forum (*Foro Ciudadano* in Spanish and *Hiritar Forua* in Basque) with the objective of "stimulating citizen participation by creating a sort of 'congress' of citizens which enables the gathering of thoughts and opinions on issues that affect the city as a whole".[2] The Forum consisted of five commissions in which participants could voice their opinions about projects concerning Irun such as economic diversification, Irun in the European context with open frontiers and its participation in the Partzuergo and the Euro Hiri. It was designed to take place over three sessions, and participants, who were required to register before the first session, came from a wide variety of backgrounds, both as individuals and as representatives of local associations. Amongst them were members of *Adixkidetuak*, an association set up by immigrants largely from Latin America as a mutual support organisation which had taken part in the Txingudi Eguna the year before, and representatives of the campaign for the integration of women into the traditional Alarde. In May, a White Paper was distributed to the public featuring some of the ideas voiced and giving details of the discussions and principal conclusions. On the day of the White Book's release, the mayor of Irun, stressed that "this forum does not shut its doors today. Rather, it is the point of departure of an irreversible road towards a more participative city".[3]

In the broader context of Bidasoa-Txingudi, however, such initiatives have remained isolated. Despite the strong interest in Hondarribia and Hendaia in matters relating to cross-frontier living, the Partzuergo and the Euro Hiri, neither of these two towns organised anything similar during the period under consideration. What is more, in the case of the Forum, it remained unclear how the concerns voiced by people in Irun would be taken up by either the municipal authorities or the Partzuergo, leaving an impression among some participants that the event was merely a half-hearted and superficial show of greater inclusiveness.

Whether or not local people will gradually identify themselves with a sense of Bidasoa-Txingudi belonging, and if so how, is hard to predict.

---

[2] http://www.irun.org/caste/foro/foropres.html.

[3] Quoted from Alberto Buen's speech on 29 May 2002.

No single factor determines the readiness of individuals to receive and digest new beliefs about the boundaries of community. What matters is the cumulative impact of a whole series of conditions. But it remains the case, so far, that identification with Bidasoa-Txingudi is of greater interest to some people than to others. For those who seek new opportunities beyond the frontier, who have ambitions for developing a business or association, or who wish to benefit from aspects of state contexts such as living in one state and working in the other or in both, Bidasoa-Txingudi becomes a relevant concept. For others, by contrast, it is less relevant, meaning that the Partzuergo's projects may benefit only a certain class of people.

The organisers of the Partzuergo justify its present structure, based on control by the majority groups in each of the three municipalities and therefore in practice excluding the left-wing Basque nationalist movement, by arguing that the public is not ready for anything more inclusive because it 'lacks information' or is 'fearful' or 'suspicious'. As we have seen from empirical observation, Bidasoa-Txingudi continues to be a highly segmented society. Divided by a state frontier and differing traditions and attitudes, by language, social origins and loyalties, its members are indeed as aware of their differences as they are of the features that they share in common. Such assertions by the Partzuergo's organisers stand in contrast, nonetheless, with the statements of some local inhabitants to the effect that "many of us have had strong contact between each other across the frontier since well before the existence of the Partzuergo". The Partzuergo's arguments effectively rule out dissent while conveniently disguising the fact that politicians within the Partzuergo have their own personal and political interests in this project that do not necessarily go in the same direction as what they preach in public.

While the Partzuergo draws on 'cultural' aspects of identity in an attempt to rally the local population in a non-conflictual way, by talking in terms of a 'Txingudi identity', it simultaneously raises new boundaries in its effort to constitute a 'Bidasoa-Txingudi people'. The Partzuergo does not go so far as to recommend certain markers over others in terms of their ability to confirm 'Bidasoa-Txingudiness', nor does it impose specific criteria for who can possess a 'Txingudi identity' and how. By positing a theoretical 'Txingudi identity', however, it implicitly raises the possibility of 'non-Txingudi identity' and 'non-Bidasoa-Txingudi people'. In this way, it opens the way for future doubts and tensions between people who think they have a 'Txingudi identity' or feel a 'Txingudi' sense of belonging and those who they think do not. By engaging in this way in the same dialectic that it seeks to shun, the

Partzuergo runs the risk of reproducing a pattern of inclusion and exclusion.

Significantly, popular support for the Partzuergo emerges in moments when all three towns are threatened by an outside force, as in the case of the possible extension of the airport, or when there are general economic benefits to be obtained for the area, for example through efforts to develop business and tourism and resolve traffic problems. Does this mean that the Partzuergo should concentrate more on 'practical' areas such as business, tourism and transport rather than on talk of 'culture' and 'identity' in order to gain local support? It is difficult of course to avoid concerns with 'identity' and 'culture' altogether, since any social initiative inevitably leads to self-questioning on the part of its participants: 'why are we doing this?' and '*who* are *we*?' But perhaps such questions are something for individuals, in their engagement with the activities of the Partzuergo, to ask themselves, rather than have the Partzuergo both ask and answer the questions for them.

To ignore the choices that individuals make in relation to identity constructions, by instead viewing identity as a group phenomenon, carries with it the risk of accepting and supporting an attempt by someone else to exercise power at a group level over the individual. Just as naming implies an attempt to exercise power over the thing or person being named, using notions of 'identity' as a means of defining someone amounts to an attempt at control and appropriation. Or, putting things another way: to include someone under a particular label without regard for whether or not that person wishes or feels entitled to be included is as much an exercise of power as is the refusal to accord an identity to someone who wishes or feels entitled to be included under that identity label. Examples of how 'identity' is used in Bidasoa-Txingudi in order to impose a way of thinking and behaving on a group of people are provided by the conflict surrounding the Alarde. At a broader level, an insidious strategy is the assertion of Basque, French or Spanish 'identity' as a way of rallying or excluding people under specific labels or headings.

Certainly, it is only by going beyond current boundaries that the Partzuergo can succeed in winning wide-ranging popular support for its project. But if the Partzuergo wants to be genuinely inclusive, a long-term recipe for its success should include an opening-up to a popular plurality by accepting the contributions of local people to the decision-making process, and by taking a conscious decision to disengage from the dialectic of a 'need' for 'identity' and 'culture', in order precisely to avoid getting involved in the drawing up of the type of markers and boundaries that we have seen in operation in this book. The same goes for any project, including that of the EU, concerned with achieving its goals on the basis of an image of popular legitimacy.

An Anthropologist in the Basque Country:
An Elaboration on Theoretical Considerations

What is Anthropology?

"I suppose that, as an anthropologist, your interest in the Basque Country will be to look for ethnic expression, as this is the main focus of anthropology, isn't it? Origins, customs, and now nationalism... But, you know, you must take into account the fact that there aren't just the nationalists. This is a very plural society: there's nationalism and non-nationalism and, what's more, the nationalists, as such, are not the whole picture. And the Basque case must not be regarded as being unique. Rather, it is singular."[1]

Personal conversation with a Professor of Law at the University of the Basque Country. July 2000, San Sebastian.

As a social anthropologist conducting research in the Basque Country since 1998, I had to grapple repeatedly with the challenge of explaining what I am doing and why. Was I there to explore the alleged uniqueness of the Basque people, or to shed light on their supposedly mysterious origins? Was I compiling a catalogue of customs, linguistic peculiarities or physical types? Was I delving into the emotional roots of the Basque nationalist movement and the motives of those who continue to follow a path of violent confrontation? Such questions, from the many different people with whom I mixed and interacted, were entirely comprehensible in a society that has witnessed a steady stream of speculation and affirmation about the nature and essence of Basque identity.[2] But they mistake the wider and deeper scope of anthropological investigation. This section then is an attempt to go beyond such superficial understandings in order to explain the process and purpose of anthropological analysis.

Since much talk about 'the Basques' is centred around 'their' mysterious origins and physiological and linguistic characteristics, it is not surprising that the anthropologist's interest in them should be understood to be motivated in this way. As is revealed by the professor's comment to me at the

---

[1]   Translated from Spanish by the author.

[2]   For critical reviews of these in the anthropological discipline, see MacClancy (1993a), Zulaika (1996, 1998), Aranzadi (2000) and Bidart (2001).

beginning of this section, anthropology often continues to be largely mis-conceived amid popular reifications of 'ethnic groups' and 'primordiality'. Questions that I was often asked in casual conversation about my research – such as "so what is it that the Basques want?" and "do they really think they will get independence?" – reflect this erroneously all-encompassing under-standing of identity (see also Brubaker, 2002; Brubaker *et al.*, 2002). Implicit in this approach is the dubious notion of 'authentic culture' arising from an *a priori* system of essential meanings, which for any serious social study is analytically useless.

Broadly, the aim of the anthropologist is to analyse the cultural processes through which people define themselves and behave. It is in moments of social tension and conflict that cultural expressions come out most starkly (MacClancy, 1993b:85), as individuals and groups struggle to impose their understandings of symbols over those of others. This is what makes themes such as nationalism attractive to scholars. Over the latter half of the twenti-eth century, nationalism, together with a modern notion of ethnicity, has become the focus of extensive sociological and anthropological research. As such, it was a logical assumption on the part of many people to whom I spoke about my work that my interest in the Basque Country would be to study 'the nationalists'. When I explained that my interest was not specifi-cally to look out for expressions of ethnic groupness or to focus on 'the nationalists', I often received a confused response from my interlocutors, who asked what could then be my object of study.[3]

An anthropological study of issues of identity in the Basque Country is incomplete and misleading if it focuses solely on political claims regarding the existence and defence of a Basque nation, as this entails a neglect of actual experience and marginalises those not accepting or feeling excluded from such a notion. Nor can an anthropological study focus only on traditional manifestations of some kind of Basque community, since this would fail to recognise that expressions of group belonging are a mixture of continuously invented, reinvented and appropriated cultural markings, achieved through continuous interaction with one's surroundings accentuated by the fast pace of the communication-intensive world in which we live. As a reflexive disci-pline, social anthropology has a crucial role to play in shedding light on changing modes of social interaction and attitudes to the spaces in which people live (Augé, 1994; 1995).

Contemporary anthropology is distinguished from other disciplines by its em-pirical approach and its attempt to avoid theoretical presuppositions. Much

---

[3] As Brubaker has also noted, in spite of all deconstructivist attempts, "everyday talk, policy analysis, media reports, and even much ostensibly constructivist academic writing routinely frame accounts of ethnic, racial and national conflict in groupist terms as the struggles of ethnic groups, races and nations" (2002:163). In the Basque case, a similar tendency is noted by Watson (1996b:3-10).

social science research is directed toward testing formal theories, whereby the researcher approaches the object of research with a preconception of what he or she expects to find. This method has been much criticised for its ethnocentrism. Modern anthropological research, by contrast, remains largely concerned with the small scale, reflecting the idea that a concentrated focus is appropriate for acquiring a full understanding of the human being in his or her social entourage. The usefulness of anthropology within the social sciences lies precisely in this speciality. Small communities and structures are linked to more encompassing social and political formations (Burawoy *et al.*, 1991). Anthropology puts a human face on the various domains in which people interact, such as economics and politics, in a way that other disciplines rarely are able to do. By carrying out a microanalysis of society and politics, one can begin to understand the wider picture.

The anthropologist carries out ethnographic work involving long periods of fieldwork, with all that this entails: learning the local language, adapting to the area, carrying out interviews, getting involved in activities with local inhabitants and thereby acquiring a deeper knowledge of the local society (Spradley, 1980). Participant observation, the research method that marks anthropology from the rest of the social sciences, is a data-collecting technique, which allows the researcher to study people in their own space and time (Rabinow and Sullivan, 1987). Such a task requires complete open-mindedness on the part of the anthropologist, who has in effect to strive to become a *tabula rasa* that will take in whatever is found. This means that the anthropologist does not look for specific manifestations, following already formed ideas of what 'identity' is. Only after an adequate amount of time spent gaining familiarity with the social environment can the anthropologist decide which informants merit further analysis and which courses of investigation are worth pursuing (Spradley, 1979). Nor must the anthropologist arrive with a certain ideological state of mind, which would lead her not only to impose her own set of values, but also to favour the point of view and lifestyle of a certain group of people within the field, while neglecting the consideration of others and remaining insensitive to the power games being played out. Such an approach would only stunt the scope of interpretation and produce excessively biased results. Unfortunately, however, cases of such political bias are not rare, particularly in the study of the Basque Country.

Rather than supporting or criticising notions of Basque uniqueness and difference, my interest lay in looking beyond and beneath them to discover how such notions are used in the context of social interaction. This is the task of the social anthropologist, to probe into the construction by the group of individuals that form and live a culture of the essential elements that go into the formation of this culture.

Let us focus first on the misperceptions of the role of the anthropological discipline. Taking as my starting point the remark by the professor of law whom I quote at the outset, I briefly explore here the basis for his assumptions regarding both the nature of anthropological research and the preconceptions that he feared I might have about the Basque Country. I build on this to review the perceptions of both outsiders and insiders of 'nationalism' and the consequences of this for an understanding of ethnic identity in the Basque context, and analyse their effect in the broader context of social interaction.

I show how 'nationalism' is one of a number of elements that determine how people interact, construct and express their sense of self. In order to build and maintain these elements, the individual must adapt his or her use of the social environment in an appropriate manner. This becomes a symbolic manifestation of what a person wants to say about him or herself. For example, the pleasurable sensation associated with the use of space in conformity with one's identity can turn into 'discomfort' when individuals find themselves in spatial situations that do not correspond to their view of themselves (e.g. Ardener, 1993:1-3). Such negative space connotations can result in self-imposed restrictions on individuals' social interaction, creating one of the many symbolic boundaries used by a person as part of their expression of who they are.

Anthropology is above all the study of people as social beings, how they interact and give meaning to their world. As such, anthropologists are concerned with providing a qualitative account, stressing the importance of the particular in the search for descriptive explanatory generalisations about the way a society works. Anthropology aims to achieve a fuller understanding of the individual as a social being. It looks at its object of study as a whole, seeking to understand how individuals make their own place within the social context through their relationships with each other.

Nonetheless, despite the evolution of the discipline over the hundred and fifty years, misunderstandings persist regarding anthropology's nature and objectives. This is partly due to its origins in the colonialist era, as the study of those peoples 'discovered' and brought under European authority. Focusing on 'other civilisations' of peoples different from the largely white European 'us', early anthropologists set out to analyse customs, rituals, kinship systems and other organisational structures with a view to gaining a systematic understanding of the make-up and functioning of other cultures. Culture was largely understood along the lines of Tylor's definition as "that complex whole which includes knowledge, belief, art, morals, law, custom, and many other capabilities and habits acquired by man as a member of society" (1871:1). Such a definition made it possible to generalise about large configurations of people, such as 'the Samoans', 'the Hottentots', 'the Inuit' and 'the Javanese', all united by their "webs of shared significance" (Geertz, 1973:5).

In the post-colonial era, the self-assertion of peoples previously dominated by European colonial powers led to a reassessment among social anthropologists of their methods and objectives. This took place against a background of soul-searching among social scientists about the possible contribution of academics to the essentialisation of the peoples under study, who by being viewed as 'different' to members of the society to which the academics belonged were fashioned into some exotic 'Other', detached from the 'normal' and 'civilised' 'us' of the world of the academics. Anthropology, in particular, was criticised for its tendency to maintain an egocentric and ethnocentric approach to its object of study. In response, and recognising the redundancy in a rapidly changing modern world of classifying peoples and cultures into neat units and structures, anthropologists engaged in a re-thinking of their discipline, focusing on their own notions of self in their relationship with the traditional object of study.

During the same period, amid the crumbling of European colonialism and resulting proliferation of nation-states, 'Western' and 'non-Western' societies acquired equal status as objects of research. Cultures in Southern Europe and the Mediterranean area became a focus of anthropological interest, which then spread to the rest of the continent. This process contributed to the growth of an anthropology of 'complex societies', within which an appreciation of the intricacy of cultural formations challenged a unitary view of culture that stressed boundedness, continuity and homogeneity (Werbner and Modood, 1997:91). In parallel, anthropological theory was marked by a shift in focus from 'system' to 'practice', accompanied by an interest in agency and in the actors' point of view. This resulted in a further dismantling of the notion of the 'cultural whole', associated with a distrust of unifying, homogenising forms of anthropological writing, forcefully expressed in such critical texts as James Clifford's and George Marcus's *Writing Culture* (1986).

In this context, the concept of culture came to be re-defined as a web of shared but continuously negotiated and contested meanings. Central to this contested environment are such elements as language and power, ideology and consciousness. Culture is the result of social interaction, since it is people, in their relations with each other, who produce and negotiate meaning. Understood in this way, the concept recognises that social groups are themselves 'culturally' constructed. Thus Terence Turner saw culture as "collective forms of social consciousness arising in the context of historical social processes" (1993:417). Culture is a "political process" (Wright, 1994:26), in which some meanings are always imposed at the expense of others (Bourdieu, 1991). Culture then is necessarily studied in interaction, whereby human beings, as members of society are not only influenced by each other but individually interpret and manipulate cultural symbols in their social and material context.

Such a shift in anthropological focus has gone hand in hand with a revised approach to the 'object of study',[4] which now becomes a reflection of our-

---

[4]   Bourdieu has since gone further by insisting that social scientists rethink the idea of subjectivity versus objectivity (e.g. 1991:224-227). Science, he argues, is not a neutral 'field' but yet another context of symbolic struggle which results in social scientists' construction of a particular version of the 'reality'.

selves and how we define who we and others are. More recently, the concept of 'Europe' and its construction in the minds of the inhabitants of the continent and within the institutions of the EU have become a focus of interest.[5] So, while still concentrating on ground-level research, anthropology moved "beyond the community" (Boissevain, 1975) to become concerned with larger issues such as centre-periphery relations, economic development and the formation of the state and the nation.[6]

Anthropology in the Basque Country

The development of anthropological studies in the Basque Country reflects these trends. Douglass's *Death in Murelaga* (1973) and Bidart's *Le Pouvoir Politique à Baigorri* (1977) are each concerned in their own way with the local and its wider implications for the exploration of issues of identity and nationalism in an economically developing and politically polarising environment. Ott's *The Circle of the Mountains* (1981), focusing on a rural community in the isolated hinterland of Iparralde, is a classic example of anthropological interest in a small community in what was then seen as one of the backwaters of ethnic and traditional Europe. Against the background of the advent of democracy in Spain, Heiberg looks at expressions of Basque nationalism in a small town in Hegoalde and their consequences for an understanding of the processes of constructing a modern notion of the Basque nation (*The Making of the Basque Nation*, 1989). Although her work has since been criticised for its oversimplification of complex relations between inhabitants of the Basque Country on ethnic lines, it is an example of the kind of anthropological work produced in the 1970s when nationalism and political violence had captured the attention of anthropologists and social and political theorists as part of a general context of change in the configuration of nation-states following the independence of ex-colonial societies and the self-affirmation of so-called minority ethnic groups. Zulaika's *Death and Sacrament* (1989) is another milestone in the development of this approach, focusing on local cultural processes in an effort to understand violence in the name of nationalism.

Urla's *Being Basque, Speaking Basque...* (1987), dealing with the role in the construction of a modern Basque identity of the language policy of the Basque government in the early 1980s, introduces a different set of sociopolitical debates to those of the anthropologists just mentioned. The establishment of a Basque government as part of Spain's transition to democracy following the death of Franco led to a process of Basque institutionalisation with a view to 'remedying' the past and constructing a firm sense of Basqueness – or cultural sovereignty – through language planning. Such a process

---

[5] E.g. Shore, 2000; Bellier and Wilson, 2000; Bellier, 1994; Goddard, Llobera and Shore, 1994; Wilson and Estellie-Smith, 1993; Shore and Black, 1992; Abélès, 1996.

[6] E.g. Grillo 1980 and MacDonald, 1993.

has had consequences for self-understanding in a Basque context and the modern formation of Basque identity/identities. Urla's work demonstrates how politics of language and politics of identity can become one. However, in order to portray a clear and accurate picture of a social situation, it is crucial to look at all the actors within this context. This is what I felt was lacking in much of the social anthropological research carried out in the Basque Country, where the tendency towards categorisation and homogenisation of people into groups is still observable. For example, Laborde (1996), describing a bertsolari championship in the stadium of Tolosa in Hegoalde in 1995, identifies this event in ritual terms as an expression of Basque identity. While those attending may well share a certain view of their Basque identity and culture, I question whether the 'Basqueness' being celebrated at this event can be equated with a reified 'Basque identity', as such an assumption fails to take account of those who may not identify with this event but do identify with other symbols which they consider to be Basque.

Taking the approach of a political scientist, Itçaina (2002) sought to find a pattern in the experience of Basque identity over time based on his interpretation of four so-called configurations of identity. His first configuration consists of what he describes as a traditional sense of identity, characterised by a strong attachment to the Basque language and to Catholic values (euskaldun fededun), an identity "which is not questioned" (2002:3). His second involves a political understanding of Basque identity that moves away from an attachment to Catholic values and towards Basque nationalist values, personified by individuals who, though not native Basque-speakers, deliberately set out to learn the language (euskaldun berri), and by the so-called Basque patriot (abertzale). His third configuration involves a kind of compromise between the first two configurations in which 'Basque identity' accommodates itself to other less absolute values. Finally, his fourth configuration attempts to explain the nature of identification with Basqueness today among people not caught up in a nationalist discourse by citing a combination of utilitarianism with an emotive attachment to Basque symbols unconnected with nationalist projects. Despite stating that any notion of Basqueness exists only thanks to individual and collective interaction with other notions of identity (2002:1), however, he approaches his analysis of 'Basque identity' exclusively from the *outside*.

In taking these approaches, both Laborde and Itçaina fail to go beyond generalities to examine individual and interpersonal interpretations of the significance of Basque symbols and expressions of identification with them. Thus, they participate in the reification of the ethnic group by treating it as a natural and fixed reality of central importance in social life. The same approach is evident in the symbolic struggle between members of the Basque community over 'Basqueness'. Rather than addressing individual issues of identity and belonging, many participants in this symbolic struggle resort to commonplaces and platitudes in their analysis of who qualifies as 'Basque'.

Theoretical Elaboration of the Concepts of Identity and Boundaries

By treating identity as the result of an agglomeration of different shifting boundaries, I go beyond past primordial and essentialist notions of identity that prevent any effective, sympathetic and all-encompassing understanding of identity expression in real-life settings. Building on existing work relating to the conceptualisation of identity in the social sciences, I focus on the use of markers and boundaries as tools for the formation and the analysis of individual expressions of identity and social interaction. In order to put my approach into context, I present a more elaborate overview here of how the term identity has been used in past academic research in the discipline of social anthropology. While not an exhaustive review of all the relevant literature, this outline is intended to present the theoretical foundations on which my approach to identity in this book is based.

Although identity is widely understood in the social sciences today as a construction that evolves out of a sense of social belonging (Barnard and Spencer, 1996:292), different theoretical approaches still continue to affect the way in which the concept is understood and used, not only by social scientists but also by politicians and ordinary people. In everyday communication for instance, we generally tend to talk about identity as that which defines who we are as individuals and as members of certain social groups adhering to certain values and customs. At a group level, identity is often seen as being linked to nationality or ethnicity. On the interpersonal level, we talk of identity in relation to all sorts of different statuses, as a teenager, for example, or as a mother or painter. On the cultural/value level, we use the word to refer to our way of perceiving the world and living in a certain way. This can relate to a religious creed, for example, or simply to personal experiences and interests. Altogether, these different 'identities' define a person individually, with some assuming more importance in some situations and contexts than in others, as for example when a Muslim journalist assumes his identity as a parent in going to his children's school to talk about their progress. However, these different 'identities' presuppose fixity, imposing the notion of immutability. Used in this way, the word 'identity' fails to encompass all the different 'identities' of a person or to question the possibility of individual interpretation of these. It also fails to make a difference between how the person is viewed by others in contrast to how the person views himself.

The term identity has become imprecise in academia too, varying in its meaning according to discipline, subject and context. This has led some social scientists to go so far as to declare it undefinable. According to

Brubaker and Cooper, it has been used in so many different ways for different interests and purposes that it has become too ambiguous, torn between "hard" and "soft" (2000:2) meanings and between essentialist connotations and constructivist qualifiers, to usefully serve the requirements of social analysis. Brubaker points out the need "to break with vernacular categories and common-sense understandings" (2001:15) of both identity and ethnicity. In shifting my focus towards markers and boundaries, I do not discard the term identity entirely but simply seek to avoid being dragged into the misunderstandings and confusions that arise from its widespread use.

Social theory approached identity in terms of symbolic interactionism, whereby the self, emerging from its encounter with the social world, can be understood by examining its place in the social context (Mead, 1934). Social interaction was deemed a key aspect in the analysis of individual and collective identity (Heider, 1958). Weber, one of the fathers of modern (and interpretative) sociology was equally concerned with the issue of identity in the modern world, although he talked of *Persoenlichkeit* (personality) rather than identity (1968). For Weber, an understanding of modern identity involved a coherent and measured acceptance and assumption of social stimuli. Later, Freud proposed to see individuals as conceivers of the self according to the cognitive models of personality or moral character available within the range of their experience.

Anthropologists have most frequently employed the term 'identity' to refer to this idea of selfhood in a loosely Eriksonian way (Erikson, 1972), properties based on the uniqueness and individuality which makes a person distinct from others. Identity became of more interest to anthropologists with the emergence of modern concerns with ethnicity and social movements in the 1970s. This was reinforced by an appreciation, following the trend in sociological thought, of the manner in which the individual is affected by and contributes to the overall social context. At the same time, the Eriksonian approach to identity remained in force, with the result that identity has continued until recently to be used in a largely socio-historical way to refer to qualities of sameness in relation to a person's connection to others and to a particular group of people.

This ambiguous and confusing approach to identity has led on occasion to rather restrictive interpretations of the concept, following two more or less opposite tendencies. The first favours a primordialist approach which takes the sense of self and belonging to a collective group as a fixed thing, defined by objective criteria such as common ancestry and common biological characteristics. The second, rooted in social constructionist theory, takes the view that identity is formed by a predominantly political choice of certain characteristics. In so doing, it questions the idea that identity is a natural given, characterised by fixed, supposedly objective criteria. Both approaches need to be understood in their respective political and historical contexts. While they have been criticised, they continue to exert an influence on approaches to the conceptualisation of identity today.

The first approach treats identity as fundamentally a group phenomenon, binding group members together on a basis of exclusive common characteristics. Identity here is understood as denoting a fundamental and consequential sameness among members of a group. Viewed in this context, identity is invoked as something allegedly deep, basic and foundational. This has led to certain conceptualisations of ethnic identity, such as Herder's influential neo-romantic concept of the *Volk* as a unity of blood and soil. While it has been severely criticised (e.g. Thompson, 1989:21-48), it has remained an element of theoretical discourse.

To most proponents of modernisation in the 1960s, assertions of ethnic identity feeling were seen as backward and anachronistically attached to traditional values. Ethnic groupness continued to be associated with objective sociobiological criteria. With the emergence of political conflicts in which issues of ethnicity played a central role, this approach led to an acceptance of objective and perceived differences between social groups as a basis for the construction of group distinction and consequently of political mobilisation. Ethnic groups were seen as the product of political myths. In this vein, Smith has defined them as made up "of people whose members share a common name and elements of culture, possess a myth of common origin and common historical memory, who associate themselves with a particular territory and possess a feeling of solidarity" (1986:15).

While moving towards a subjective approach to ethnic identity, as a politicised cultural identity, these so-called instrumentalist theories still gave ethnic groupness an essentialist quality. By associating it with political strategy-making, overflowing sometimes into violence, ethnic groupness was also often given negative connotations. This has caused in many cases a return to a rather primordialist view of ethnic groupness, as the ethnic group is understood to be fighting for its distinctive values. This has also been in spite of Weber's own clear distinction between the race and ethnicity, whereby the former is taken to be unconscious belonging to a biological group, and the latter subjective and consciously defined. Ethnic identity often continues to be confused with ideas of race and general biological criteria, maintaining the understanding of individual identity as something permanent and fixed.[7]

---

[7]   Based on my personal experience, the fact that we are often asked in everyday social interaction: "Where are you from?" is quite telling. This question presupposes an answer along the national line, a question about which country one is from, which is supposed to equal one's nationality. This supposes territorial origins and national adherence to be the most fundamental aspects of who a person is. This belonging is essentially 'proved' by our possession of a passport or 'identity card'. The popularised discourse of ethnicity and identity linked together also explains why saying that one has several nationalities or does not speak the language of the nationality often

Another approach to identity, and consequently to ethnicity, interprets the concepts as deriving from a sense of self formed out of an awareness of distinctiveness, of difference to Others. The anthropologist Barth was a pioneer in this approach in his analysis of ethnic identity (1969). In this way, ethnic identity could be understood as formed on the basis of what is chosen and agreed (we want to be like this, we feel different to them on the basis of things we believe we have in common) rather than as a collection of fixed types (blood, language, history, character). This notion of ethnic boundaries provides a way of understanding how a sense of organisation and order in a social environment and a sense of group membership is developed and sustained amidst surrounding change. They assist people in their creation of bonds based on shared ideas and emotions as part of a group in contrast to others, to such an extent that it is not necessary for them to know each other personally (Anderson, 1983).

Some anthropologists of the 1970s concentrated on the social and political role of symbols. Abner Cohen, for example, defined symbols as "objects, acts, relationships or linguistic formations that stand *ambiguously* for a multiplicity of meanings, evoke emotions, and impel men to action" (1974:23). He and others saw culture as made up of symbols interpreted by individuals and used for their expression of the self. Geertz (1973) worked on the idea of culture as a particular symbolic system promoted by a social group, assisting the group in its way of thinking and looking at the world. As a set of symbolic statements, culture shapes and gives meaning to human perceptions and behaviour. And rather than the meanings of symbols being fixed or given, they are inter-subjectively created by the members of the group together. As such, they are a source of group negotiation. Geertz views this negotiation of meaning as fundamentally a social process which occurs, "not in the head, but in that public world where people talk together, name things, make assertions, and to a degree understand each other" (1973:213).

Over the following decades, identity came to be seen as an object of personal struggle in social and political studies (e.g. Calhoun, 1994). Hall (1995) maintained that the challenges of the modern world result in making identity a central concern in people's lives, and the need to find one's roots becomes indispensable (Beck, 1992). What occurs then, Hall and Calhoun have argued, is a politics of difference, whereby group identities assert

---

causes so much confusion. Often, in the attempt to make some sense of this confusion, interlocutors ask, 'well, where were you born?' as if this will help to provide an answer. For the past two centuries, nationalism has had a great influence on how we define ourselves, associating personal identity closely with nationality. Likewise, confusion is sometimes caused when one expresses attachment to an ethnic identity instead, but does not stereotypically look like this ethnic group or was not born in its particular area.

themselves in opposition to perceived pressures of homogenisation and, in doing so, assume roles in the political arena.

Subsequent studies focused on the relationship between ethnicity and nationalism. Horowitz, for example, examined how ethnic identity becomes reinforced when competing with other identities (1985). Similarly, Wallman suggests that differences between social groups become ethnic boundaries "only when heated into significance by the identity investments of the other side" (1986:230). Hechter (1975), more specifically, looked at ethnic identity in the context of internal colonialism and perceived suppression by a dominant identity. Glazer and Moynihan have treated identity as a politicised social fact, whereby social change and new political challenges are seen to bring about self-consciousness (1975:7). Their concern with boundaries then was between communities, and how these are considered as necessarily oppositional, occurring as a reaction between one social system and another (Wallman, 1978:205).

However, this means that in general, despite attempts since Barth to de-essentialise the notion of the ethnic category, it still often remains understood as characterised by primordial criteria and as a politicised cultural homogeneous group. The concept of ethnicity remains bound up with tradition, folklore and nationalist ideology.

But if the anthropologist treats the ethnic group as a politicised cultural group, as A.P. Cohen does (1994a; 1998), how does the anthropologist fit in those people who feel, in the case of the Basque Country, for example, Basque, but do not have any political awareness of their 'Basqueness'? Or is the socio-cultural group to be regarded as an ethnic group of its own? This is how Shore (1993) for example analysed the Italian Communist Party and its members: as an ethnic group with its own web of shared meanings, special customs, ways of speaking, behaving, and choosing and using symbols. The same can be said about the various political groupings which claim to be the 'real' Basques.

But the concept of the ethnic group is problematic because it is too restrictive. It sustains a reification of personal identity as bound to the 'ethnic' group. As Calhoun noted, "there are always internal tensions and inconsistencies among the various identities and group memberships of individuals" (1994:28). Terms like 'group', 'category' and 'boundary' still connote fixed identity, and the ability of individuals to express their own notions of the self is ignored.

A.P. Cohen, as one of the most outspoken critics of the idea that ethnic identity can be generalised to all members of the group, argued that ethnicity is continually reconstructed on the collective level thanks to the individual members of the group (1994a; 1994b). He pointed to the need to be aware of the individual variations that can exist within an ethnic group, talking of boundaries as things that acquire meaning in the minds of individuals (1985:12; 1994a; 1994b; 1998). While Barth suggested that the boundaries between groups are of primary definitional importance, Cohen drew attention to the risk of erroneously thinking that the understanding of these boundaries is equally shared by all members of the group. Members have their own ways of defining their membership and understanding their ethnic group and they express this through their own use of symbolic boundaries. They may share many common characteristics of a prototypical ethnic identity, but not all (Mahmood and Armstrong, 1992). Ethnicity thus becomes a construct conditioned not only by inclusive/exclusive external boundaries but also by the existence of internal boundaries drawn up by members of the ethnic group in relation to each other, and thus is perpetuated by the different visions and experiences of both members and outsiders, whether they are in agreement or not.

While Cohen called for a focus on individual consciousness in the use of ethnic boundaries, Douglass, Lyman and Zulaika (1994) also pointed to the possibility of a lack of internal cohesion in the ethnic group, drawing attention to the internal problems of minority groups such as Chicanos, Asians and American Indians in the United States. These groups use categories to define who is a 'faithful' member and who is not, talking in disparaging terms of those who show too much willingness to integrate into the dominant culture (1994:70-2). Douglass, Lyman and Zulaika thus showed that boundary-drawing also takes place within the ethnic group and not just in relations with outsiders. The same thing has been noted in the case of the Basques, where attitudes to the notion of a Basque 'ethnic identity' are far from consensual. There are tensions between nationalist and non-nationalist Basques (Heiberg, 1980, 1989; Douglass *et al.*, 1994), as well as between different kinds of Basque nationalists, with some believing they are more 'genuine' than others.

In a broader context, social scientists are confronted with the challenge of dealing with the multitude of social and cultural experiences acquired today in the context of globalisation. As Said points out, "no one today is purely one thing" (1993:407). Caglar has also noted that since the 1980s at least, the world has been marked by what she called "unprecedented translocal flows" of people, capital and technology (1997:169), whereby people of different cultures mingle and mix, producing a whole new set of values and reference points. Responding to the questions regarding the self and identity in an age of 'globalisation', 'homogenisation', 'mass culture' and 'extensive communication', social scientists have made numerous attempts to break with tendencies to define identity as something fixed and functional and to move away from reifications of group identity. In an attempt to accommodate those people who increasingly define themselves in terms of multiple national attachments and who feel at ease with different subjectivities, Kershen (1998), Caglar (1997), Modood and Werbner (1997) and others, rather than questioning the use of the word 'identity', have sought to adapt

their analytical approach by presenting identity as something fluid, changing and multi-dimensional. Pieterse (1995) for example, described 'hybridisation' as "the ways in which forms become separated from existing practices and recombine with new forms in new practices" (1995:84) and, as
such, offering "revolutionary antidotes to essentialist notions of culture,
identity and ethnicity" (Caglar, 1997:172).

Reflecting the increased mobility of people across state and national territories, the concept of the 'transnational' has been developed to describe the
'identity' of these people whose experience of self is affected by their high
mobility and consequent intake of a great variety of cultural symbols. It
seems to me, however, that these alternative definitions continue to be
based precisely on those foundations from which they claim to move away.
The ideas of hybridity or creolisation continue to presuppose some kind of
'cross-over', or accommodation of various whole and fixed parts. Furthermore, experiences of 'transnationalism' entail different things for different
people, such that the term, in my opinion, ceases to have analytical value.

Among others, Werbner and Modood (1997) put forward the idea of 'multiple identity', whereby an individual builds up and expresses a range of
identities based on personal experience. Examining the idea that a person
can have more than one group allegiance at the same time, Sangrador
(1996) and Moreno (1997) discussed the ability of regional populations in
Spain to feel a sense of 'national identity' in some cases and of more narrow
collective identities in other cases. In the Basque context, respondents were
asked about the 'possibility' of feeling Basque and something else, such as
'also' or 'equally' 'Spanish' or 'also' or 'equally' 'European'. While demonstrating the possible compatibility of several social, cultural and political attachments at the same time, these accounts, however, shed no light on
the formation and everyday expression of identity. In evoking the concept
of 'multiple identity', they continue to assume that 'identity' is a root base
and that the various identifications are fixed and uniform in their nature
rather than fluid and eclectic. Again, these new concepts of identity appear
to me as mere covers for an understanding of identity as a mish-mash of
different fixed identities.

Discussions of identity use the term with different meanings, from fundamental and abiding sameness, to fluidity, contingency, negotiated and so on.
Brubaker and Cooper note a tendency in many scholars to confuse identity
as a category of practice and as a category of analysis (2000:5). Indeed,
many scholars demonstrate a tendency to follow their own preconceptions
of identity, following more or less the frameworks listed above, rather than
taking into account the mechanisms by which the concept is crystallised as
reality. In this environment, some analysts, such as Brubaker and Cooper,
have suggested doing away with the concept completely (2000:1). Others,
by contrast, have sought to introduce alternative concepts in an attempt to
capture the dynamic and fluid qualities of human social self-expression.

Hall (1992, 1996), for example, suggests treating identity as a process, to take into account the reality of diverse and ever-changing social experience. Cuche (1996), Guibernau and Rex (1997) and Passerini (1998; 2000) introduce the idea of identification, whereby identity is perceived as made up of different components that are 'identified' and interpreted by individuals.

Shifting the Focus: Symbolic Boundaries

One of the first challenges for the researcher wishing to carry out empirical research in this area is to identify an appropriate analytical tool. It is in response to this requirement that I chose in my fieldwork to use the concept of boundaries for exploring 'identity'. In the same way that Barth approached 'ethnicity', advocating a focus on the boundary "that defines the group rather than the cultural stuff that it encloses" (1969:15), I wish to shift the focus of analytical study from identity to the boundaries that are used for purposes of identification. If identity is a kind of virtual site in which the dynamic processes and markers used for identification are made apparent, boundaries provide the framework on which this virtual site is built.

While the term 'boundary' is familiar in the social sciences, particularly as used by Barth and his followers in the domain of social anthropology, it has largely been employed in the context of attempts to understand group definition (e.g. Kershen, 1998; Lamont, 1992). So for example Heiberg (1980:45), for her analysis of Basque society, draws on Barth's concept of social boundaries which she describes as providing "the interfaces for the necessary process of social classification and ordering. They are the means by which those who are perceived as 'similar' are separated from those who are perceived as significantly 'different'". She notes that "a system of social boundaries is as complex, fluid and, at points, contradictory as the social structure of which it forms part" (1980:45). However, once again, it turns out that what she is concerned with is groups within Basque society,[8] when she says "the nature of this boundary and the *cultures* which it marks and separates have altered radically over the last 100 years or so" (1980:46. My italics).

Cohen (1992; 1994a; 1994b; 1996; 1998) went beyond Barth and his followers such as Heiberg by concentrating on how the idea of community belonging is differently constructed by individual members, how individuals within the group conceive ethnic boundaries. My approach to boundaries differs from both Barth's and Cohen's approaches in that my concern is with how individuals express a sense of self in social interaction.[9] Sökefeld

---

[8]   As noted in Chapter Three, Heiberg distinguishes between 'Basques' and 'Basques anti-Basques', following the terminology of her informants in the Basque Country (1980; 1989).

[9]   Other scholars have come close to my idea by talking of personal symbolic interpretation and strategy-making for the expression of personal identity (Lévi-Strauss,

(1999) proposes a similar approach in his account of personal construction of self in an area of northern Pakistan characterised by a plurality of conflicting identities.

As a non-directive and flexible analytical tool, the concept of boundaries helps both to map and to define the changeability and mutability that are characteristic of people's experiences of the self in society. I take as my point of departure the idea that, while identity is a volatile, flexible and abstract 'thing', its manifestations and the ways in which it is exercised are often open to view. Identity is made evident through the use of markers such as language, dress, behaviour and choice of space, whose effect depends on their recognition by other social beings. This is something long recognised in the social sciences. I wish to go further by pointing out that, while markers help to create the boundaries that define similarities or differences between the marker wearer and the marker perceivers, their effectiveness depends on a shared understanding of their meaning. In a social context, misunderstandings can arise due to a misinterpretation of the significance of specific markers. Equally, an individual can use markers of identity to exert influence on other people without necessarily fulfilling all the criteria that an external observer might typically associate with such an abstract identity.

To give an example, a person wearing a policeman's uniform may not be a policeman but simply be dressed up as such for a fancy dress party. In order to capture the deeper meaning of the dress marker, and its consequences for the wearer's identity, it is necessary to see how it is used by the wearer and how it is interpreted by other people. Were the wearer to stand in the street directing traffic, the marker would become a clear boundary between him and other people, defining him as a policeman and eliciting a corresponding response from drivers. If, on the other hand, he is seen dancing at a party, his policeman's uniform will not be taken as part of an exclusive boundary defining him as a policeman, but rather as part of an inclusive boundary placing him in the same group as other people at the party wearing fancy dress. That isn't necessarily the end of the matter, however. Reactions to this person's choice of fancy dress may vary among the other people at the party. Another person might assume, for instance, that the man dressed as a policeman feels an affinity for the police force. On this basis, if this second

---

1977; Camilleri, Kastersztein, Lipiansky *et al.*, 1990; Bourdieu and Wacquant, 1992a; 1992b). They acknowledge that people employ different 'strategies' in order to display their notions of self, in such a way as to enable the process of identity formation and affirmation to be observed. Douglass, Lyman and Zulaika (1994:11) put forward the idea that, consciously or unconsciously, a person 'activates or disactivates' different aspects of his or her public sense of self, in accordance with the situation of the moment, creating and expressing identity through association, resistance or rejection of other people and symbols. This, however, remains to be demonstrated empirically.

person has an antipathy for the police, he may act aggressively towards the man dressed as a policeman: the dress marker creates a boundary separating two people who otherwise might have been united by it, even if the second person's assumption is not a true reflection of the first person's intention or attitude. Still further permutations can be considered, if for example the wearer of the policeman's uniform has adopted it deliberately to mislead people around him, for example to conduct a robbery.

In this way, we see that identity becomes merged with, and depends on, identification. Boundaries can be inclusive or exclusive depending on how they are perceived by other people. An exclusive boundary arises, for example, when a person adopts a marker that imposes restrictions on the behaviour of others. An inclusive boundary is created, by contrast, by the use of a marker with which other people are ready and able to associate. At the same time, however, an inclusive boundary will also impose restrictions on the people it has included by limiting their inclusion within other boundaries. An example of this is the use of a particular language by a newcomer in a room with people speaking various languages. Some people may understand the language used by this person, while others may not. Those who do not understand it might take the newcomer's use of this particular language merely as a neutral sign of identity. But they might also perceive it as imposing an exclusive boundary that is meant to mark them off from her. On the other hand, those who do understand the newcomer's language could take it as an inclusive boundary, through which the new-comer associates herself with them to the exclusion of the other people present. Equally, however, it is possible that people who do understand the newcomer but who also speak another language may not want to speak the newcomer's language and so see her marker as an imposition and a negative boundary. It is possible that the newcomer is either aware or unaware of this, depending on whether she herself knows other languages or is con-scious of the plurilingual quality of the people there and is respectful of it or not.

Anthropologists have already noted how symbols can be appropriated by individuals in ways that have meanings different from those originally or conventionally intended (e.g. Willis, 1977; Douglas and Isherwood, 1979; Miller, 1995; Appadurai, 1996). The symbolic and social context in which individuals find themselves is used and interpreted differently by them for the construction of their uniquely personal sense of identity. At the same time, the individual's sense of self is influenced by his or her surroundings. And as the symbolic and social context changes, so do the person's sense of self and his or her desires of how to be understood by others (Cohen, 1998:23-33; Douglass, 1999:38-9). People can manipulate boundaries to their own individual advantage and refashion their selves in a variety of ways at different moments in time.

My observation of this in my field research led me to consider the possibility that, contrary to conventional views of identity as homogeneous within a given social or ethnic community, people may be selective in their appropriations of different aspects of identity according to circumstances. While this is not a new discovery in the social sciences, this basic recognition is essential for beginning to understand how people with different notions of the self and different views and attitudes and categorisations of others can interact with relative harmony in otherwise sometimes tense socio-political situations. People make their own personal niches within society through a careful choice of interactions with others and public presentations of their selves (Goffman, 1967).

An individual's identity is a reflection of the ability consciously or unconsciously to apply a multiplicity of boundaries, with the adoption of any one boundary at any particular time implying belonging to a social group or idea within that particular boundary and distance from or rejection of those outside it. A person may use different boundaries at different moments, depending on the situation and the objectives of social interaction. Some boundaries are more easily moved, or 'switched', than others. In the case of language, for example, a person who knows Basque may choose to speak it with other Basque-speakers in one context but not in another. A person who does not know Basque may choose to learn it, thereby adding a potential new marker to the range of possible boundary choices available to him. Alternatively, such a person can choose to demonstrate his sense of Basqueness by adopting other boundary markers, such as style of dress or taste in music. In addition, some people may adopt and apply the same boundaries for different purposes and with different results in a range of different contexts.

My focus on the individual is justified by the need to appreciate that each individual contributes to the collectivity. By taking identity as made up of an infinite variety of symbolic boundaries played out by individuals at different times and under differing circumstances within society, we can begin to answer the question of what is identity.

Theoretical Elaboration of Frontiers and Borders

Frontiers are classically associated with the notion of the modern nation-state. The frontier is generally regarded as a physical demarcation, defining where the territory of one state ends and that of another begins. They are, according to political scientist Malcolm Anderson, "the basic political institution: no rule-bound economic, social or political life in advanced societies could be organised without them" (1998:4). As a representation of the territorial limits of the state, the frontier has also conventionally been understood as the circumscription of the territory within which the residing population feels identified with the state and shares in a 'national' identity. Geographers have played an important role in opening the way for this appreciation of border areas as locations with a social and political dynamic very different from that of non-frontier zones (Prescott, 1987). Their analysis has helped political and social scientists to appreciate the frontier as having a particular role in the formation of a sense of difference between populations on either side of it and in the creation of the 'nation' in line with the state of which either side forms part.

The international border often has a peculiar quality of no-man's land. It is a space that is 'betwixt and between' two distinctly culturally marked territories. The frontier, as a mere transit point, presents itself as what Augé (1995) has called a *non-lieu*, a non-place that is not culturally defined (1995:34) but rather a social space of its own (1995:82). Lavie and Swedenburg see in border zones sites of "creative cultural creolisation, places where criss-crossed identities are forged out of the debris of corroded, formerly (would-be) homogenous identities", and where one experiences the "feeling of being trapped in an impossible in-between" (1996:15).

Indeed, a particular characteristic of borders as social spaces is the way in which local populations live with the state frontier as a factor in their daily existence. This has led to the concept of 'border identity' as some kind of unique sense of self found amongst inhabitants of border areas (Wilson and Donnan, 1998).[10] As a space where two or more states meet and end, the border is an area in which the presence of the state in the human landscape is particularly evident. Elements that identify the state, from the language of road signs and advertisements to the style of urban architecture and the uniforms of state officialdom, are visible in abundance until they suddenly cease at the frontier. This makes it starkly evident to the person crossing that he or she is going from one particular space to another. Just as in ritual passages, this change in context obliges the individual to reflect on his or her position in relation to the changing environment (Van Gennep, 1960).

In the political sciences, concerned as they are more with the larger political and institutional consequences of frontiers, borders in Europe have traditionally been regarded as mere peripheral zones, assumed to have a 'static' or 'frozen' quality (Anderson, 1996). As from the late 1980s, however, the Schengen Agreement of the EU brought about a change in the nature and perception of borders. Many border areas have become sites of active economic and cultural interchange (Ricq, 1992; Leresche, 1995). This has aroused new interest among both state and institutional political theorists and policy makers. With the breakdown of border controls, local institutions and organisations on either side of frontiers have begun forging stronger links of cross-border cooperation. This trend has been particularly encouraged by

---

[10]   See also project consortium on 'Changing Identities, Changing Nations, Changing Stories in European Border Communities' on http://www.borderidentities.com funded by the EU Fifth Framework Programme.

financial assistance from the EU, in the form of the INTERREG programme specifically geared in the economic development of peripheral regions and border areas (O'Dowd and Wilson, 1996:12-3). This new dynamism of border areas has prompted some theorists to talk of an erosion of the sovereignty of the modern nation-state, from above by the construction of Europe, and from below by the greater self-assertion of localities and other sub-national authorities (Loughlin, 1994). As discrete socio-economic areas providing fertile ground for different cultural, economic and political discourses and as potentially new dynamic areas in the wider context of the EU, European borders have lately attracted increasing interest on the part of researchers in the political and economic sciences and legal studies.[11]

Borders are interesting not just as sites permitting the construction and interplay of competing national identities but as contexts in which to explore both the multivocality and the multilocality of place. Place after all, is given meaning by human interpretation. It acquires a multiplicity of meanings through diverse and often competing views of the geographical landscape, which, at the end of the day, is inherently social. While the frontier is and remains a real dividing line in political and social terms, it also has significance in symbolic terms as a boundary relevant to individuals in their construction and expression of personal identity. Crossing the frontier means different things to different people. While some people are very much aware of moving from one context to another, others can remain largely unaware of it. In some cases, this can be a source of frustration for people who regard the frontier as an important line of demarcation. Cohen, for example, comments on how he would wish English people to be more conscious of the fact that they have crossed some kind of boundary and entered another social context when they come from England to Scotland. This remark is illustrative of the different and often competing use of symbols. I add to Cohen's remark that it may not be so much a question of English people being unaware of their crossing the border but rather of actually not wanting to recognise it, as part of their self assertion in what they believe to be their space.

While frontiers and borders define the limits of contiguous societies, boundaries are abstract divisions which appear routinely not just between cultures but between individuals who, despite sharing similar cultural markers, interpret these abstract divisions differently. By looking at how boundaries are transformed by individuals, we can begin to understand the qualitative and diverse nature of collective boundaries. While frontiers are political spaces objectively marking which state the areas on either side belong to, boundaries are subjective referents of the frontiers. As a 'social fact', the frontier is given meaning when a person consciously or unconsciously makes it into a sym-

---

[11]   Examples for the Basque Country: Letamendia *et al.* (1994); Cambot (1998); Jáuregui *et al.* (1997).

bolic boundary (Cohen, 1998) in his or her personal symbolic struggle as part of the socio-cultural context.

Anderson (1996), in a review of the changing use of the concepts of frontier, border and boundary in the political sciences, makes a clear distinction between the three. In his definition, the frontier applies not only to the precise demarcation line where two State jurisdictions meet, but to the area around it (1996:8-9). In this way, he understands the frontier as a zone of contact in which neighbouring populations maintain relations of contiguity. The border, by contrast, is taken by Anderson to mean both the demarcation line and the zone around it, marked by the changing presence of the relevant states, while the boundary is used to refer to the actual line of delimitation (1996:8-9).

These definitions stand in stark contrast to the definitions attributed in the anthropological discipline. Anthropology makes a distinction between frontiers and borders as matters of physical political fact and boundaries as matters of consciousness and experience. I follow Cohen (1994a; 1994b; 1998) in my use of the terms frontier, border and boundary as conceptual tools, limiting the term frontier strictly to its geographical and legal applications as a delimitation of state jurisdictions and using border to refer to the area on and close to the frontier whose landscape is affected by the presence of man in all its different ways. As for the term 'boundary', following Cohen, I use it as a basis for social differentiation. Contrary to the other terms, which are specific and geographical, a boundary is abstract and symbolic and individually interpretable. Using this concept of boundaries as symbolic manifestations of difference, we can analyse how certain people see and act within a certain reality of space, such as that of the frontier or the border and their social world in general.

Borders in Anthropological Study

In the social sciences, the study of borders in Europe has only recently attracted the attention of researchers.[12] This can largely be related to the broader debate about globalisation and the demise of the nation-state as the preeminent political structure of modernity. As the realms of society, culture, politics and economics become increasingly boundless and translocal, the analysis of notions of the self in the context of discrete cultural units and neatly identifiable socio-political groupings has been brought into question. Nonetheless, the physical structures of territory and government remain an everyday reality, continuing to influence and assist in people's construction of the self. Borders are key vantage points from which to view the processes of building and redefining the states, nations and transnational networks, which comprise

---

[12] For a review of border studies in the social sciences see Donnan and Wilson (1994; 1999).

the new Europe. Anthropologists' concern with the study of the human being in society inevitably leads them to focus on these particular and singular spaces.

The anthropologists Cole and Wolf (1974) and the historian Sahlins (1989) played a pioneering role in the appreciation of borders as sites of interest for the social sciences. Their work served to underline the importance of borders as instrumental in the construction and expression of identity. In the Italian region of Alto Adige, Cole and Wolf (1974) noted how the inhabitants of the two neighbouring villages, one traditionally German-speaking and the other Romance-speaking, had retained their sense of different identity despite being affected by the repeated shifting of the Austrian-Italian frontier during the two World Wars. Long after the political boundaries of the Austrio-Hungarian Empire had disappeared, cultural boundaries continued to divide the two villages in spite of the fact that they are now both situated within the territory of the Italian state. In everyday encounters, Cole and Wolf noted, the inhabitants of the two villages played down their differences. Yet, once in the company of their own cultural group, those of each village were quick to resort to stereotypes to explain the actions of their neighbours.

Sahlins (1989), in his study of the construction of state national identity in the Cerdanya, straddling the Franco-Spanish frontier to the East of the Pyrenees, noted how the existence of the frontier served to reinforce the formation of separate French and Spanish identities by providing a boundary across which to view the people on the other side. He observed how the inhabitants used the frontier for their own convenience, sneaking across it in order to avoid conscription and other civic obligations. This shows that the border is not just an imposer of difference, but can be used by the local inhabitants to their own advantage. From this, Sahlins proposed a model of national identity based on instrumental manipulation. When it was in their interest to associate themselves with their cross-border neighbours, local inhabitants asserted their common Cerdans identity. When it was in their interest to deny any involvement with their neighbours, for instance in situations of rivalry or political divisions, or when comparing the lifestyle, economic progress and cultural 'openness' of the contrasting state contexts, they emphasised their state national identity. With this case, Sahlins demonstrated how state national identity develops not only through the nationalisation projects of the state, but also through the interests of the local inhabitants. By incorporating the border into their social psychology over the centuries, they came to see each other as French or Spanish first and Cerdans and Catalan-speaking second; "their national disguises ended up sticking to their skin" (1989:269). From this, Sahlins has suggested a bottom-up approach to the construction of state national identity which remains relevant to analyses of identity in many border areas today.

With the recent transformation of frontiers, particularly in the EU, borders are recognised today as "meaning-making and meaning-carrying entities, parts of cultural landscapes which often transcend the physical limits of the state and defy the power of state institutions" (Donnan and Wilson, 1994:4).[13] Following this line of thought, recent academic analysis has focused on the "porosity", "permeability" and "ambiguity" of state borders, and on the consequences that these imply for a unified sense of state national identity (e.g. Douglass, 1998, 1999; Donnan and Wilson, 1999; Wilson and Donnan, 1998). By stressing the 'blurred' quality of borders, these anthropological accounts highlight borders as particular contexts in which people of theoretically opposed notions of identity can cohabit in many domains of daily living, thereby making the distinction between state national identities redundant. Moncusí (1999), for example, in his anthropological research in the Cerdanya, identified a unique kind of "reciprocal" relationship between the population on either side of the frontier in a symbiotic relationship that led to ambivalent attitudes towards French and Spanish identity (1999:127). In a similar vein, Leizaola (1999) focused on the phenomenon of dual nationality in the rural Basque border area to demonstrate the 'ambiguity' of French and Spanish national identity for some of its inhabitants and who, with such an ambiguity, claim to feel at home on either side of the frontier.

Common to the accounts of both Moncusí and Leizaola is the idea that when a common ethnic culture straddles a frontier, border inhabitants enjoy a special bond among themselves that over-rides any state boundary. It remains for me to point out however that this 'sense of community' regardless of the border depends on the other processes of political and cultural boundary-drawing of the people's identity. Some people who, despite meeting the so-called ethnic criteria that make them automatically part of the 'Basque community', may not identify with Leizaola's understanding of what this is. Such differences and disparities – and political tensions thereof – have been made evident throughout the ethnographic accounts in this book.

---

[13] In his study of the influence of the frontier in a borderland village in Nafarroa, anthropologist Douglass had already pointed out how local inhabitants had a utilitarian concept of the frontier. Not only did they use the frontier to their own advantage, for smuggling, shelter from state authorities and the like, but also, in other circumstances, ignored its existence, going back and forth and entertaining family, friendly and professional relations across it (Douglass, 1977).

An Anthropologist in the Basque Country: Methodology

Inevitably, the qualitative account of the anthropologist reflects her own "consciousness" (Cohen, 1994b:230). The researcher's culture and upbringing will affect her relationship with her informants, the treatment of the issues at stake and her interpretation of behaviour and events. It is necessary then for the anthropologist to consider her own understanding of herself before engaging in this sort of research and finally, in the analysis, to take into account the potential influence on other people of her presence.

The anthropologist cannot escape being identified by the cultural and historical contexts of the groups to which she belongs any more than the individuals studied can separate themselves from their groups. "Understanding", wrote Gadamer, "always implies a pre-understanding which is in turn pre-figured by the determinate tradition in which the interpreter lives and shapes his prejudices" (1979:158). "The history of the individual is never", asserts Bourdieu, "anything other than a certain specification of the collective history of his group or class" (1977:86).

My own upbringing has enabled me to experience different lifestyles and witness different ways of thinking and behaving, thereby facilitating my adaptation to different cultural environments and varying ways of social interaction. Born of an English father and a French mother, I have lived as a child with my family and as an adult on my own in six different countries. As a result, in addition to English and French, I am fluent in Spanish. While moving around, however, I have regularly returned to the home of my maternal grandmother in Iparralde during the holidays. As an undergraduate student of anthropology at Edinburgh University, I focused on the Basque Country, carrying out exploratory fieldwork in Hegoalde and eventually focusing on local political relations in a village in a rural part of Iparralde. Around this time, I also began taking lessons in Basque, initially following a summer course in Hegoalde and then other courses in Iparralde.

Through these activities, I became conscious of a world of Basque social and political life of which I had been unaware as a French-speaking child and teenager on holiday, not paying much attention to the fact that Basque people switched to French to include me in their conversations. I gradually came to form part of a network of people active around the issues of modern Basque culture and politics, while at the same time remaining slightly detached due to my personal life abroad. These experiences have helped me to acquire a sensitive appreciation of the local culture in all its facets, including not only Basque cultural and political movements but also the experiences of those inhabitants not so engaged in these trends. This I believe puts me in a good position to approach this study in its most just light (Marcus, 1998).

A certain detachment is necessary in order to ensure an unbiased recording of events and unemotional and strictly scientific analysis. It is fundamental for the researcher to remain neutral, avoiding the temptation to identify too much with the actors under study (Hastrup and Hervik, 1994). The anthropologist must be able to understand issues from the inside and empathise with people's experiences and points of view. By taking part in social interaction, the researcher is able to make sense of it. At the same time, however, a balance between subjectivity and objectivity is required (Bourdieu, 1977). From my own personal experience and sense of self, I believe I have been able to empathise with the various experiences and visions of the different people with whom I have dealt without becoming too deeply involved or judgemental. I believe that this has been crucial in my attempt to produce an unbiased and objective interpretation of events in the field.

As someone coming into the area from outside, I became aware of the need felt by the people whom I met to situate me within a context. My ability to draw on my possession of a wide range of markers and boundaries assisted me in my own identity construction in relation to people around me. So I also engaged in the play of identity. For instance, I realised that both my Basque roots and non-Basque origins served me as markers and potential boundaries. Knowing that my grandmother was Basque helped some people to place me in a familiar context. Often I found it opened doors more easily. When introducing me to people, some individuals would mention the fact that my grandmother came from a village close to their own, a piece of information that served for them as an important reference point, helping me to gain access to some kind of common 'club'. I learnt from these experiences to exploit this characteristic of mine, and to drop it propitiously during preliminary contacts with some informants to gain the necessary further openness on their part. This happened, for example, when I went to interview another municipal councillor of Hendaia at his home. Sensing his reserve after I had introduced myself simply as a researcher with an unusual name from a foreign university, I switched to Basque and explained my own family attachments to the rural hinterland after I had heard him chat to his son in Basque on the phone and mention in passing that his father was born in a village not far from mine. From that moment on, the formality of the interview was thawed.

In Hegoalde, where many people are not familiar with the rural parts of Iparralde, I noticed that mentioning my attachments there often gave me an exotic aura. It seemed to many people that there was something 'authentic' about being from this rather secluded area of the Basque Country, which appeared to many to evoke serenity and simplicity, compared to the more stressful urban and nationalistic ambience of the coastal area of Hegoalde where they lived. When conversing with Basque-speakers, my French Basque accent was welcomed by many in Hegoalde as 'much softer' than their own. It appears to me that this image was again related to their idea of 'authenticity', of a Basque ideal devoid of the political connotations which they felt the Basque language had now acquired in Hegoalde amid political debates and the spread of the standardised Basque language, Batua. With hindsight, I recognise now that if I did not make much effort during this fieldwork period to adapt my way of speaking to those around me, it was precisely because I noticed these often positive reactions.

In general, I also noticed that mentioning my Basque connections helped people to understand better my interest in carrying out research in the Basque Country. It appeared that such connections provided a legitimate justification for my research interest. When I sometimes introduced myself simply as an English researcher, I encountered perplexity and reserve. I suspect that many people, particularly those without nationalist affiliations, thought that my academic interest in the Basque Country was most likely to lie, as assumed by the law professor quoted in the first annex, in a fascination for the somewhat trendy subject of 'nationalism', and that I therefore had no interest in looking at 'ordinary', less sensational, experiences. As a result, some people living peacefully on what they believed to be the margins of Basque politics could not understand why I should want to talk to them. In such situations, I had to explain clearly my personal background and my status as an academic researcher aiming to approach local issues in a neutral and apolitical way, with 'nationalism' far from being my sole or primary research interest.

At other times, by contrast, to present myself as English first had its own advantages. It provided me with completely different markers from others around me and thus exempted me, as an outsider, from political categorisation. Only on one occasion did the fact of saying I was English have an adverse effect, when it prompted some particularly extreme supporters of the 'minority' discourse to take it as a negative boundary, expressing their dislike of the English, both in relation to the situation in Northern Ireland and as the embodiment of everything to do with globalisation, anglicisation, dominating discourses and the hierarchisation of languages.

Since language plays a central role in the formation, interaction and expression of identity, it was valuable for me as a researcher, to be able to shift between the different languages. I am fluent in French and Spanish, and have a fair knowledge of Basque. Speaking Basque enabled me to gain access to a part of the Basque world from which I would otherwise have been excluded. For elderly euskaldun zaharrak, or mother tongue Basque-speakers, not involved in politics, the fact that I could speak Basque was often both welcome and surprising, prompting many to open up to me more easily as they felt there was a common bond between us both in our ability and enjoyment of speaking Basque and desire to understand each other in this language.

My ability to speak Basque won positive reactions from Basque-speakers in the nationalist community, amongst whom the discovery that I, as an outsider, had made the effort to learn Basque, often helped to win respect. On numerous occasions, it even gained me a form of honorary membership of local Basque society. So, for instance, some newly made friends in the left-wing nationalist circle in Hondarribia categorically declared me 'euskaldun', stating that "although you are English, you are from here".

But my efforts to learn Basque sometimes had an adverse effect, notably amongst local inhabitants who had no interest in Basque nationalism or who were actively opposed to it and who took my interest in learning Basque as a sign that I must have different attitudes to them and perhaps even that I had nationalist sympathies. In such circumstances, I had once again to explain my personal background and scientific interest in learning the language, at times arousing in response an attempt on the part of my interlocutors to justify their own lack of interest.

With other people, by contrast, I often found it best to stick to French or Spanish, rather than to speak Basque, which might be taken as a politically motivated move on my part. In situations of this sort, the national language provides a relatively neutral mode of communication compared to Basque. It does not impose on the informant any seemingly Basque nationalist insinuations. Furthermore, in Iparralde, it is relatively uncommon still to hear people of my age speaking Basque. It would therefore be considered much more 'normal' for me to initiate the conversation in the state national language. This need to alter my mode of communication according to the speakers and the context also shows how, as the ethnographer, I am an element within the social interaction I am examining.

While by definition present within the context of what I saw and heard in the course of my field observations, I nonetheless sought in accordance with anthropological practice to neutralise the impact of my own presence as far as possible in order to avoid influencing the interaction of the subjects of my study. Through participant-observation, the anthropologist can also acquire a deeper knowledge and thorough understanding of the social group under study. Directed interviews and the gathering of statistics provide only a partial picture. In order to acquire 'scientific' (Pérez-Agote, 1986; 1999) understanding of the social being, the researcher needs to take time to go beyond initial impressions.

Through experience, I learned to avoid asking direct questions such as "Do you feel Basque? How? What are your political views?" Because of the delicate nature of the issues at stake, such questions were likely to be unproductive or even counter-productive. Instead, I let people react to me in their own way, revealing in the process many interesting expressions of boundaries. Thereby, I avoided frustrating situations in which, were I to ask a direct question which seemed obvious and unproblematic to me, I would only receive a vague and ambiguous answer.

Both Heiberg (1989:x) and Urla (1987:5) mentioned finding their social mingling restricted to a large extent to a certain segment of the population; in Heiberg's case to the Basque nationalists (whether she means Basque nationalists in general or sympathists of a certain branch is unclear) and in Urla's case to those 'traditionally' Basque (as opposed to the Spanish immigrants). Heiberg noted that during her fieldwork in the mid to late 1970s, it was difficult to be acquainted with both "nationalists" and "non-nationalists" at the same time: "Free movement from the nationalist camp to the non-nationalist one was permitted", she says, but not so easily the other way round (1989:x). Heiberg carried out her research at a politically extremely tense moment when distrust between different political camps was particularly acute. Urla, carrying out her research at the turn of the 1980s, explains that "Castellanos[1] and Basques are strongly polarised in the community", which meant that she found it difficult to establish a similar relationship with both of them (1987).

My experiences have been rather different. Two decades after Urla and Heiberg's research, I found the social and political divide in Bidasoa-Txingudi to be less clear-cut. I found it not uncommon, even in seemingly very 'traditional' Basque families proud of a long list of Basque surnames and residence in the same house over several generations, to find family members married with people coming from outside the Basque Country. Even in such families, too, the political affiliations may be starkly opposed. Some of the members may be supporters of the moderate and traditionalist Basque nationalist party EAJ, others more radical Basque independentists, while still others may proclaim themselves supporters of Spanish or French parties, or even reject any involvement in "all this political stuff".[2] So while social relations between people do follow certain patterns according to place of origin, time lived in the area and local experiences, I found evidence of at least some basic mingling which makes suggestions of polarised ethnic categorisation difficult to accept. Secondly, despite the tensions caused by ETA's continued violence and the differences in the reactions and interpretations of political parties in relation to nationalism and violence, I found it possible to mingle with different kinds of people whose political allegiances, if any, were not always clear. In my own activities in the area, I found myself mingling in different social

---

[1] Castellano literally means Castilian. Heiberg uses it to refer both to a person who speaks 'Castilian', or Spanish, as a mother tongue, and who does not have Basque ancestors. In my field research, I did not hear the word used in this way. Rather, I only heard it used as an alternative name for the Spanish language.

[2] Statement picked up from various informants in the field.

circles, many of which were interconnected. In doing so, I was able to observe friendships between people of varying political tendencies. For instance, when I took Basque lessons with AEK in Hendaia, I was introduced to a certain social circle of people of more or less Basque militancy. I met some of these people again in other circles that were more 'French' in the local political and cultural sense of the word.

My personal appearance and style of dress also helped me to integrate in different social circles. The way I dressed was broadly neutral in relation to trends in the Basque Country. Going to Basque festivities, I could have dressed in a similar way to other participants, for example by wearing one of the various t-shirts adorned with Basque logos, in an attempt to fit in. That would have been appreciated by Basque nationalists, but it would have been inconvenient for me if I had then encountered someone from a different social and political circle. Amongst members of left-wing nationalist circles in Hegoalde, I think that my different style of dressing was simply taken as part of my personal 'identity' as a young woman coming from outside the Basque Country.

On some occasions in Hegoalde, when people with whom I conversed in Spanish did not know who I was, many simply assumed I was French. This in itself was interesting since it came out that French was the immediate 'other' thought about. It also permitted me to experience what it must be like to be treated as a French person by some of these people. It made me the butt of many jokes about 'gabachos' even when the people knew that I was not just, or not entirely French, but something more complicated than that. In other cases, some people remained rather reserved with me until they found out that I was not exactly 'French', when the comments about French people which they had until then abstained from making would come out. So I inadvertently found myself participating in the play of identity, using some boundaries rather than others depending on their possible value to me as a researcher. In this way, I was able to function both as an insider and as an outsider.

Since it was important for me to witness different social interactions, I mingled in all sorts of circles, becoming a kind of social chameleon. To some people, my presence in different situations, say at a late-night bar frequented by left-wing nationalist sympathists in Irun after having been in a tranquil tea-room earlier in the day with local people not involved in Basque politics at all, may have appeared rather peculiar. Even some people to whom I had already explained what I was here to do would appear surprised at seeing me in different contexts, indicating the degree to which identity is polarised by the political situation in the Basque Country. Reactions to my presence varied. A left-wing nationalist militant of Hendaia, for instance, with whom I had become quite friendly after a few interviews to the point where our frequent bumping into each other at various events became a running joke for him, once mentioned that he wondered whether I was not some kind of spy. Other less direct and initially more reserved people would inquire about me to other people who had more information about me.

It is seldom easy to explain clearly to people in the field what one's research is about (Rose, 1990; Davies, 1999). I attempted to make my explanations basic. As is evident from some of the observations made above, people had different interpretations of what my research study could be about. Usually, in casual conversations, I simply said my research was about "life in the area, relations between the inhabitants of the three towns since the existence of the cross-border cooperation agreement, issues of identity, behaviour, what the Partzuergo is doing, what do people think about it and how are they affected by it". As I gradually became an accepted member of some social circles, some people came to forget what I was actually there for. This was often very convenient since it meant that they were not on their guard as to how they behaved and expressed themselves in front of me. At other times, however, it was less advantageous as people I came to know well sometimes forgot that inviting me to certain events or introducing me to certain people would be of interest to me. Again, this may have reflected a misconception of the nature of my anthropological interest.

Many people active in the Basque left-wing nationalist movement gave me an exceptionally warm welcome on hearing about my research interests, reflecting what I found was a general enthusiasm among Basque militants at any expression of interest in the Basque Country. Numerous took it upon themselves to introduce me to their friends and contacts, to show me around and to bring me to their various social events. Many also took pains to give me their version of the history of the Basque Country, an important subject for Basque culturalists and nationalists given what they believe to be the indispensability of knowing 'one's own history', particularly in opposition to the versions predominantly provided by Spanish and French intellectuals. I was often invited to visit small villages in the rural hinterland, homes with collections of ancient artefacts and the workshops of people who practised a traditional craft or some eminent Basque scholar of local history. In addition to demonstrating the important role that 'tradition' plays in Basque identity, such invitations say something about the local understanding of anthropology and the supposed nature of the anthropologist's interests. Zulaika noted a similar phenomenon, observing that "even today, when asked about their mysterious origins, queer language or terrorist separatism, Basques are likely to feel compelled to enact the ethnographic person as created by anthropology" (1998:95).

I always felt welcomed into people's social lives and sometimes invited to share intimate aspects of their existence. Most of the time, there were no questions about who I knew and associated with at other times, since discretion seemed to be a general unspoken rule in the area. It was possible for me then to appear in a place and hang out with people there without being asked what I had been doing earlier in the day. This felt rather strange to me at first, but soon I realised that I was not going to be asked and so often there was no point in telling people since when I did, it was rarely taken as a cue for further conversation.

While at times there were clear limits to the extent to which some of my informants really confided in me, others were very open, in a manner for which I am extremely grateful, as such relationships, in addition to maturing into strong friendships, provided me with additional insights. In selecting certain incidents as examples of emblematic significance, I have endeavoured to respect the privacy of individuals concerned by preserving their anonymity.

Defining the Field

Choosing a fieldsite was relatively easy. Having decided that my interest lay in covering a border area where I could observe the interaction of different notions of identities among the inhabitants of Iparralde and Hegoalde, I wanted to find a modern urban community that reflected the cosmopolitan lifestyle common across Europe today. I was not looking for an 'authentic' Basque community that had somehow managed to survive, preserving intact a language, culture and social structure that is foreign to most Basques today. On the border, the most obvious place was the area formed by Irun, Hondarribia and Hendaia, since the rest of the border area in the Basque Country consists of mountains with only small towns or villages.

I had no preliminary knowledge of the area, having only been through it a few times on my way from a place on one side of the frontier to somewhere else on the other. Like many passing visitors and tourists, I knew Irun only as a point of transit, getting off one train and onto another, and as a place providing the last opportunity to purchase Spanish products before entering French territory, just as I knew Hendaia for its beach and Hondarribia for its picturesque old fishing quarter and medieval centre.

In order to become familiar with the area, I lived between two and three months in each town. I carried out my fieldwork in several stages, suspending it at regular intervals in order to return to my academic base and so to shift from practice to theory and back again (Briggs, 1986). This helped me to reflect on the observations made in the area in an appropriately objective-subjective fashion. Coming back to the field at regular intervals also made me notice change (Wengle, 1988). I became aware of the Partzuergo and its relevance to local life when I first arrived in the field. Soon, it became evident that the Partzuergo had a particular role in the locality, both reflecting local life and having a certain impact on it. My regular returns to the field over a space of three years allowed me to notice changes in the elaboration of the Partzuergo's activities and in the evolution of people's behaviour and attitudes.

My first period of fieldwork lasted three months, during the autumn of 1999. During this time, my aim was simply to get a good general understanding and impression of life in the area. Arriving in the field at the beginning of October, I based myself in Hendaia, where I rented a flat by the beach area. In order to facilitate my integration in the area, I began my fieldwork by doing an internship in a local business. I chose Sokoa for two main reasons: Firstly, I knew that it held an important though ambivalent position in Hendaia and Iparralde as a beacon for Basque nationalist aspirations. Secondly, as also both an investor and employer in Hegoalde, it is a good example of cross-frontier business cooperation and of a kind of border living.

My internship in Sokoa lasted three weeks. I spent the first week and a half in the office building, helping out with administrative work and generally observing interaction around me, how people related to each other and the languages they used. At lunch time, most of the staff would go and eat in the general canteen open to the workers of all the other businesses and factories in the area. This was then an opportunity to observe the employees of these other businesses, most of which were transport agencies or small production companies. As I spoke Basque, however, I found myself being invited to go to lunch by a particular group of four people who enjoyed speaking Basque to each other and shared certain Basque nationalist reference points.

I then moved on to the factory, where I assisted employees unloading material from lorries, assembling spare parts on conveyor belts and packaging office chairs for shipping. I also took part in a few union meetings. As I went about this work, I was able to build friendly relationships with employees. Many of my conversations with people took place informally as we went about our work. My time at Sokoa also helped me to get to know people whom I was later to meet in other contexts, in Hendaia, Irun and Hondarribia. I also became friends with Elisa, the receptionist, who introduced me to some of the nightlife of Irun, and with Sébastien, a factory worker, who showed me the more tranquil social life of Hendaia.

During this first period of fieldwork, I took part in a variety of activities in the area, which helped me to access different social circles in the three towns. Three times a week, I took evening classes in Basque at the Hendaia branch of AEK. This brought together people living in Hendaia, some of whom had come there from Hegoalde, of different ages from late teens to early sixties, all eager to learn Basque, many having forgotten it at an early age. Our teacher was a young native Basque speaker, whose parents were originally from Hegoalde but lived near Hendaia and who had been educated in French schools. She lived with her partner in his hometown of Irun. This experience with AEK, besides improving my Basque, enabled me to access the local social circle of supporters of new, modern notions of Basque culture and language revival.

Keen also to continue with my personal artistic interests alongside research, I attended ceramic classes twice a week in a centre funded by the municipality of Irun. There, I encountered a very different group of people, mainly women from middle-class backgrounds who worked part-time or not at all. Only two of the group of twenty could speak Basque or French. From our informal chats, and my observations, as we went about our activities, I gathered that most of them spent the bulk of their time in and around Irun and Hondarribia, rarely crossing the frontier into Iparralde. This experience opened up yet another aspect of local society, more Spanish-speaking, hardly motivated by Basque politics and with a more Spain-centred lifestyle. Many of the people had relatives from other regions of Spain, and significantly referred to place names in the Basque Country in different ways. For example, they referred to Donostia, as the capital of Gipuzkoa is known in Basque, as "SanSe", short for San Sebastian.[3]

In December 1999, I took an internship in one of Hendaia's two supermarkets, Stoc. I worked there for two weeks, stacking shelves and serving customers from behind the counter. Stoc and the other local supermarket, Champion, 500 metres down the road, are branches of supermarket chains present throughout France. They are also regular meeting-places for local people, who come to shop and chat with each other and with the supermarket employees. Old people, in particular, came every day to purchase their daily requirements. Employees were often acquainted with many of the regular customers in other ways, as neighbours, relatives, or childhood friends. Working at Stoc provided me with a framework in which to study Hendaia's inhabitants and to witness their interaction with Spanish-speaking people, as the supermarket also attracted customers from Irun, Hondarribia and other places in Hegoalde. It also provided me with an absolute contrast, culturally and linguistically, to Sokoa.

At the time I worked there, Stoc employed over thirty people. Two thirds lived in Hendaia and the rest in nearby villages in Iparralde. Six originally came from other parts of France and had settled in the locality for economic or family reasons. The manager originally came from north-east France and had been at this store for approximately two years. Only three members of staff spoke a little Basque. By contrast, about twenty spoke Spanish more or less fluently, in some cases because their parents were from Hegoalde and in some cases as a result of speaking to Spanish customers. Two years earlier, the management of Stoc had organised Spanish lessons for its employees in order to be able to deal more effectively with the great number of Spanish customers, but only a few took them. By contrast, the management had shown no interest in promoting the use of Basque among its staff. When AEK launched its campaign to encourage the use of Basque in

---

[3]   This, however, is also found amongst Basque-speakers in Iparralde. I heard some people in Hendaia for example talk about "Saint Sé" when speaking in French.

commercial establishments, Stoc did not participate.[4] During the time that I was at the store, I observed how some people who came from Hegoalde tried to speak French to the staff, but others spoke in Spanish or sometimes Basque. Some of those who spoke Spanish admitted to me that if they had known that the supermarket employees could speak Basque, they would have opted for Basque instead.

My internship at Stoc took place a few weeks before Christmas. This meant that there was a particularly high influx of people from Hegoalde. On two days that were public holidays in Spain but not in France, Stoc extended its opening hours in order to take advantage of an expected increase in business. Many more people from Hegoalde came to shop on those days, stocking up on French cheeses, yoghurt and especially 'chatka', a Russian delicacy of crabmeat that was being sold at a greatly reduced price.

During my first period of fieldwork in Hendaia, I noticed that articles in the local papers often mentioned the Partzuergo and its cultural activities. At that time, the formalisation of the cross-border cooperation agreement had just been celebrated. Realising the relevance of the Partzuergo's aspirations and activities for my research, I got in touch with members of its staff, interviewing some of them, and began finding out more about its activities. A few weeks after my arrival in Hendaia, the fourth annual Txingudi Eguna provided an opportunity to observe the Partzuergo in action. Through contacts made there, I was able to attend some of the Partzuergo meetings held to discuss its magazine Bidasoa-Txingudi. Thus I observed how the conceptualisation of the magazine took place and how the participants interacted in the process.

I also made contact with the cultural consultancy Maîtres du Rêve. Their work for the Partzuergo involved contacting local cultural associations and public figures to gather information about the area. I joined them on three of their interviews, with the president of the association of shopkeepers in Hendaia and representatives of two environmentalist associations of Hendaia, Txingudi Ecologie and Hendaye Environnement. By being present during these interviews, I was able to observe how Maîtres du Rêve went about obtaining material for the eventual writing up of a history of Bidasoa-Txingudi and laying out of a cultural itinerary. It was also interesting for me to observe how the interviewees responded to Maîtres du Rêve.

I returned to my academic base in January 2000 to work on the data I had obtained so far, going back briefly to the field during the Easter holidays in order to carry out interviews with the mayors of Irun and Hondarribia, municipal councillors, technicians of the Partzuergo and a selection of ordinary inhabitants. Planning my next period of fieldwork for the follow-

---

[4]   Interview with teacher of AEK in Hendaia, 21 December 1999. When I asked the secretary of Stoc about this campaign, she replied that she had not known about it.

ing summer, I arranged with the director of Txingudi Telebista to work as a volunteer journalist during the summer months. Contact with officials from the DATAR,[5] a French government-run agency dealing with territorial management involved in the monitoring of cross-frontier initiatives such as the Partzuergo, provided me with more in-depth knowledge about French government policies with regard to local and regional initiatives of cross-frontier cooperation. A visit also to the French Ministry of Culture further supplied me with information on the government's views on regional language development.

I returned to the field in June 2000 for my second phase of fieldwork. This time I settled in Irun and began working as a volunteer journalist for Txingudi Telebista.

Through my local news coverage and interviews, I was able to glimpse the wide range of social, cultural and political goings-on in the area. At the same time, from the inside of Txingudi Telebista, I was able to observe how this television enterprise functioned, how its employees interacted and, through their work, contributed in their own way to the construction of new local spatial concepts and notions of local identity. My greatest contribution to the television's work was in extending news coverage in Hendaia. In doing so, I helped Txingudi Telebista to give more substance to its name as the television of Txingudi.

As a member of the television team, I was also able to experience at first hand situations which I would not otherwise have been able to witness. I encountered hostility to Txingudi Telebista on the part of some sections of the local population, such as left-wing Basque separatists who dislike most non left-wing Basque nationalist media, or people in Hondarribia who despised Txingudi Telebista as one of the media organisations perceived as meddling in their Alarde, and specifically as an Irun organisation. So boundaries were drawn up between Txingudi Telebista and some local inhabitants despite its Irun, Hondarribia and Hendaia-englobing name.

Through my work in Txingudi Telebista, I became closely acquainted with Ana Grijalba Martinez, the wife of the director, and ended up living with her parents, with whom I became very close. Ana, having learnt Basque in her youth, is fluent in this language, but she is indifferent to the idea of Basque nationalist identity. As a journalist for the local television channel, she and her husband occasionally suffered harsh criticism from some radical Basque nationalists. At the same time, in Hondarribia, a local representative of the left-wing Basque nationalist party, whom I had interviewed, gave me much hospitality, inviting me to her house and to meet her children of a similar age to me. Thanks to them, I was introduced to their social circle. Many of their

---

5   Abbreviation for *Délégation à l'aménagement du territoire et à l'action régionale.*

friends were closely linked to or members of the left-wing Basque separatist youth group Haika (now Segi).

While I shifted easily from one context to the other, meeting various people in different contexts throughout the day, it became clear to me that there were clear boundaries between these different worlds. In February 2001, Ana Grijalba and another journalist colleague from Txingudi Telebista were featured on a list produced by the Irun branch of Haika, of people whom they proclaimed to be 'enemies of the Basque people'. One evening, when I was having a drink in Muara, the social club of the left-wing Basque nationalist movement in Hondarribia, I asked a friend who I knew to be an active member of this youth circle why this list had been drawn up. He answered that he had not been aware of it. He knew that I had worked at Txingudi Telebista and that I lived with the parents of Ana. The conversation on this subject simply did not go any further. Another example is illustrated by my encounter at a bertsolari competition (a Basque improvised recital context) organised by AEK in Hondarribia. I was invited to go by a member of the Hondarribia town council representing EH. Sitting beside her and her friends, I recognised a few rows below me a close friend of mine who happened also to be a municipal councillor in Hondarribia, but representing EA, the moderate independentist Basque nationalist party. I went up to him to greet him and have a chat. When I answered his question about who I had come with, the expression on his face turned stony and he made no comment. When I went back to my seat, the person who had invited me made no reference to my acquaintance with the other councillor.

I remained in the field until October 2000, thus witnessing how inhabitants of Irun, Hondarribia and Hendaia adapted their lifestyle to the summer. Many people took holidays during August but remained in the area, adapting to the presence of tourists and enjoying the numerous local fiestas, the open bars of Hondarribia and the beach of Hendaia.

I returned again to the field in January 2001, this time to live in Hondarribia for three months. I rented a room from a woman who came from a family of Hondarribian fishermen and lived alone in a small flat in an old neighbourhood near the fishing port of Hondarribia. This enabled me to integrate better into community life in Hondarribia than I had been able to do until then. Every day, I took coffee in a café called Gaxen, where local women and young families came for brunch or an afternoon snack. This café contrasted to Muara where I also occasionally went. Alongside it, Gaxen looked quaint with its framed posters of sea- and landscapes and watercolours on whitewashed walls in an ambience of new age and folk music. As a result, in Hondarribia as in the other places where I lived, I moved within different socio-cultural, political and linguistic milieus.

During this period, I stopped taking Basque lessons at AEK in Hendaia and carried on instead with the Basque government's own Basque language teaching system, HABE, provided by the municipality of Hondarribia (there was no AEK branch in Hondarribia). My aim was to see how different HABE was to AEK and who in Hondarribia would attend Basque lessons and for what motivations. Attending these lessons served also as a way of meeting more residents of Hondarribia. As in Hendaia, the age of the pupils ranged between seventeen and seventy-five. Most participants lived in Hondarribia but originally came from other parts of Hegoalde. All of the pupils I talked to mentioned speaking Basque as an important factor in community feeling in Hondarribia, citing this as one of their prime motivations for learning it. In this way they sought to acquire a marker which would favour their inclusion in the Basque language boundary of Hondarribia.

In order to observe how the Partzuergo worked from the inside, I arranged in February to carry out voluntary work in its offices for a month. At the time, the Partzuergo's technicians were located in different places, with two in offices in Irun and one in Hendaia. For reasons of practicality for the Partzuergo, I worked with the technician in Hendaia. I took part in various meetings between technicians of the Partzuergo and local councillors and association representatives. Again, as a temporary member of the Partzuergo technical team, I was able to assume a different status from that of anthropologist. My work for the Partzuergo required me to make contact with local people and introduce myself as a representative of the Partzuergo. It was interesting then to observe people's behaviour towards me as such.

Every day I would cycle from Hondarribia, through Irun, to the office in Hendaia. Every morning and evening, along this route, I was faced with the opposite flow of traffic of people driving to work from Hendaia to Irun or Hondarribia, or from Hondarribia to Irun. Because of the change in my working hours, I was obliged to stop taking my Basque lessons in Hondarribia, which had been in the mornings. Instead, I took evening classes with AEK in Irun, which opened to me yet another social context.

In February 2001, the campaign began for municipal elections in France, due to take place in March. All around me the various issues of concern to Hendaia's inhabitants were being voiced, leading sometimes to tensions and conflicts I would not have been able to observe otherwise. I attended public debates, political rallies and press conferences, interviewed candidates in their homes and generally took part in gossip with inhabitants in various contexts. Through my continued contact with Txingudi Telebista, I was also able to organise a television programme where, every night, we invited a candidate to explain his or her electoral programme.

Five groups, or lists, of candidates were competing in the elections. Raphaël Lassallette, who had served as mayor since 1981, had chosen not to stand again. He designated Kotte Ecenarro to take his place as leader of the coalition Hendaye Plurielle. Most of them had stood with Mr. Lassallette before. The other three lists included the left-wing Basque nationalist group Biharko Hendaia, headed by Robert Arrambide; two non-aligned groupings, one led by local entrepreneur Jean-Baptiste Sallaberry and the other, with a more right-wing tendency, by local businesswoman Carmen Hiribarren; and finally the Green party, led by a French teacher at the Hendaia ikastola, Serge Lonca. With the exception of Ms. Hiribarren, the leaders of these lists had already served on the municipal council in the minority. After the first round of two-stage elections,[6] a Socialist councillor who was initially on Mr. Ecenarro's list, Christian Butori, broke away to form his own list which he claimed would be genuinely 'left-wing'. He joined forces with the local Green Party to form another group together with a few more individuals with Communist sympathies. What was particularly interesting for me to note was that his new list did not appear to me to be any more plural or left-wing than Mr. Ecenarro's. While it included the Green party, together with members of the PS, there were no Basque nationalists.

In France, 2001 was the first year that residents not of French nationality but from another country of the EU could vote in municipal elections. It was interesting to note then how all of the lists in these elections included at least one person of Spanish nationality, in an effort to show open-mindedness to the changing demographic character of Hendaia and the increased numbers of residents of Spanish nationality.

Also noteworthy was the fact that all the lists mentioned the Partzuergo in their manifestos, though with varying degrees of frequency. The two non-aligned groupings mentioned it only briefly, saying that "it is something that must be approached very slowly. Little by little". What exactly was meant by that remained rather vague, even after I asked for elaboration. The head of one of these lists, Mr. Sallaberry, explained to me that "for many Hendaians, the Partzuergo can be quite scary. Hendaians are still concerned about the particular sociocultural character of their town and find the idea of Hendaia being more open to people from the other side of the frontier quite daunting". As for Biharko Hendaia, it reiterated its demands for a popular referendum on the Partzuergo and for it to be open to all political parties in the locality, effectively proposing the Partzuergo as some sort of cross-frontier parliament.

When the elections finally took place, the counting of votes at the town hall was an exciting moment, with many Hendaians waiting there to hear the results in an atmosphere of apprehension and suspense. Never had I seen the main square, the Place de la République, so lively. Mr. Ecenarro's list ended up winning with a majority, with the lists of Ms. Hiribarren, Mr. Sallaberry and Mr. Butori in the minority. Biharko Hendaia did not receive enough votes to have even one representative on the municipal council. Discussing afterwards with various local inhabitants the reasons for its demise, I was

---

[6]　There are two rounds in French municipal elections. After the first round, all those parties or lists which have not obtained more than a certain minimum of votes are excluded from the second and decisive round.

told that some people who usually voted for Biharko Hendaia had not appreciated the fact that, in the particularly tense period at the time, one of its candidates should be a Basque political refugee from Hegoalde. After counting, many people, irrespective of their support for different lists – apart from supporters of Biharko Hendaia, whom I did not see present – went off to one of the two main bars nearby, Café de la Poste and Café de la Bidassoa.

A month later, the next big excitement in the area was the coming through of the Korrika, AEK's marathon around the Basque Country. Taking part in the local organisation of the event with AEK, I was able to experience it from the inside.

Towards the end of April, I returned to my academic base to resume writing up my research. However, since this time, I have regularly returned to Bidasoa-Txingudi in order to check facts and to attend specific events. So in September 2001, I was present for the fiestas of Hondarribia, in October for some of the Partzuergo's events, and again in November 2001 and January 2002 for interviews. I was able to see what Bidasoa-Txingudi 'looked like' now that the euro was established as the common currency of both France and Spain. For local inhabitants going regularly back and forth across the frontier, life was made much less complicated in terms of carrying money around. In January 2002, interviews with Alain Lamassoure, local member of the European Parliament[7] and former Minister of Foreign Affairs who has been a pioneer of cross-frontier relations between the region of Aquitaine and Nafarroa and Euskadi, and Pablo Barros, Spanish Consul in Bayonne, revealed more about the point of view of the French and Spanish governments on the Partzuergo and other local initiatives of cross-frontier cooperation. While they both expressed a positive view of it, supporting it as part of a forward-looking and dynamic process, each of them intimated the need for sustaining close central governmental control of its development.

I returned to Bidasoa-Txingudi again in April 2002 for the Easter celebration in Hondarribia. More interviews with local figures with whom I had not yet had the opportunity of speaking were carried out until mid 2003.

Interviewing

Interviewing forms an important part of doing ethnography because of the valuable, culturally significant information that it provides. It serves as an ideal complement to participant observation since it enables the interviewer

---

[7] At the time of writing, he was also vice-president of the *communauté d'agglomération du BAB*, an initiative between the municipalities of Bayonne, Anglet and Biarritz to jointly manage certain urban issues, and which has undertaken the cross-frontier cooperation plan of the Euro Hiri with the town of San Sebastian.

to check what people say they do against what they actually do (Burawoy *et al.*, 1991). Both interviewing and participation are essential for obtaining a thorough grasp of the role of the individual informant as social actor (Crapanzano, 1992; Fowler and Hardesty, 1994).

I interviewed a large and varied selection of people in Bidasoa-Txingudi, including key players in regional and governmental institutions, and studied the political, social and economic visions of people in the locality at a wider level. Amongst local inhabitants, I interviewed people mainly aged between 20 and 85, who understood and lived out the local space and their sense of self in different ways. The aims of these interviews varied. Sometimes, they were purely to obtain factual information about a specific subject, be it a political group, an organisation, or some activities. On other occasions, they were to obtain the opinion of informants on certain issues which affected them. I asked them to explain certain things to me, according to how they understood and defined them, and to recount to me certain experiences and situations. My interview techniques varied accordingly. Above all, I was concerned that informants feel free to express what they saw as important to them. My interviews were therefore largely open-ended and semi-directed.

When possible, I also did informal interviews in order to allow the informant to feel more at ease and less self-conscious. These 'interviews' took place while carrying out daily activities, such as taking a drink in a bar, helping with household chores, serving behind the counter at the local supermarket, or assembling bits of ironwork in the factory. This helped to create a closer relationship with the people concerned (Kvale, 1996).

I used a tape recorder only when doing formal interviews. Sometimes, judging from the situation that the tape recorder could have a negative effect on the informant's ability to relax and open up, I refrained from taping and instead took notes from the conversation as precisely as possible, which I later wrote up, always striving to record as closely as possible what I re-membered my informants saying, how and in which context (Agar, 1986; Briggs, 1986). Many of my informants' quotes are *verbatim*, while others are the product of my notes and memory.

Not all of my informants' names are real. When describing the private, intimate life of some of my informants, I felt it necessary to preserve their anonymity by using invented names. These invented names nonetheless aim to reflect the cultural aspect of the person. So for example, if the person had a Basque name common to Iparralde, then I would replace it with another one common to that side of the frontier.

References

Abélès, M., "La Communauté européenne: une perspective anthropologique" in *Social Anthropology*, 1996, 4 (1), p. 33-45.

Abélès, M. & Bellier, I. & McDonald, M., *Approche anthropologique de la Commission européenne*, Brussels: European Commission, 1993.

Agar, M., *Speaking of Ethnography*, London: Sage, 1986.

Alonso, A.M., "The Effects of Truth: Re-presentations of the past and the imagining of the community" in *Journal of Historical Sociology*, 1988, 1 (1), p. 33-57.

Alvarez Junco, J., "The Nation-Building Process in Nineteenth-Century Spain" in C. Mar-Molinero and A. Smith (eds.), *Nationalism and the Nation in the Iberian Peninsula*, Oxford: Berg Press, 1996.

Anderson, B., *Imagined Communities. Reflections on the Origin and Spread of Nationalism*, London: Verso, 1983.

Anderson, M., "European Frontiers at the end of the twentieth century: an introduction" in M. Anderson and E. Bort (eds.), *The Frontiers of Europe*, London: Cassell, 1998.

Anderson, M., *Frontiers: Territory and State Formation in the Modern World*, Oxford: Polity, 1996.

Apaolaza, T., *Lengua, Etnicidad y Nacionalismo*, Donostia: Cuadernos de Antropología, 1993.

Appadurai, A., *Modernity at Large: Cultural Dimensions of Globalization*, Minneapolis: University of Minnesota Press, 1996.

Aramburu, A., *Los Orígenes del Alarde de San Marcial. Las milicias forales*, Donostia: Caja de Ahorros, 1978.

Aramendi Arzelus, A., "Projet de Coopération Transfrontalière de l'Eurocité Basque Bayonne-Saint Sébastien" in http://www.basque-eurocite.org, 1998.

Arana Goiri, S., "La Pureza de la Raza" in *Bizkaitarra*, 1895, No. 24, 31 March.

Aranzadi, J., *El Milenarismo Vasco*, Madrid: Taurus, 2000.

Aranzadi, T., J.M. Barandiarán and M.A. Etcheverry, *La Raza Vasca*, San Sebastian: Auñamendi, 1959.

Ardener, S., "Ground rules and Social Maps for Women: an introduction" in S. Ardener (ed.), *Women and Space: Ground Rules and Social Maps*, Oxford: Berg, 1993.

Augé, M., *Non-Places: introduction to an anthropology of supermodernity*, London: Verso, 1995.

Augé, M., *Pour une anthropologie des mondes contemporains*, Paris: Aubier, 1994.

Azcona, J., *Etnía y nacionalismo vasco. Una aproximación desde la antro- pología*, Barcelona: Anthropos, 1984.

Ayuntamiento de Irun, *Irún a vista de grulla*, Irun: Ayuntamiento de Irun, 1991.

Barnard, A. and J. Spencer (eds.), *Encyclopedia of Social and Cultural Anthropology*, London: Routledge, 1996.

Barth, F., *Ethnic Groups and Boundaries*, Oslo: Bergen, 1969

Basabe Prado, J.M., *Euskaldunak. La Etnía Vasca*, San Sebastian: Ekor, 1985.

Beck, U., *Risk Society: towards a new modernity*, London: Sage, 1992.

Bellier, I., "Une culture de la Commission européenne? De la rencontre des cultures et du multilinguisme des fonctionnaires" in Y. Mény, P. Muller and J. C. Quermonne (eds.), *Politiques Publiques en Europe*, Paris: L'Harmattan, 1994.

Bellier, I. and T.M. Wilson, *The Anthropology of the European Union*, London: Routledge, 2000.

Berger, B.M., "Foreword" in E. Goffman, *Frame Analysis*, New York: Harper and Row, 1986.

Bidart, P., *La singularité basque*, Paris: Presses Universitaires de France, 2001.

Bidart, P., *Le pouvoir politique à Baigorri*, Bayonne: Ipar, 1977.

Billig, M., *Banal Nationalism*, London: Sage, 1995.

Boissevain, J. and J. Friedl, *Beyond the Community: Social Process in Europe*, The Hague: Department of Education Science of the Netherlands, 1975.

Borneman, J., *Belonging in the Two Berlins: Kin, State, Nation*, Cambridge: Cambridge University Press, 1992.

Bourdieu, P., *Language and Symbolic Power*, Cambridge: Harvard University Press, 1991.

Bourdieu, P., *Outline of a Theory of Practice*, New York: Cambridge University Press, 1977.

Bourdieu, P. and L. Wacquant, *Réponses: pour une anthropologie réflexive*, Paris: Seuil, 1992a.

Bourdieu, P. and L. Wacquant, *An Invitation to Reflexive Sociology*, Chicago: Chicago University Press, 1992b.

Briggs, C., *Learning How to Ask: a sociolinguistic appraisal of the role of the interview in social science research*, Cambridge: Cambridge University Press, 1986.

Brighty, D., "State and Region: the Spanish Experience" in *Briefing Paper New Series*, 1999 (3) June, The Royal Institute of International Affairs.

Brubaker, R., "Ethnicity without Groups" in *Archives européennes de sociolo- gie*, 2002, XLIII [2], p. 163-189.

Brubaker, R., "Cognitive Perspectives" in *Ethnicities*, 2001, 1 [1] (April), p. 15- 17.

Brubaker, R. and F. Cooper, "Beyond 'Identity'" in *Theory and Society*, 2002, 29 [1], p. 1-47.

Bullen, M., "Bordering on Chaos: Culture, Gender and Identity" in *Session 2: Culture and Identity: Imagining New Frontiers for Euskal Herria, First International Symposium on Basque Cultural Studies.* Institute of Basque Cultural Studies: London, 2002.

Bullen, M., "Gender and Identity in the Alardes of Two Basque Towns" in W. Douglass *et al.* (eds.) *Basque Cultural Studies*, Basque Studies Program, Reno: University of Nevada, 2002, p. 149-77.

Bullen, M., "Las Mujeres y los alardes de Hondarribia e Irun" in *Bitarte*, 1997, (11).

Burawoy, M. *et al.* (eds.), *Ethnography Unbound: Power and Resistance in the Modern Metropolis*, Los Angeles: University of California Press, 1991.

Caglar, A. S., "Hyphenated Identities and the Limits of 'Culture'" in T. Modood and P. Werbner (eds.), *The Politics of Multiculturalism in the New Europe: Racism, Identity and Community*, London: Zed Books, 1997.

Calhoun, C., "Social Theory and the Politics of Identity" in C. Calhoun (ed.), *Social Theory and Identity Politics*, Oxford: Blackwell, 1994.

Cambot, P. "Commentaire du Traité de Bayonne du 10 mars 1995 relatif à la coopération transfrontalière entre collectivités territoriales" in M. Lafourcade (ed.), *La Frontière franco-espagnole: lieu de conflits interétatiques et de collaboration interrégionale* Actes de la journée d'études du 16 novembre 1996, Biarritz: Presses Universitaires de Bordeaux, 1998.

Camilleri, C., J. Kastersztein, E.M. Lipiansky *et al.*, *Stratégies identitaires*, Paris: Presses Universitaires de France, 1990.

Clifford, J., "Diasporas" in *Cultural Anthropology*, 1994, 9, [3], p. 302-38.

Clifford, J. and G. Marcus, *Writing Culture*, Berkeley: University Press of California, 1986.

Cohen, A., *Two-Dimensional: an essay on the anthropology of power and symbolism in complex society*, London: Routledge, 1974.

Cohen, A.P., "Boundaries and Boundary-Consciousness: Politicising Cultural Identity" in M. Anderson and E. Bort (eds.), *The Frontiers of Europe*, London: Printer Press, 1998.

Cohen, A.P., "Boundaries of consciousness, consciousness of boundaries. Critical questions for anthropology" in H. Vermeulen and C. Gowers (eds.), *The Anthropology of Ethnicity. 'Beyond Ethnic Groups and Boundaries'*, Amsterdam: Het Spinhuis, 1994a.

Cohen, A.P., *Self Consciousness: An Alternative Anthropology of Identity*, London: Routledge, 1994b.

Cohen, A.P., "Self-conscious anthropology" in J. Okely and H. Callaway (eds.), *Anthropology and Autobiography*, London: Routledge, 1992.

Cohen, A.P., *The Symbolic Construction of Community*, London: Tavistock Publications, 1985.

Cole, J.W. and E.R. Wolf, *The Hidden Frontier: Ecology and Ethnicity in an Alpine Valley*, London: Academic Press, 1974.

Collins, R., *The Basques*, Paris: Perrin, 1986.

Consorcio Transfronterizo Bidasoa-Txingudi. *Estatutos del Consorcio*, Irun: Adebisa, 1998.

Conversi, D., *The Basques, The Catalans and Spain: alternative routes to nationalist mobilisation*, London: Hurst, 1997.

Crapanzano, V., *Hermes' Dilemma and Hamlet's Desire: on the epistemology of interpretation*, Cambridge: Harvard University Press, 1992.

Cuche, D., *La notion de culture dans les sciences sociales.* Paris: La Découverte, 1996.

Davies, C.A., *Reflexive Ethnography: A Guide to Researching Selves and Others*, London: Routledge, 1999.

Del Valle, T., *Korrika: rituales de la lengua en el espacio*, Barcelona: Ediciones Anthropos, 1988.

Descheemaeker, J., "La Frontière dans les Pyrénées basques (organisation, antiquité, fédéralisme)" in *Eusko Jakintza*, 1950, IV, p. 127-78.

Devereux, G., *Essais d'ethnopsychiatrie générale*, Paris: Gallimard, 1970.

Die Erde, *Beiträge zur Humangeographie* (special issue on Borders), Heft 1. Berlin: Gesellschaft für Erdkunde zu Berlin, 2002.

Donnan, H. and T.M. Wilson, *Borders: Frontiers of Identity, Nation and State*, Oxford: Berg Press, 1999.

Donnan, H. and T.M. Wilson, *Border Approaches: Anthropological Perspectives on Frontiers*, Boston: University Press of America, 1994.

Douglas, M. and B. Isherwood, *The World of Goods: towards an anthropology of consumption*, London: Allen Lane, 1979.

Douglass, W.A., "Fronteras: La Configuración de los Mapas Mentales y Fisicas en el Pirineo" in *Globalización, Fronteras Culturales y Políticas y Ciudadanía*, VIII Congreso de Antropología, Santiago de Compostela, 1999.

Douglass, W.A., "A western perspective on an eastern interpretation of where north meets south: Pyrenean borderland cultures" in T.M. Wilson and H. Donnan (eds.), *Border Identities: nation and state at international frontiers*, Cambridge: Cambridge University Press, 1998.

Douglass, W.A., *Muerte en Murélaga: el contexto de la muerte en el País Vasco*, Barcelona: Barral Editores, 1973.

Douglass, W., S.M. Lyman and J. Zulaika, *Migración, etnicidad y etnonacionalismo*, Bilbao: Universidad del País Vasco, 1994.

Eguren, E., *Antropología*, Paper presented at First Congress of Basque Studies, 1918, p. 321-32.

Eriksen, E.O. and J.E. Fossum, "Democracy through strong publics in the European Union?" in *ARENA Working Papers*, 2001, WP 01/16.

Etchaniz, M. and M. Estomba, A. Puche (eds.), *Txingudi*, Gasteiz: Eusko Jaurlaritza, 1999.

Erikson, E.H., *Adolescence et Crise. La quête de l'identité*, Paris: Flammarion, 1972.

Erikson, E.H., *Identity and the Life-Cycle*, New York: W.W. Norton, 1959.

E.T.A. (Euskadi ta Askatasuna) *Documentos*, Donostia: Hordago, 1979.

Euro Cité, *Livre Blanc de l'Euro Cité*. Bayonne, 2000.

Euskal Kultur Erakundea, *Enquête sociolinguistique au Pays Basque*, Ustaritz: Euskal Kultur Erakundea, 1996.

EUSTAT *Educación, Euskera y Cultura – Euskera – Encuesta Sociolingüística de Euskal Herria*, http://www.eustat.es/spanish/estad/temalista.asp?tema=184, 1996.

Fairén Guillén, V., "Contribución al estudio de la facería internacional de los valles del Roncal y Baretons" in *Principe de Viana*, 1946, 7, p. 271-96.

Fernández de Casadevante Romaní, C., *La Frontera Hispano-Francesa y las Relaciones de Vecindad: especial referencia al sector fronterizo del País Vasco*, Leioa: University of the Basque Country, 1989.

Foster, R., "Making National Cultures in the Global Ecumen" in *Annual Review of Anthropology*, 1991, 20, p. 235-60.

Foucault, M., "Nietzsche, Genealogy, History" in D. Bouchard (ed.), *Language, Counter-Memory, Practice: Selected Essays and Interviews*, Ithaca: Cornell University Press, 1977.

Fowler, D. and D. Hardesty (eds.), *Others Knowing Others: perspectives on ethnographic careers*, Washington: Smithsonian Institution, 1994.

Fusi Aizpúrua, J.P., *España. Autonomías*, Madrid: Espasa-Calpe, 1989.

Gadamer, H.-G., *Truth and Method*, London: Sheed and Ward, 1979.

García, S. and H. Wallace, "Conclusion" in S. García (ed.), *European Identity and the Search for Legitimacy*, London: Pinter, 1993.

Geertz, C., *The Interpretation of Cultures*, New York: Basic Books, 1973.

Gellner, E., *Nations and Nationalism*, Oxford: Oxford University Press, 1983.

Gilmore, D.D., *Hacerse Hombre: concepciones culturales de la masculinidad*, Barcelona: Paidos, 1994.

Glazer, N. and D. Moynihan, *Ethnicity: Theory and Experience*, Cambridge: Harvard University Press, 1975.

Gleason, P., "Identifying Identity: A Semantic History" in *Journal of American History*, 1983, (69) 4 March, p. 910-31.

Goddard, V.A., J.R. Llobera and C. Shore (eds.), *The Anthropology of Europe: Identities and Boundaries in Conflict*, Oxford: Berg, 1983.

Goffman, E., *Interaction Ritual. Essays on face-to-face behavior*, New York: Pantheon Books, 1967.

Gomez-Ibánez, D.A., *The Western Pyrenees: Differential Evolution of the French and Spanish Borderland*, Oxford: Oxford University Press, 1975.

Greenwood, D., "Continuity in Change: Spanish Basque Ethnicity as a Historical Process" in M. Esman (ed.), *Ethnic Conflict in the Western World*, Ithaca: Cornell University Press, 1977.

Greenwood, D., *Unrewarding Wealth: the commercialisation and collapse of agriculture in a Spanish Basque town*, Cambridge: Cambridge University Press, 1976.

Grillo, R.D., *"Nation" and "State" in Europe: Anthropological Perspectives*, London: Academic Press, 1980.

Guibernau, M. and J. Rex, "Introduction" in M. Guibernau and J. Rex (eds.), *The Ethnicity Reader. Nationalism, Multiculturalism and Migration*, Cambridge: Polity Press, 1997.

Hall, S and P. du Gay, *Questions of Cultural Identity*, London; Thousand Oaks, Calif: Sage, 1996.

Hall, S., "New Cultures for Old" in D. Massey and P. Jess (eds.), *A Place in the World? Places, Cultures and Globalization*, Oxford: Oxford University Press, 1995.

Hannerz, U., "The World in Creolisation" in *Africa*, 1987, 57, p. 546-59.

Haritschelar, J., "De quoi je me mêle" in *Enbata*, 2001, No. 1694: 8.

Haritschelar, J., *Être basque*, Toulouse: Privat, 1983.

Hastrup, K., and P. Hervik (eds.), *Social Experience and Anthropological Knowledge*, London: Routledge, 1994.

Hechter, M., *Internal Colonialism: The Celtic Fringe in British National Development, 1536-1966*, Berkeley: University of California Press, 1975.

Heiberg, M., *The Making of the Basque Nation*, Cambridge: Cambridge University Press, 1989.

Heiberg, M., "Urban Politics and Rural Culture: Basque Nationalism" in S. Rokkan and D. Unwin (eds.), *The Politics of Territorial Identity: Studies in European Regionalism*, London: Sage, 1982.

Heiberg, M., "Basques, Anti-Basques and the Moral Community" in R.D. Grillo (ed.), *"Nation" and "State" in Europe: Anthropological Perspectives*, London: Academic Press, 1980.

Heider, F., *The Psychology of Interpersonal Relations*, New York: Wiley, 1958.

Hobsbawm, E. and T. Ranger, *The Invention of Tradition*, Cambridge: Cambridge University Press, 1986.

Horowitz, D.L., *Ethnic Groups in Conflict*, Berkeley: University of California Press, 1985.

Intxausti, J., *Euskara: la langue des Basques*, Donostia: Elkar, 1992.

Itçaina, X., "Les affiliations croisées: la circulation des interprétations autour des identités basques", Exposé présenté au Colloque sur l'Identité, Poitier, Maison des Sciences de l'Homme, Janvier, 2002.

Jacob, J.E., "The French Revolution and the Basques of France" in W. Douglass (ed.), *Basque Politics: A Case Study in Ethnic Nationalism*, Reno: University of Nevada Press, 1985.

Jaureguiberry, F.B., *Le basque à l'école*, Pau: Université de Pau et des Pays de l'Adour, 1993.

Jauristi, J., *La tradición romántica. Leyendas vascas del siglo XIX*, Madrid: Taurus, 1986.

Keating, M., "How historic are historic rights? Competing historiographies and the struggle for political legitimacy" in *Actas do Simposio Internacional de Antropoloxía 'Etnicidade e Nacionalismo'*, Santiago de Compostela: Consello da Cultura Galega, 2001, p. 45-81.

Kerexeta Erro, X., *Dime de qué alardeas.* http://www.alarde.org/a6/dimedeque/alardeas.html., 2001.

Kershen, A.J. (ed.), *A Question of Identity*, London: Aldershot, 1998.

Kertzer, D.I., *Ritual, Politics and Power*, London: Yale University Press, 1988.

Kvale, S., *Interviews*, London: Sage, 1996.

Laborde, D., "Des concours d'improvisation poétique chantée en Pays Basque, ou comment construire une identité culturelle" in *Canadian Folklore Canadien*, 1996, 18, (2), "Identity Transactions", The Folklore Studies Association of Canada.

Lamont, M., *Money, Morals, and Manners: the culture of the French and American upper-class*, Chicago: Chicago University Press, 1992.

Larronde, J.-C., *El Nacionalismo Vasco: su orígen y su ideología en la obra de Sabino Arana-Goiri*, San Sebastian: Ediciones Vascas, 1977.

Lavie, S. and T. Swedenburg (eds.), *Displacement, Diaspora, and Geographies of Identity*, Durham and London: Duke University Press, 1996.

Lefèbvre, T., *Les modes de vie dans les Pyrénées atlantiques orientales*, Paris: Armand Colin, 1933.

Leizaola, A., "'Hacerse Francés'. Nacionalidad y Ciudadanía en el area fronterizo en Euskal Herria" in *Globalización, Fronteras Culturales y Politicas y Ciudadanía*, Santiago de Compostela: VIII Congreso de Antropología, 1999.

Leizaola, A., "Muga: Border and Boundaries in the Basque country" in *Europaea, Journal of Europeanists*, 1996, II (1): 91-102.

Leresche, J.-P., "L'État et la coopération transfrontalière, un monde complexe d'adaptation à l'Europe" in J.-P. Leresche and R. Lévy (eds.), *La Suisse et la coopération transfrontalière: repli et redéploiement?*, Zurich: Seismo, 1995.

Letamendia, F., "Régime institutionnel et coopération transfrontalière. La comparaison entre le nord et le sud est-elle possible?" in J. Palard (ed.), *L'Europe aux Frontières. La coopération transfrontalière entre régions d'Espagne et de France*, Paris: Presses Universitaires de France, 1997.

Letamendia, F., *Les Basques: un peuple contre les États*, Paris: Seuil, 1976.

F. Letamendia, J.L. De Castro, A. Borja and J. Palard (eds.), *Cooperación Transfronteriza Euskadi-Aquitania (aspectos políticos, económicos y relaciones internacionales)*, Bilbao: Universidad del País Vasco, 1994.

Letamendia, P., *Nationalismes au Pays Basque*, Bordeaux: Presses Universitaires de Bordeaux, 1987.

Lévi-Strauss, C., *L'identité*, Paris: Éditions Grasset et Fasquelle, 'Quadrigue', 1977.

Loughlin, J., "Nation, State and Region in Western Europe" in L. Bekemans (ed.), *Culture: the building stone of Europe 2002 (Reflections in Western Europe)*, Brussels: Presses interuniversitaires européennes (P.I.E.), 1994.

MacClancy, J., "The Predictable Failure of a European Identity" in B. Axford, D. Berghahn and N. Hewlett (eds.), *Unity and Diversity in the New Europe*, Oxford: Peter Lang, 2000.

MacClancy, J., *Anthropology, Art and Contest*, Oxford: Berg, 1997.

MacClancy, J., "Bilingualism and Multinationalism in the Basque Country" in C. Mar-Molinero and A. Smith (eds.), *Nationalism and the Nation in the Iberian Peninsula*, Oxford: Berg Press, 1996.

MacClancy, J., "Biologically Basque, Sociologically Speaking" in M.K. Chapman (ed.), *Social and Biological Aspects of Ethnicity*, Oxford: Berg Press, 1993a.

MacClancy, J., "At Play with Identity in the Basque Arena" in S. MacDonald (ed.), *Inside European Identities*, Oxford: Berg Press, 1993b.

Macdonald, S., *Inside European Identities: Ethnography in Western Europe*, Providence, RI: Berg, 1993.

Mahmood, C. and S.L. Armstrong, "Do Ethnic Groups Exist? A Cognitive Perspective on the Concept of Cultures" in *Ethnology*, 1992, 31 (1), p. 5-12.

Marcus, G.E., *Ethnography Through Thick and Thin*, Princeton University Press, 1998.

Martiniello, M., *L'ethnicité dans les sciences sociales contemporaines*, Paris: Presses Universitaires de France, 1995.

Mead, G.-H., *Mind, Self and Society*, Chicago: Chicago University Press, 1934.

Michelena, L'Abbé, *Hendaye: son histoire*, Hendaye: Les Éditions du Mondarrain, 1997.

Miller, D., *Acknowledging Consumption*, London: Routledge, 1995.

Modood, T. and P. Werbner (eds.), *The Politics of Multiculturalism in the New Europe: Racism, Identity and Community*, London: Zed Books, 1997.

Moncusi Ferré, A., "De la frontera política a la frontera cotidiana en una comarca del pirineo" in *Globalización, Fronteras y Ciudadanía*, VII Congreso de Antropología, Santiago de Compostela, Spain, 1999, p. 119-128.

Moreno, L., *La Federalización de Espana: poder político y territorio*, Madrid: Siglo Ventiuno, 1997.

O'Dowd, L. and T.M. Wilson (eds.), *Borders, Nations and States: Frontiers of Sovereignty in the New Europe*, Avebury: Ashgate Publishing, 1996.

Ott, S., *The Circle of the Mountains*, Oxford: Clarendon Press, 1981.

Palard, J. (ed.), *L'Europe aux frontières. La coopération transfrontalière entre régions d'Espagne et de France*, Paris: Presses Universitaires de France, 1997.

Passerini, L., "The last identification: why some of us would like to call ourselves Europeans and what do we mean by this" in B. Stråth (ed.), *Europe and the Other and Europe as the Other*, Brussels: Peter Lang, 2000.

Passerini, L. (ed.), *Identitá cultural europea: idee, sentimenti, relazioni*, Firenze: La Nuova Italia, 1998.

Payne, S., *A History of Spain and Portugal*, Madison: University of Wisconsin Press, 1973.

Peillen, D., "Frontières et mentalités en Pays Basque" in M. Lafourcade (ed.), *La frontière franco-espagnole: lieu de conflits interétatiques et de collaboration interrégionale*, Actes de la journée d'études du 16 Novembre 1996, Bayonne: Presses Universitaires de Bordeaux, 1998.

Pérez-Agote, A., "La politización de la identidad colectiva", Conferencia pronunciada dentro de la celebración de la Primera Cátedra de Sociología en España, Facultad de CCPP y Sociología, Universidad de Complutense de Madrid, 27 Febrero, 1999.

Pérez-Agote, A., "La identidad colectiva: una reflexión abierta desde la sociología" in *Revista de Occidente*, 1986, No. 56, Enero.

Persson, H.-Å. and I. Eriksson, "Introduction" in H.-Å. Persson and I. Eriksson (eds.), *Border Regions in Comparison*, Lund: Studentliterratur, 2000.

Pieterse, J.N., "Globalisation as Hybridisation" in M. Featherstone and S. Lash (eds.), *Global Modernities*, London: Sage, 1995.

Portu, F., *Hondarribia: notas históricas y curiosidades*, Hondarribia: Ayuntamiento de Hondarribia, 1989.

Prescott, J.R.V., *Political Frontiers and Boundaries*, London: Unwin Hyman, 1987.

Preston, P.W., *Political/Cultural Identity: Citizens and Nations in a Global Era*, London: Sage, 1997.

Puche Martínez, A., *El Socialismo en Irun*, Irun: Ayuntamiento de Irun, 2001.

Rabinow, P. and M. Sullivan (eds.), *Interpretive Social Science: a second look*, Berkeley: University of California Press, 1987.

Ricq, C., "Les régions frontalières et l'intégration européenne" in *Livre Blanc de l'Assemblée des régions d'Europe*, Zaragoza, 1992.

Risse, T., "How Do We Know A European Public Sphere When We See One? Theoretical clarifications and empirical indicators", paper presented for the IDNET workshop "Europeanization and the Public Sphere", European University Institute, Florence, 20-21 February 2002, http://www.fu-berlin.de/atasp/texte/pi5s1otn.pdf.

Rodman, M., "Empowering Place: Multivocality and Mutlilocality" in *American Anthropologist*, 1998, 94 (3), p. 640-56.

Rodríguez Gal, L., *Lo que el rio vió*, Bilbao: Biblioteca de la Gran Enciclopedia Vasca, 1975.

Rose, D., *Living Ethnographic Life*, London: Sage, 1990.

Sahlins, P., *Boundaries*, Berkeley: University of California, 1989.

Said, E., *Orientalism*, New York: Pantheon Books, 1978.

Sangrador García J-L. (eds.), *Opiniones y Actitudes No. 10. Identidades, Actitudes y Estereotipos en la Espana de las Autonómas*, Madrid: Centro de Investigaciones Sociológicas, 1996.

San Martín, J., "Bidasoa-Txingudi: Hidronomia zehatz kokatzearen aldeko txostena" in *Euskaltzaindiaren lan eta agiriak*, 1998, 1, 43.

Saragueta, F., *El Consorcio Transfronterizo Bidasoa Txingudi: Las Relaciones Transfronterizas en el Entorno Vasco*, Preparation for Candidacy to PhD in Law. Unpublished Paper, 2000.

Shore, C., *Building Europe: The Cultural Politics of European Integration*, London: Routledge, 2000.

Shore, C., "Ethnicity as revolutionary strategy: Communist Identity Construction in Italy" in S. McDonald (ed.), *Inside European identities*, Oxford: Berg, 1993.

Shore, C. and A. Black, "The European Communities and the construction of Europe" in *Anthropology Today*, 1992, 8, (3) June.

SIADECO (Sozio-Ekonomi Ikerketa Elkartea) *Étude Sociolinguistique à Hendaye*, October, 1999a.

SIADECO *Euskararen Erabilpen Erreala Leku Publikoetan*, Hondarribia, 1999b.

Smith, A.D., *The Ethnic Origin of Nations*, Oxford: Blackwell, 1986.

Smith, M. and L. Guarnizo (eds.), *Transnationalism from below*, London: Sage, 1998.

Sökefeld, M., "Debating Self, Identity, and Culture in Anthropology" in *Current Anthropology*, 1999, 40, (4), August-October, p. 417-31.

Spradley, J.P., *Participant Observation*, New York: Holt, Rinehart and Winston, 1980.

Spradley, J.P., *The Ethnographic Interview*, New York: Holt, Rinehart and Winston, 1979.

Stråth, B. (ed.), *Europe and the Other and Europe as the Other*, Brussels: P.I.E.-Peter Lang, 2000.

Tambou, O., "Le Consorcio Bidasoa-Txingudi: premier organisme public franco-espagnol de coopération transfrontalière" in *Quaderns de Treball*, 1999, No. 32.

Tejerina Montana, B., *Lengua y Nacionalismo*, Madrid: Centro de Investigaciones Sociológicas, 1994.

Terradas, I. "Catalan Identities" in *Critique of Anthropology*, 1993, 10, (2 and 3), p. 39-50.

Thompson, R.H., *Theories of Ethnicity*, New York: Greenwood Press, 1989.

Turner, T., "Anthropology and Multiculturalism: What is Anthropology that Multiculturalists Should be Mindful of It?" in *Cultural Anthropology*, 1993, 8 (4), p. 411-29.

Turner, V., *The Forest of Symbols*, New York: Cornell University Press, 1967.

Tylor, E., *Primitive Culture*, London: John Murray, 1871.

Ugalde, M. de, *Unamuno y el Vascuence*, Buenos Aires: Ekin, 1966.

Uranga Gómez, M. *et al.* (eds.), *Un Nuevo Escenario: democracia, cultural y cohesión social en Euskal Herria*, Bilbao: Fundación Manu Robles-Arangiz Institutoa, 1999.

Urbeltz, J.-A., "Alardeak" in *Bertan*, 1995, 8.

Urla, J., *Being Basque, Speaking Basque. The politics of language and identity in the Basque country*, PhD thesis, University of California, Berkeley, 1987.

Van Gennep, A., *The Rites of Passage*, Chicago: Chicago University Press, 1960.

Van Maanen, J. (ed.), *Qualitative Methodology*, Beverly Hills: Sage, 1983.

Vermeulen, H. and C. Gowers (eds.), *The Anthropology of Ethnicity: 'Beyond Ethnic Groups and Boundaries'*, Amsterdam: Het Spinhuis, 1994.

Wallman, S., "Ethnicity and the Boundary Process in Context" in J. Rex and D. Mason (eds.), *Theories of Race and Ethnic Relations*, Cambridge: Cambridge University Press, 1986.

Wallman, S., "The Boundaries of 'Race': Processes of Ethnicity in England" in *Man*, 1978, 13 (2), p. 200-17.

Wastell, S., *The Salacencans: marginal Basques*, Edinburgh University, Social Anthropology department. Unpublished paper, 1994.

Watson, C.J., "Folklore and Basque Nationalism: language, myth and reality" in *Nations and Nationalism*, 1996a, 2 (1), p. 17-34.

Watson, C.J., S*acred Earth, Symbolic Blood, a cultural history of Basque political violence from Arana to ETA*, PhD thesis in Basque Studies, Reno: University of Nevada, 1996b.

Weber, E., *Peasants into Frenchmen: the modernization of rural France – 1870-1914*, London: Chatto and Windus, 1977.

Weber, M., *Economy and Society*, New York: Bedminster Press, 1968.

Werbner, P. and T. Modood (eds.), *Debating Cultural Hybridity: Multi-Cultural Identities and the Politics of Anti-Racism*, London: Zed Books, 1997.

White, W., *Learning from the Field*, London: Sage, 1984.

Willis, P., *Learning to Labour: How working class kids get working class jobs*, Aldershot: Gower, 1977.

Wilson, T.M. and H. Donnan, *Border Identities: nation and state at international frontiers*, Cambridge: Cambridge University Press, 1998.

Wilson, T.M. and M. Estellie-Smith (eds.), *Cultural Change in the New Europe: perspectives on the European Community*, Oxford: Westview Press, 1993.

Wright, S. (ed.), *Anthropology in Organisations*, London: Routledge, 1994.

Zubiaur Carreño, F.J., "Toponomía de San Martín de Unx (Navarra)" in *Cuadernos de etnología y etnografía de Navarra*, 1977, Año IX, 27, p. 415-62.

Zulaika, J., "Tropics of Terror: From Guernica's 'Natives' to 'Global' 'Terrorists'" in *Social Identities*, 1998, 4 (1), p. 93-108.

Zulaika, J., *Del Cromañon al Carnaval: los vascos como museo antropológico*, San Sebastian: Erein, 1996.

Zulaika, J., *Basque Violence, Metaphor and Sacrament*, Reno: University of Nevada Press, 1989.

Index

"Multiple Europes"

Multiple Europes is a series that aims to describe and analyse, in a historical perspective, the variety of ways in which social community and images of cohesion have been constructed in Europe. Particular emphasis is given to the idea of "nation", which, without doubt, has been one of the most persistent community categories of the last two hundred years. Various myths, memories, and historical heritages, often contradictory, always shifting, have been mobilised in the processes of community construction, and, taken together, these emphasise the multiplicity of Europe.

It is not only the processes of construction that are multiple – so too are the images of Europe that are produced as a result. Historically, images of Europe has been both utopian and dystopian. The experience of war has given rise to pacifist dreams, while atomism and disintegration have produced a longing for holism and wholeness. Indeed, the tension between war and peace, atomism and holism, is one of the most obvious elements in the construction of community in Europe. The continent's self-images have oscillated between pride and shame, between, for example, Europe as civilisation and Europe as degeneracy, and these self-images have emerged through various demarcations between Us and the Other. A crucial aspect of such demarcations is the views they project of minorities and immigrants, either as refugees from political regimes and war or as economic migrants.

Another crucial question addressed in the *Multiple Europes* series is how, since the French Revolution, with its rousing call for *liberté, égalité, fraternité*, images of social justice have been used in the construction of community, and how, in political processes, efforts have been made to minimise the evident tension between concepts like freedom and equality.

In this series, the analysis focuses on the levels of both the political, economic and intellectual elites, and the everyday, and considers these levels not only as reflected constructions, but also as unreflected practice. It is in this space between construction and practice that Europe, in its multiple forms, emerges.

Series Editor: Professor **Bo Stråth**, Contemporary History Chair, History Department, Robert Schuman Centre, European University Institute (Italy)

Recent Series Titles